THE
ALASKA CRUISE
HANDBOOK

A MILE BY MILE
GUIDE

THE ALASKA CRUISE HANDBOOK

A MILE BY MILE GUIDE

BY JOE UPTON

Coastal Publishing
Bainbridge Island, WA

The maps in this book are not to be used for navigation.

This book is sold by Princess Cruises as The Alaska Cruise Companion

2008 Edition

Coastal Publishing
15166 Skogen Lane, Bainbridge Island, WA. 98110

Illustrations by Russ Burtner and Christine Cox
Maps by Joe Upton
Design by Martha Brouwer

Photographs by Joe Upton unless noted with the following abbreviations:
AMNH - American Museum of Natural History, New York
BCARS - British Columbia Archives and Records Service.
BCRM- British Columbia Royal Museum.
CRMM - Columbia River Maritime Museum, Astoria, Oregon
MOHAI - Museum of History and Industry, Seattle.
SFM - San Francisco Maritime Museum.
THS - Tongass Historical Society, Ketchikan, Alaska.
UAF - University of Alaska, Fairbanks
UW - University of Washington Special Collections.
WAT - Whatcom County (WA) Museum of History and Art

ISBN 978-0-9794915-0-4

Printed in Korea

For
Mary Lou, Matthew,
and Katherine Anne,
mariners all.

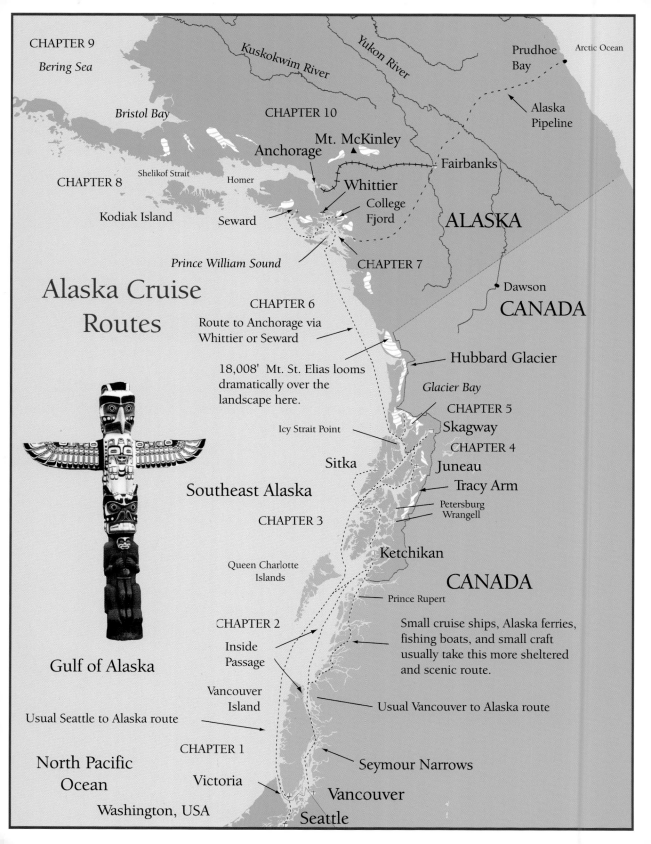

CHAPTER 9

Bering Sea

Kuskokwim River

Yukon River

Prudhoe Bay

Arctic Ocean

Bristol Bay

CHAPTER 10

Alaska Pipeline

Mt. McKinley ▲

Anchorage

CHAPTER 8

Shelikof Strait

Homer

Whittier

Fairbanks

College Fjord

ALASKA

Kodiak Island

Seward

Prince William Sound

CHAPTER 7

Dawson

CANADA

Alaska Cruise Routes

CHAPTER 6
Route to Anchorage via Whittier or Seward

Hubbard Glacier

18,008' Mt. St. Elias looms dramatically over the landscape here.

Glacier Bay

CHAPTER 5

Icy Strait Point

Skagway

CHAPTER 4

Sitka

Juneau

Tracy Arm

Southeast Alaska

Petersburg

Wrangell

CHAPTER 3

Ketchikan

Queen Charlotte Islands

CANADA

Prince Rupert

CHAPTER 2

Inside Passage

Small cruise ships, Alaska ferries, fishing boats, and small craft usually take this more sheltered and scenic route.

Vancouver Island

Usual Vancouver to Alaska route

Gulf of Alaska

Usual Seattle to Alaska route

CHAPTER 1

North Pacific Ocean

Victoria

Seymour Narrows

Vancouver

Washington, USA

Seattle

Contents

Ports and Places

TO THE ALASKA TRAVELER

On a June night in 1965, I felt a hand on my shoulder in the dark fo'c'sle of the *Sidney*, a 90' fish buying boat on which I'd just gotten my first Alaska job. I was 19.

"C'mon up, kid," Mickey, the 70-year-old mate rasped, nodding up at the pilothouse stairs, "You gotta' see this."

He was right. We were lying almost motionless in a little bight in a steep and forested shore. Ahead of us in the thin light I could make out a torrent of water, like rapids in a river, pouring out of a gap in the trees.

"W-w-we're going in there...?" I stammered, awed at the sight, inexperienced, and totally new to the Inside Passage.

"It used to be really bad" came the soft-voiced answer, "That's Seymour Narrows. There was a rock in the middle. They blew it the hell out of there."

Two days later we arrived at our cannery in a remote fishing village, to join a large fleet of workboats. It was Alaska in capital letters—we saw icebergs, eagles, and whales. And everywhere we traveled, old Mickey had a story—about the steamer that stranded there in 1920, and how the passengers just waited on shore for the next boat and kept going. About the square rigged ships that used to sail up from San Francisco to the canneries, and about the northern fisheries and working in the pack ice. Mickey shared tales from his life as a trapper, a fisherman, and a mail boat skipper. The old gentleman took me under his wing, teaching me about the lore and legends of The North.

That long season in The North and that kindly old Alaskan instilled in me a lifelong interest in northern places and history, especially the inland waterways that form the Inside Passage and Southeast Alaska.

Eventually I bought a used 32-footer and began fishing salmon, along the sheltered waterways of Southeast Alaska. In the cove where British explorer George Vancouver and his men found desperately needed shelter in 1793, my wife and I built a cabin. Nearby was a tiny, roadless, fishing settlement.

Our store and post office each floated on a log raft in the harbor; our vehicles were our outboard boats. It was a unique community, where a person could make a living fishing with an open skiff, get a piece of waterfront land with little money, and build a

home with local lumber. Our store was also a floating bar, which eliminated the nasty problem of negotiating that steep walkway down to your boat at low tide. The drinks were whiskey and water, whiskey and coke, and whiskey and Tang.

The people of the community welcomed new blood—showing us the best fishing places—and helping us build our home. Just 200 yards from our house the humpback whales hung out all summer, and at night, if it were still, we could hear them breathing as they surfaced.

In the spring we fished the windy outside coast. In the summer, we worked nearby Sumner Strait. In the fall we traveled north to the natural wind tunnel called Lynn Canal, for the 10-dollar-a-fish chum salmon. And in the long, kerosene lantern-lit winters, there was time for visiting.

And during these last three decades, in a hundred little coves up and down the coast, from the very edge of the Arctic down to Puget Sound and Seattle, when the storms came, we anchored up in our little boats, waiting for the wind to stop.

Sometimes it blew for days, and while we waited, the stories came out. The experiences of my friends, and those before them, an oral history of the coast. And in my travels I sought out the little-visited communities, the out-of-the-way places.

I was an amateur photographer, and a writer. "Write a book," my friends said, "Tell our story." One book became another, and another after that.

When I first started fishing, cruise ships were few and small. Then more ships began traveling the coast, and I designed a series of illustrated maps to better share with these new visitors the drama and beauty of The North.

When I traveled on board cruise ships, I found many passengers found it very hard to simply find out where they were as they traveled up the coast. To make it easier, I developed a route numbering system based on Seattle as Mile Zero. On many ships your position will be announced using these milemarker numbers. The book and map are keyed together with milemarker numbers in the text in bold to make it easier for you to follow your progress.

For me the books and maps are a way to share with you a sense of the mystery and the power of this place that is such a big part of my life.

So come, take this journey through this land that remains much as it was when the first explorers came through.

Left: My neighbor, 'Flea,' in his salmon fishing skiff, at Point Baker in 1974. Top: Alaska cruise ship, 1972. This was the Princess Patricia, in Wrangell Narrows. Right: Mickey Hanson and me, Southeast Alaska, 1965.

PLANNING YOUR ALASKA CRUISE

Top: The channels east of Vancouver island are spectacular. This is a small cruise ship in Desolation Sound. Below: Evening, Sumner Strait, Alaska.

"Whenever a bunch of fellows would get together, someone would start to talking about going up north...

Things were pretty much settled to the south of us. We didn't seem to be ready for steady jobs. It was only natural we'd start talking about the North. We'd bought out the Russians. We'd built canneries up there. The fellows who hadn't been up was hankering to go. The rest of us was hankering to go back.

- Mont Hawthorne in *"The Trail Led North"*

Headed "Up North?" Taking an Alaska cruise is probably one of the best travel values you'll ever find. But especially if you haven't cruised in Alaska before, here are some things to consider.

First come itineraries; there are several choices:

Seattle to Seattle round trip: Generally the most affordable cruises, these typically make two or three port calls, plus part of a day at either Glacier Bay, Hubbard Glacier, or Tracy Arm. While these are often billed as 'Inside Passage' cruises, their route usually is up the west or outside coast of Vancouver Island rather than the more interesting and scenic traditional Inside Passage through the narrower channels east of Vancouver Island. At least one ship, the *Norwegian Pearl*, travels up the outside coast on the way north, and inside waters on the way south.

Vancouver to Vancouver round trip: Until about 1996, this was about the only itinerary available. Like Seattle sailings, it offered usually three ports and glacier viewing. Modestly priced in that you didn't have to fly back from Alaska as you would with a one way cruise, and also offering the advantage of traveling both northbound and southbound up the traditional and very scenic Inside Passage, east of Vancouver Island

Vancouver to Seward or Whittier: Pioneered by Princess Cruises in 1996, and often called some variation of 'Voyage of the Glaciers,' most lines operating large cruise ships in Alaska offer some variation of this. Basically these are one way cruises either to or from Alaska, offering an additional part of a day of glacier viewing, usually at College Fjord in Prince William Sound. A particular advantage of these cruises are that they afford you an opportunity to explore interior as well as coastal Alaska. The most popular add-on itinerary is to spend a day or two in both Fairbanks and Anchorage, take one of the wonderful vistadome style railroad cars on the Alaska Railroad between those towns, combined with a one or two day stopover in the Denali or McKinley National Park area. Many families will start with a Seattle or Vancouver round trip cruise, find that it whets their appetite for more, and then follow up in later years with a one way cruise two or from Alaska combined with a week or so exploring Alaska's great interior.

Other itineraries: some small ships—see following—operate all Alaska itineraries, typically departing out of either Juneau or Ketchikan. Recently Cruise West began offering three and four day itineraries in Southeast Alaska and found them very popular. Cruise West also operates 4 and 5 night cruises in Prince William Sound, near Anchorage

Which ship? There's a lot of choice here; presently some 25 large and a dozen or so smaller ships operate on the Alaska run. Today's big Alaska cruise ships are essentially floating resorts with multiple restaurants, extensive shopping, elegant theatres, a wide variety of art, and many public spaces. Free dining (most drinks extra) is usually offered in the large formal dining rooms as well as in a large buffet area on the upper decks. The most recent trend is to charge a fee in the smaller, themed, restaurants, typically $15 - $20 a person, a modest price for the excellent food and service you will usually receive. Take some time to

When the big boys come to town... The large ships operating in Alaska, like the Sapphire Princess above, are essentially full featured floating resorts, except that you are in a new place every day! Below: The elegant theatre is typical of the detail and thought that went into the design of modern cruise ships.

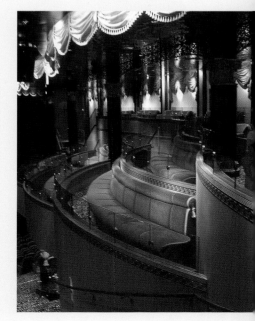

The Sea Lion, operated by Lindblad Expeditions, at 220' and about 100 passengers, is a typical small cruise ship. Below: A group from the Spirit of Oceanus, operated by Cruise West, explores the rugged shore of Tracy Arm. Opposite page: Explore your ship in the evening! This is the Dawn Princess, somewhere along the gorgeous Inside Passage.

check out the restaurant choices aboard your ship. Some ships, like the *Coral*, *Sun*, and *Dawn Princess* create a white tablecloth steakhouse in part of the Horizon Court area near the bow. With a stunning view out to the passing landscape, it is a memorable eating experience.

A very valuable feature for ships operating in Alaska is an eating or viewing area that stretches the full width of the front of the ship on an upper deck. You may find eating buffet style with a 180 degree view preferable to the traditional dining rooms, with full service and presentation, but usually little view.

THE SMALL SHIP ALTERNATIVE

Usually carrying 100 passengers or less, small ships offer a very different experience. The focus is much less on entertainment—floor shows, casino gambling, etc.—and more on the history, wildlife, and culture of the passing landscape. Many small ships have daily presentations by one or more naturalists, and have a more flexible schedule allowing them to linger, say when a pod of orcas was sighted, than the larger ships which often have tighter schedules.

The atmosphere on board is apt to be very informal, with perhaps a cocktail hour discussion of the day's activities, and ship's staff often joining passengers for meals.

One of the biggest advantages of small ship cruising is simply that they go where the big ships can't, stopping at off the beaten track towns like Petersburg and Wrangell, or poking into exquisite little coves.

In recent years most small ships operating in Alaska carry kayaks and/or Zodiacs, sturdy inflatable boats which are often launched at sites of particular interest like bird rookeries and sea lion haul outs.

Prices are usually significantly higher than for similar accommodations aboard the big cruise ships.

The major companies offering small ship Alaska cruises are Cruise West and Lindblad Expeditions, both with Seattle offices.

TRAVEL TIPS

It's only formal if you want it to be. Don't feel like you have to bring suits and dresses unless that is your style. Alaska is a very casual place, and on board your ship there are always other places to eat than the main dining room on formal night.

Bring binoculars. They are also sold on board most ships, but in any case make sure you have them. Generally on board ship, anything over 10 power might not be a good choice because of the ship's motion. Also you will find the traditional prism style 8 x 50s a better choice than smaller ones because of the wider field of view. And always bring them with you when you leave the cabin.

Bring fleece and raingear. Southeast Alaska is a rainy place. But generally the rain is of the light misting variety, so if you have a good rain jacket, you won't be bothered too much. Don't worry about rainpants unless you're determined to hike, rain or not. Many excursions offer free raingear to use. Make sure you have at least one good warm fleece that you can layer under a jacket. Especially on glacier day, it can get mighty chilly on deck.

Explore your ship early. These big ships have a lot of nifty little places to hang out and watch the passing scene. Don't discover them on the last day.

Eat where there's a view. I can't emphasize this enough, especially on ships that have a forward eating area on an upper deck. You don't have to eat in the formal dining room. Especially on your first night out of Vancouver, Whittier, or Seward, you'll be missing some truly spectacular scenery if you don't

Always look for whales. Although most ships have naturalists with a beeper who can be called to the bridge if there is a whale sighting, there are a lot of competing activities on board, and the whales may or may not be announced. Know what to look for: a puff of what looks like smoke, easily seen from a distance. It is a whale exhaling. If you know what to look for, you'll see a lot more whales.

SHORE EXCURSIONS

Alaska shore excursions are a tradition going back to the early 1900s, when passengers from the old steamer *Queen* would be rowed ashore at the foot of Muir Glacier where ladders were set up allowing them to clamber across the top of the glacier, crevasses and all. Imagine what the US Park Service would do if you tried that today!

Today at each port you are offered a wide variety of excursions and more and more cruise lines are encouraging passengers to pre-book by internet before their cruise. If you didn't, then probably you should spend some time with the shore excursions staff or materials and make your choice early in your cruise, as excursions fill up early. But if your first and second choices are full, don't despair. On the dock of each cruise port are cruise vendors offering similar excursions to those offered on board. You can generally take these excursions with full confidence. The only wrinkle is that the cruise lines will often say that they won't wait for a passenger on a 'brand x' excursion if he or she is late getting back to the ship. But the truth of the matter is that cruise ships are very reluctant to leave guests behind for any reason.

Generally I recommend that first time Alaska cruisers have at least one flightseeing experience, whether by helicopter or floatplane. If the visibility is good, a Misty Fjords flight from Ketchikan is very dramatic, and the helicopter and land on the glaciers programs offered in Skagway and Juneau are very popular. An expensive but very popular option is the flightseeing/ dogsled excursion where you land on a snowfield and go on a great dogsled ride. The dogs get sooo excited whenever a chopper lands!

The Yukon & White Pass train in Skagway is the most popular shore excursion in the state, and comes in many versions; at the least I suggest the ride up to the top of the pass and return.

If you haven't seen your quota of whales, the whale watching excursions out of Juneau are excellent, often yielding sightings of both orcas and humpbacks.

Opposite page: Beaver floatplanes at Juneau. This page: the elegant interiors of modern cruise ships reflect their status as floating resorts.

CHAPTER 1

The South End

Seattle, Mile Zero to Cape Scott, Mile 280W

*"I could not possibly believe that any uncultivated country
had ever been discovered exhibiting so rich a picture..."*

- Captain George Vancouver, upon first entering Puget
Sound, May 1792. In his *A Voyage of Discovery to The North
Pacific Ocean and Around the World*, London, 1798

This is stunning country; the drama of the mountains and the sea is everywhere; when the sun comes out suddenly after a long dreary week, the sight of Rainier looming over Seattle and Puget Sound is literally spectacular enough to stop you in your tracks.

These are big, big mountains, 6,000 footers on the west and all the way up to 14,000 foot plus on the east. Their tops are snow covered year round, and the range on the east, the North Cascades, is high enough to scrape much of the water out of the clouds as they head east. So much so that Eastern Washington seems like a different state–dry, the summers much hotter, the winters much colder.

And the ring of fire is very present here–some of the earth's great plates that form the crust meet along the ridge of the North Cascades. If you fly in or out, look as your plane gets up over the mountains and if it's clear you'll see a chain of volcanoes: Rainier, Adams, St. Helens, and Hood, stretching out of sight to the south.

And the fire is still present: after two months of throat clearing, Mt. St. Helens blew the top 1,300 feet of mountain and a cubic mile of ash into the atmosphere in May of 1980.

Much of the east side of the Sound, the Seattle - Tacoma - Everett corridor is fast paced, growing rapidly with all the attendant problems: congestion, traffic, pollution and noise.

But across the sound is very different. The old Puget Sound of cedar bungalows, forests sloping to the water's edge, driftwood fires, soaring eagles, and native settlements lingers here.

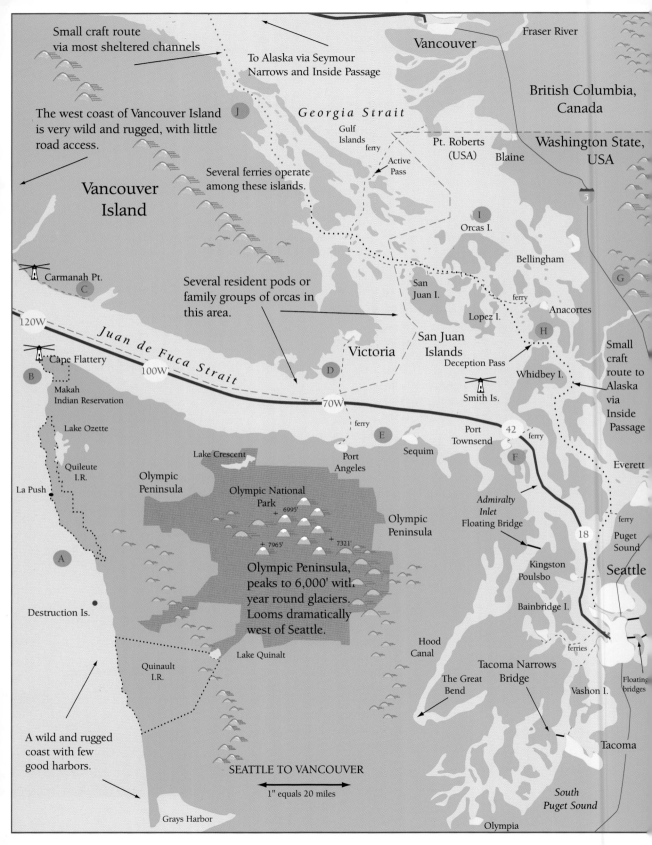

Small craft route via most sheltered channels

To Alaska via Seymour Narrows and Inside Passage

Vancouver

Fraser River

Georgia Strait

British Columbia, Canada

Gulf Islands

Pt. Roberts (USA)

Blaine

Washington State, USA

Several ferries operate among these islands.

Active Pass

ferry

J

The west coast of Vancouver Island is very wild and rugged, with little road access.

Vancouver Island

I

Orcas I.

Bellingham

Carmanah Pt.

C

Several resident pods or family groups of orcas in this area.

San Juan I.

ferry

Anacortes

120W

B

Cape Flattery

Juan de Fuca Strait

100W

Lopez I.

H

Smith Is.

Deception Pass

Whidbey I.

San Juan Islands

Small craft route to Alaska via Inside Passage

Makah Indian Reservation

Victoria

D

70W

Lake Ozette

Quileute I.R.

La Push

Lake Crescent

Port Angeles

ferry

E

Sequim

Port Townsend

42

ferry

Everett

F

Olympic Peninsula

Olympic National Park

+ 6995'

Olympic Peninsula

Admiralty Inlet Floating Bridge

ferry

Puget Sound

A

+ 7965'   + 7321'

Olympic Peninsula, peaks to 6,000' with year round glaciers. Looms dramatically west of Seattle.

Kingston Poulsbo

18

Seattle

Destruction Is.

Bainbridge I.

Quinault I.R.

Lake Quinault

Hood Canal

ferries

Floating bridges

Vashon I.

The Great Bend

Tacoma Narrows Bridge

A wild and rugged coast with few good harbors.

Tacoma

SEATTLE TO VANCOUVER

1" equals 20 miles

South Puget Sound

Grays Harbor

Olympia

ALONG THE WAY
Seattle to Cape Flattery

A - The outside coast of Washington State is easily the most rugged shore of the lower 48 states. There is little road access, and much of the shore is Indian reservations. In most places along the northwest section, the only way to get down to the actual shore is via several miles of very rugged trail. But the walk is worth it: at the end are spectacular beaches with off-shore rocks, arches, and spires, and hemmed in on either end by high and dramatic headlands.

B - In recent years the Makah tribe has sought and received permission to conduct a tribal harvest of gray whales, spurring protests by several whale conservation and environmental groups.

C - The West Coast Trail, originally built as an aid to shipwrecked mariners. Today a challenging hiking trail with crude suspension bridges, and vertical ladders in and out of ravines. Not for novices! 4-7 days, no services, and no way out except at either end.

D - Pedder Bay. In the 1970s and 80s orcas used to congregate here and hunters, seeking to capture them for sale to public aquariums set their nets here around Orca schools. Orca capture was banned in British Columbia in 1986.

E - Rain shadow effect. In the Pacific Northwest, weather generally comes from the southwest, off the ocean. However, the mountains of the Olympic Peninsula are high enough to scrape the rain out of the passing clouds. This rain shadow creates a micro climate in the Sequim area which is much sunnier and drier than in Seattle.

F - Entrance to Puget Sound. Strong tide rips here and heavy seas when wind and tide are opposed to each other. The big cross sound ferry here frequently cancels trips when the seas build too high. Before World War II three forts here guarded the entrance with big bore cannons.

G - North Cascade mountain range. A forty mile wide band of extremely rugged mountains, whose foothills extends west to the edge of the urban Tacoma - Everett corridor. Only three year round roads cross this range, which are frequently closed in winter with heavy snows and avalanches. These mountains scrape most of the moisture out of the eastward flowing clouds, creating the much much drier and hotter (colder in the winter) climate of eastern Washington.

H - Deception Pass—narrow, steep sided, tide wracked, with a high bridge over it, Northwest boaters have learned to read their tide tables carefully here.

I - Matia Island, one of Washington state's exquisite marine parks, some of which are for the exclusive use of boaters in kayaks or other non motorized craft.

J - Small craft route north—winding through the most sheltered channels.

Top: Point Wilson, Mile 42, the transition between sheltered and more open waters. Below: Campsite at Matia Island State Park, in the San Juan Islands. With just room for a few boats at the dock, and a few campsites and picnic tables, it is a perfect spot for overnight visitors who come by kayak and small craft.

SEATTLE
The Emerald City

Ferries

Each morning tens of thousands of commuters cross the generally calm waters of Puget Sound from sleepy bedroom communities 'across the water' to their work places along the busy Tacoma-Everett corridor. Particularly for those who walk on, it can be a very pleasant arrangement. The ferry takes you right to downtown Seattle, where, if you are lucky, work is just a brisk walk away. For those who must drive on, the commute is a bit more tedious as you might have to get in line an hour or more before sailing. But with wireless internet, food, and espresso service, commuting by ferry is becoming an excellent way to get to work without the hassle of freeway travel. Above: Seattle skyline with North Cascade range beyond, seen from Eagle Harbor, Bainbridge Island. Right: Seattle is a city of readers; this is the well known Elliott Bay Book Store in Pioneer Square.

When travelers took the train between New York and Boston, and walked on cobblestone streets, the entire Pacific Northwest was thickly forested from mountain to shore, and the only settlements were natives, living easily on the products of forest and sea.

Seattle's first settlers trudged ashore in the pouring rain in November of 1851, The families had braved the rigors of the Oregon Trail, had a stormy trip up the coast by boat. "And for this?" they might have said, as they found out what they had traveled all that way for: a half finished cabin on the edge of the gloomy forest with scowling, half clad natives as a welcoming committee.

Less than a month later a small schooner dropped anchor in front of the settlers and offered them $1000 for a load of fir pilings from the forest behind the settlement, and the industry that was to drive

the region far into the 20th century, logging and sawmilling, was born.

A century later, the Boeing Aircraft Company was the biggest game in town as it prepared to usher in the jet age with the plane management bet the future of the company on: the 707.

Twenty five years after that, a new industry that would truly transform the region and the world was beginning just east of Seattle: computer software and the amazing rise of Microsoft.

Today Seattle has a broad based economy where Boeing and Microsoft are still the employment leaders, and a very outdoor oriented population. A climate that allows either skiing or sailing on almost any day from Thanksgiving to Easter and a dress code where bluejeans and a clean shirt will get you in almost anywhere, has made Seattle and the Northwest very popular with young professionals.

Does it really rain all the time? Actually New York (43" annually) and Kansas City (50") are a both a lot wetter than Seattle's average 38 inches. It's just that Seattle's is often spread out over more days.

There's lots of public art in this city. As you can see from the custom manhole cover below, the cultural influence of Northwest native culture is very strong.

Pioneer Square
This area of First Avenue, at the southern end of downtown is an eclectic collection of galleries, shops, ethnic restaurants, the excellent Gold Rush Museum, and lots of street art. Additionally the highly recommended Seattle Underground Tour begins just off the square. When this part of Seattle was regraded to allow for better movement of streetcars and sewage, the streets were lifted a whole floor. The old building fronts are still there, in sort of this weird nether world.

A few well regarded restaurants: Ivar's Acres of Clams, on the waterfront, McCormick and Schmick's, 1103 First Ave, Anthony's Pier 66, waterfront, and Dragonfish Asian Cafe at 722 Pine St.

Pike Place Market is probably the most varied food and craft market on the west coast. Also there are some great places to eat here, overlooking the sound. Exciting!

Seattle Art Museum, on First Avenue, downtown, just finished up a major renovation. Many permanent and rotating collections. Highly recommended.

Fishermen's Terminal & Ballard Locks – Much of the Alaska fishing fleet is based in this area of fresh water lakes connected to the salt water of Puget Sound by the locks. On summer weekends there is a lot of action at the locks and the nearby restaurants.

Waterfront & Aquarium – Seattle's waterfront is a hopping place, Right below downtown, it is a collection of shops, restaurants, and excursion vessel docks. The Blake Island tour with salmon dinner and Native American dancing is highly recommended. The IMAX feature on Mt. St. Helens at the Aquarium is excellent.

Museum of Flight, between downtown and the airport, has a recent addition with stunning WWI and II dioramas.

Experience Music Museum in the Seattle Center, downtown. Wonderful historical exhibits and hands on activities, with excellent section on Seattle's own wild and groovy Jimmy Hendrix.

Olympic Sculpture Garden at the north end of the downtown waterfront is a 3 acre spread with graceful sculptures overlooking the water. Opened 2007.

GREAT SHORT TRIPS

Olympic Peninsula Loop

Bainbridge ferry to Kitsap Peninsula, to Hood Canal Bridge to Port Angeles, to Forks, and La Push. Return same way or via Queets and Olympia. Alternate stop at Hurricane Ridge S. of Port Angeles. 1-? days

North Cascades Loop

I-5 north to Burlington, east on North Cascades Highway to Okanogan, follow Columbia River S. to Wenatchee, then Rt. 2 over Stevens Pass back to I-5. Don't miss Winthrop and Levenworth. 2 days.

Victoria Clipper

Day trip from Seattle waterfront to downtown Victoria, truly an exquisite destination.

Vancouver by Train

This is a wonderful day trip–Amtrak, leaves around 7:45, cruises along the shore of Puget Sound and up through gorgeous farm country, arrives 11:30. Explore Vancouver and return on the 6 pm dinner train!

Mt. St. Helens

Day trip to Mt. St. Helens National Monument–four hours each way, but dramatic vistas and wonderful visitors center.

The Outer Coast

Very few places around the US shore are as remote and wild as the Northwest coast of Washington.

Above: Cannon Beach, Oregon, an easy day drive from Seattle. Below: Diablo Dam, on the Skagit River, near the North Cascades Highway. Opposite: Pike Place Market, one of Seattle's most exciting places.

Where Once They Logged...

Top: Fir logs ready for sawing in a Puget Sound mill, circa 1900. The quality and size of the timber in the northwest awed the east coast lumber entrepreneurs that started mills there. Opposite page: Port Blakely, Bainbridge Island around 1880. Notice the size of the timbers the ship is loading into its stern ports, probably 20"x24," 50 or 60 feet long. To get such timbers today would be extremely difficult. UW MSCYUA 6560 Right: Timber office, Port Gamble, WA. The sawmill town here was established by two brothers from East Machias, Maine, in 1865. Missing their home, they made this community around the mill a replica of the town they had left behind. SFM F12.21.725m

When the timber barons came to Puget Sound, it was not just the trees that awed them–they were used to big doug firs on the California and Oregon coasts, but it was the harbors! Because on those bold coasts the ships could only get in to load lumber in the best of conditions because there were hardly any harbors worthy of the word.

In places there was wonderful timber but no harbors at all–ships had to run a cable from their mast to the dock while they lay at an exposed mooring, and tediously receive lumber by cable, steam up in their boilers, ready to leave immediately if the weather deteriorated.

But in Puget Sound it was the combination of good harbors and protected waters next to great stands of trees that created the vast timber economy that was to dominate the region for its first hundred years. Port Blakely, Port Madison, Port Gamble, Port Ludlow, and other sheltered sleepy coves became the destination of ships from all over the world as big mills and little towns sprang up to harvest the great trees and load them aboard ships.

LILBE
HAMBURG

ding large timbers for

TODAY THEY COMMUTE

Just 15 minutes from the ferry to downtown Seattle, West Port Madison is one of Puget Sound's many exquisite harbors. Bottom: Morning commuter ferry pulling into the dock at Kingston, 15 miles northwest of downtown Seattle, with Mt. Rainier in the background. Not a bad view for your morning commute!

Over time the great stands of timber around the sawmill towns were cut, and many mills closed or relocated to less valuable land where logs cut in more distant forests could be brought by tug and barge.

As the logging and mill jobs disappeared, workers from across the sound discovered the pleasures of having summer homes in the waterfront communities of Kitsap County, on the west side of central Puget Sound. A 'Mosquito Fleet' of small steamboats sprang up to move people and freight back and forth. Then as Seattle grew, more and more families discovered the value of living 'across the water,' with the primary worker commuting on the fleet of larger and faster ferries.

Seattle's growth really took off in the 1990s, and the traffic across the two Lake Washington bridges and along the region's freeways became more and more intense, furthering the interest in homes across Puget Sound. Today families here have to travel further and further to find housing they can afford and, it is not uncommon for people to travel 45 minutes or more to the ferry dock to wait to get on the ferry for the 35 minute or hour plus ride to downtown Seattle, depending on the run.

Seattle itineraries depart from the waterfront, site of all the action in the 1897-98 Yukon gold rush, when it was crowded with men seeking passage north to make their fortune and merchants trying to make their fortune selling supplies...

Have a look at the steeply sloped waterfront north of the city. In really wet winters, these hillsides get super saturated and the homes occasionally slide to the bottom.

A few miles north of the Edmonds ferry terminal on the east at **mile 19**, Port Susan, and Everett harbor open to the right or east of your ship. Over the bluff here is The Boeing Aircraft Companies big plant, home to the amazingly venerable 747, 777, and now the new "Dreamliner," the fuel efficient 787.

Small craft headed to Alaska like to stay in the narrowest waters, and unless the tides and the weather forecast are both perfect, usually branch off here, taking a scenic, but more winding route up to the San Juan Islands and then on into Canada. A favorite stop for these boats is **La Conner**, a very picturesque small town located along the shores of the Swinomish Slough. This area is all very fertile bottomland, part of the Skagit River delta. Hundreds of acres are planted in flowers, and a popular event each spring is the Tulip Festival.

At **mile 39**, the Point Wilson Lighthouse, your ship and the landscape make a major change. Just south of here is the **Deadly Triangle**, where the cannon from three forts once created an overlapping field of fire, though which no enemy ship could pass unscathed.

Point Wilson is the intersection between the sheltered waters of Puget Sound and the much wider and windier waters of the Strait of Juan de Fuca. It was somewhere around here that Captain George Vancouver, the English Navy Captain who first

The Boeing Aircraft Company, circa 1915, when lightweight Sitka spruce was a major structural component. MOHAI 9274A Bottom: A footbridge leads to a private island in Port Madison, on Bainbridge Island, directly across from Seattle.

Passenger Tip

You'll probably be busy, exploring the ship, unpacking, meeting up with friends, etc. But the Point Wilson area, beginning around mile 37, is a major transition, so you should be ready to have a look around. Typically, once your ship gets moving at full speed, it will be traveling around twenty miles an hour, so figure less than two hours to get up to the Point Wilson area.

Above: Sleepy Coupeville, on Whidbey Island. Small craft bound to Alaska or the San Juan Islands often take a route to the east of Whidbey.

Mile 40: Point Wilson lighthouse marks the transition from sheltered to more open waters.

explored and charted much of the northwest coast made his famous observation on page 17 which history proved correct.

There is a lot of tide here; look for tide tips close to the point, as well as sea lions and seals having a nice supper on the salmon which are swept by the tide close to the point.

The landscape changes dramatically at Point Wilson. Narrow Puget Sound opens up to the wide Strait of Juan de Fuca. Most large cruise ships leaving Seattle for Alaska will turn to the west here, staying to the right or north side of the traffic lanes as they parallel the Washington coast, along the US-Canada border.

On the bluff to the west at **Mile 38** is **Port Townsend**, a decidedly Victorian town with a wonderfully eclectic flavor. Realtors had really gotten excited in the 1880s when for a time it looked as if The Northern Pacific Railroad would select PT (as it is known locally) as its western terminal. But after a geography check, the NPRR wisely chose Tacoma instead. So while Seattle and Tacoma boomed, Port Townsend grew at a much slower pace, with Victorian style houses perched on the steep hills around town with commanding views of the intersection of Puget Sound and Juan de Fuca Strait.

If you look closely, just north of town, and south of the lighthouse at Point Wilson, you'll see what looks a bit like a New England college campus. This is Fort Worden, one of three major US Army facilities situated on the three points overlooking the entrance to Puget Sound. The fields of fire from their hidden cannon formed a killing zone to prevent enemy ships from enter-

ing Puget Sound. Today the cannons are gone but the forts are available for rent and are busy with many functions year round from soccer tournaments to sea kayaking symposiums.

About six hours after your ship leaves Seattle, you'll be at the place that sailors truly dreaded, before the advent of electronic aids to navigation. For decades, "Lost off Cape Flattery without a trace" was the epitaph for too many ships. This was the entrance to the Strait of Juan de Fuca, an area of strong currents, and frequent fogs. Captain Cook, exploring the coast, never found this ten mile wide entrance, wisely staying out of the fog near the coast.

The consequences of a navigational error were severe; the coasts of northwest Washington and Vancouver Island were fringed with reefs, isolated spires, and rocks. The surf was almost always heavy and any ship caught in its grip would be quickly destroyed.

Tugboat skippers knew how sailing masters felt about the entrance to the strait, and in those days before good radio communications, would patrol the entrance, hoping to pick up a big square rigger, anxious about the weather and looking for a tow up the strait to its final destination.

So many ships were lost along the British Columbia shore north of Cape Flattery that a trail was constructed along the very

Above: Downtown Port Townsend is full of exquisite buildings like this one. Below: This community is a major center for wooden boat enthusiasts. with several active boatyards.

Mt. St. Helens:

Volcano watchers knew something big was happening on Mt. St. Helens, that spring of 1980. It had started months earlier when a stark black blotch of fresh ash appeared on her pristine snowy coat one morning.

Then came the rumblings and steam and ash venting: after 138 years of sleep, the volcano, 80 miles south of Seattle, was waking up.

Safety zones were set up, access limited, and evacuations begun for the owners and operators of a few remote wilderness lodges on spectacular Spirit Lake. One crusty lodge owner stayed. "The mountain would never hurt me," he said.

Then something more ominous began to happen—the mountain bulged substantially, as if something were building up inside. But no one expected the events of May 18.

With the power of a nuclear bomb, the top 1,200' of the mountain simply disappeared, blown into the sky with a cubic mile or so of ash, knocking flat thousands of acres of prime big two and three foot diameter fir trees.

Apparently the inside of the mountain had been filled with lava and gas, all under tremendous pressure, until, like popping the top on a shaken soda, an earthquake ripped the mountain open, and everything exploded. Roger Werth Photo

Tacoma Narrows

When the Tacoma Narrows Bridge opened in the spring of 1940. residents were thrilled. But shortly thereafter it began exhibiting very unusual behavior—oscillating so badly on windy days that sometimes you would lose sight of the car ahead of you because of the motion of the bridge deck. Heavy gravel trucks were parked on the bridge on windy days to reduce the motion until a better way could be found to handle the problem.

It wasn't enough—just four months after it opened, on a day when its action was so violent that drivers abandoned their cars and ran, 'Galloping Gertie,' as she had become known, shook herself to pieces and fell into the gorge.

Since then parts of two of Washington's floating bridges (in water too deep for regular bridges), have broken up and sunk in stormy weather. It's hard on bridges here. MOHAI PI0793

THE SAN JUAN ISLANDS

"A place in the San Juans" was the ultimate for northwesterners–a little waterfront bungalow somewhere among the large and small islands of this sleepy archipelago, just 50 miles north of Seattle, but a world away. With four major islands served by ferries out of Anacortes, and dozens of smaller ones, they are a major destination for vacationers. In recent years the price for all land has shot up, and a bit of a two tier society has developed with teachers and other workers finding it very hard to find affordable places to buy. It is also a place where the pace of life in the winter slows way down, especially on the smaller islands. There are a number of summer camps here where generations of Northwest families have sent their children.

Above: "Waterfront fixer upper"–wouldn't it be a dream to find a place like this for a modest price? Actually it is one of the cabins at Cape Four Winds, a boys and girls camp that has changed little over the years. Right: Seal and classic sailboats, West Sound, Orcas Island.

The crew of this schooner which went ashore on a Washington beach south of Cape Flattery was lucky; they survived. Had they gone ashore 60 or 70 miles further north, on the rocky shore of Vancouver Island, their ship would have broken apart in the surf on the rocks, and few would have made it ashore. Puget Sound Maritime Historical Society 2727-3

Passenger Tip

There's a lot to do aboard ship your first night out, but this landscape is really worth seeing. Find a place in the front part of your ship with a good view forward and just sit for a bit and look at the changing scene.

rugged shore of Vancouver Island, north of the entrance to the Strait. At intervals cabins were built, stocked with food and firewood and a telephone to the nearest lighthouse.

The straits also marks the place where the coast road ends, on both sides, cut off by the rugged geography. From here to the north on the Vancouver Island side, there are a few small towns, but only reached by long and twisting roads heavily used by log trucks.

THE WILD WEST COAST OF VANCOUVER IS.

The overnight passage from Seattle takes you to a very different land. Gone are the waterfront homes, a road that follows the shore, lights at night, buildings or other signs of man seen by day.

The west coast of Vancouver island is very rugged, open to the full force of the storms that drive in off the North Pacific. It is also almost completely isolated from the busy east coast—only a couple of roads penetrate the difficult interior of the island, essentially upgraded logging roads, winding and potholed.

For most of the 20th century, the economy here was almost totally resource driven. Salmon, herring, halibut, and timber. You were either producing them, processing them, or supporting the folks who did.

With few roads, the canneries and fish processing plants were scattered in remote coves, only accessed by boat and floatplane. All winter long the plants would sleep, tended by just a caretaker and perhaps his family. Then in the spring boats would bring

The native and often Asian cannery workers and for the busy months of the herring and salmon season.

Bunkhouses, processing equipment and messhalls would come alive while the fish ran. Then in the fall, the workers would return to their homes in the few larger towns and the fish plants would settle in for the long and quiet winter.

For the loggers, only the western slopes of the coast mountains of Oregon and Washington have growing conditions rivaling that of the west coast of Vancouver Island. The great forests of fir, hemlock, cedar, and spruce that created the lumber economy of the Pacific Northwest, are here, too.

The hard part was access. Unlike the Oregon and Northern California coasts, the west coast of Vancouver Island is penetrated by many deep, winding, and sheltered inlets. However, the country was steep and very rugged, and except in a few places, totally without roads.

Heavy equipment was barged into remote inlets, and winding roads carved out of the difficult landscape to access the thick forest. In a few places the forest was steep enough close to the shore that the trees, when felled expertly, would slide neatly down into the water. But in most, a network of rough roads would be carved out of the difficult landscape, and so called high point logging set up, whereby a system of winches on the ground and pulleys hung from high trees could transport logs to a central loading point for the truck or trains.

In addition to the industrial style logging–big trucks, tugs and mills, there was opportunity here for the small scale operator as well. Cedar shingles, used both for siding and roofs on houses

Top: Isolated West Coast beach–few beaches here have any road access. Truly committed surfers might have to hike for hours through rugged terrain to try out a new beach. Below: West coast harbor entrance; mariners tread carefully here as in stormy weather seas sweep across the narrow entrance and getting in can be very dangerous and sometimes impossible.

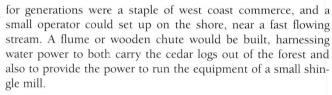

Above: Street scene; downtown Ucuelet. When salmon trolling seasons got shorter and shorter, some fishermen brought their boats ashore and looked for other work. Below: Making do with what you have: beached fishing boat turned into a house, Tofino.

for generations were a staple of west coast commerce, and a small operator could set up on the shore, near a fast flowing stream. A flume or wooden chute would be built, harnessing water power to both carry the cedar logs out of the forest and also to provide the power to run the equipment of a small shingle mill.

CHANGES COME TO THE WEST COAST

If someone had told a West Coast logger or fishermen in the boom years of the 1950s that a new economy would come to the coast, based on whale watching, kayaking, eco tours, and vacationers, chances are he might have fallen over backwards laughing in disbelief. Back then the life was so rough, so rugged, so remote from anything not connected immediately to the business at hand–logging and fishing–that a change of that dimension seemed totally out of the question.

Yet this is exactly what happened. The salmon stocks that the West Coast fishermen depended on slumped badly in the 1970s and 1980s, due to a combination of mismanagement–overfishing–and damage done to salmon habitat. At the same time a growing awareness by the native tribes and commercial fishermen of the ecological damage of certain logging practices led to logging restrictions.

What had seemed like an endless bounty in the 1950s became closed logging camps and shorter and shorter fishing seasons three decades later. 'What will happen to us?' was a refrain up

THE FLOATING TOWNS

There were of course no towns nor facilities of any kind in these remote inlets where the logging took place. The landscape was too steep in many places to set down the buildings that a full scale logging camp required: mess halls, bunkhouses, equipment sheds, blacksmith shop, and the like.

Besides, it made little sense to go to the trouble of building a town in a remote inlet that would just have to be moved when the inlet was logged.

The solution was to build whole little floating towns, complete with houses for couples, schools, stores, and gardens: all floating! And when that inlet was logged, a tug was called and the whole town towed, slowly, very slowly... to the next inlet.

Right: Abandoned floating home with trollers, Milbanke Sound, 1972. Top: narrow gauge logging railroads were often built to move logs from woods to mill or to the water. UW 10954

and down the West Coast as the traditional mainstays of coastal income, fishing and logging, changed dramatically.

Few expected or anticipated what happened next. A growing urban population and a culture more attuned to the outdoors suddenly became aware of the dramatic beauty of this coast. Within a few years remote fishing outports like Tofino and Ucuelet transformed themselves to offer services to the new visitors: urbanites with money in their pockets and a keen desire to experience and explore this hitherto almost forgotten corner of British Columbia.

And the rough weather that made mariners so cautious about this coast brought another unexpected contingent: the surfers. Just south of Tofino is 10 miles of beach, broken by rugged headlands, but providing probably the best and reasonably accessible surf on the BC coast.

Along with the surfers were the kayakers, particularly seeking places like the myriad Broken Islands in Barkley Sound. Outfitters here both rent epquiment and offer expeditions, where they provide the food, set up the tents, etc. for more upscale clients. North of the Barkley Sound - Tofino area the settlements become rare, the visitors, fewer. Visitors here are apt to be hardy yachtsmen, sportfishermen, or particularly adventuresome kayakers, for whom a passage along the west coast of Vancouver Island is an epic journey. In the Nootka area, a local freight boat, the *Uchuck III*, offers a service to drop kayakers off at remote locations and pick them up days or weeks later.

Logging continues in some of the winding inlets, though at a slower pace than in previous decades. But for the most part the land is wild and lonely. .

The new coastal economy is more based on recreation and second homes than extractive industries like commercial fishing and logging. Top: Fishing resort, Ucuelet - you can either stay on board or in the lodge on shore. Below: Surfers at Long Beach, south of Ucuelet wear wet suits even in summer. Opposite page: Sea kayaking is a major activity in Barkley Sound and the lower British Columbia coast. Tcp photo from Pacific Rim Paddling.

VICTORIA

Victoria's inner harbor is dominated by the Provincial Parliament, above, and the big Empress Hotel. Statue on right is Queen Victoria.

Your ship docks just a few blocks from Victoria's inner harbor, a "don't miss" spot dominated by the Empress Hotel and the classic architecture of the buildings housing the provincial legislature. This is a city that also truly celebrates its maritime heritage—look for the brass plaques around the top of the inner harbor's sea wall across from the Empress that commemorate people like Miles and Bea Smeaton, who battled Cape Horn in their 38-footer as well as their crew John Guzwell, who circled the globe in a homemade 26-footer.

While Vancouver—just 75 miles to the NW—is a totally cosmopolitan modern city with a heavy sprinkling of Asian immigrants, Victoria seems a bit more like a taste of Olde England. The British fondness for gardens is especially evident in the many private and public gardens and plantings that line its streets.

Originally settled when a Hudson's Bay Company trading post was established here in 1843, this city and Vancouver Island became a crown colony in 1849. Ten years later another colony was established on the mainland to support the many prospectors that had arrived with the 1858 Fraser River gold strike. Eventually the two colonies merged to form what is today British Columbia and Victoria became its administrative capital, while Vancouver became the industrial center.

Today, though separated by 75 miles of water and

islands, the two are intimately liked with regular ferries (Vancouver bound ferries leave from Sidney, about 20 miles NE of downtown Victoria) as well as big twin-engine floatplanes that go downtown to downtown.

What to see: Fortunately, many of Victoria's attractions are centered around the harbor:

The Royal British Columbia Museum is one of the best small museums you'll ever encounter. If you want to see Northwest Native culture up close, this will be probably your best opportunity. While the tribes in British Columbia are distinct from those along the areas of Coastal Alaska that you will be traveling through, their art such as totem poles share many of the same themes.

The Empress Hotel was part of a series of large and very notable resorts built by the Canadian Pacific Railway. Make a point of visiting the restored lobby, where afternoon tea is a major local event.

Across the harbor are the seaplane docks and the booking and boarding area for **whale watching tours**. This area is particularly suited for seeing orcas or killer whales.

12 miles from downtown are **Butchart Gardens**, which has become one of the most visited sites in the province. What is now a stunning 50 acre showpiece had rather humble beginnings. In 1904 Jennnie Butchart, whose husband operated a cement plant near the site, got tired of staring at the ugly scar in the land that his limestone quarrying operations left. She brought in a few plants to spruce up the area, one thing led to another and now hundreds of thousands of visitors come to see her handiwork.

Known in Canada as First Nations, the native tribes of British Columbia have a colorful cultural heritage. This clan house is on the grounds of the Royal British Columbia Museum, a truly excellent facility located near the Empress Hotel, just off Victoria Harbor. The large totem display area is open to the street and is easy to view, even in the evening when the museum is closed.

VANCOUVER

Like most Northwest coast cities, forest products played a huge part in Vancouver's history, with big square riggers waiting to take lumber to Asian, Australian, and Pacific ports as soon as it could be milled. It still continues today–you'll cross the Fraser River entering the city. Look down and most likely you'll see BC's premier product, logs, (some say marijuana is the province's biggest export...) traveling by barge or raft to a sawmill or a waiting ship.

With one of the best harbors on the coast, good road and rail connections, it quickly developed into Canada's premier west coast port as well. With a dramatic mountain and waterfront setting, the city became one of the favorite spots in the British Empire within a few decades of being founded, as evidenced by the many large and elegant Victorian era homes.

In more modern times, concerns about what would happen in Hong Kong after the mainland Chinese took over in 1997 led to the arrival of large numbers of Chinese immigrants, many of whom brought substantial personal wealth with them. The result is a noticeably multi-ethnic city with the second biggest Chinatown in North America.

Opposite: Granville Island, close to downtown is a delightful place with many places to eat and a huge market. Top: Cruise ship at Canada Place, one of two cruise terminals. Bottom: Make sure you take time to walk around Chinatown, on the waterfront, a few blocks east of Canada Place.

Opposite: there are some gorgeous buildings downtown here. Top: in the early evening, a big cruise ship heads out toward the Lion's Gate Bridge and the journey to Alaska. Below: Street art at Canada Place.

Around town: Many of the sights are easily accessible from where your ship docks. Within walking or short taxi distance is much of the city core with almost unlimited shopping and dining. There is also a subway/elevated rail system called the Skytrain which makes getting around fairly simple.

A few blocks east of Canada Place is **Gastown**, where the city was first settled, and today is an eclectic neighborhood of old warehouses made into restaurants, artist's lofts, condos, and all manner of shops.

Chinatown is a few more blocks to the south (consider a taxi) and its size reflects Vancouver's popularity with Asians. This is the real thing: If you don't read Chinese, make sure your menu has English as well. With the waters of Georgia Strait and the North Pacific close at hand, many restaurants feature live tanks from which patrons may select their meal.

Visitors and Vancouverites alike are indeed fortunate that its founders set aside the 1,000 or so acres that today is **Stanley Park**. It features restaurants, a zoo, the ubiquitous totems, but most of all a stunning waterfront setting right next to downtown. A popular walk leads through the park to a dramatic overlook at Lion's Gate.

Take the foot ferry to **Granville Island** on False Creek. Granville Island is a combination of a farmer's and craftsmen's market, with restaurants.

Within walking distance west of Granville Island is the **Vancouver Maritime Museum**, whose showpiece exhibit is the brave little steamer *St. Roche*, which much of her epic two year Vancouver to Newfoundland transit frozen into the Arctic ice.

If you didn't get Victoria–consider a quick trip–floatplanes leave from just west of Canada Place and fly over the scenic waterways of the Gulf Islands and land in the harbor–right downtown!

CHAPTER 2

The Wilderness Begins

Vancouver, B.C., Mile 95, to Alaska Border, Mile 575W

"Tracing shining ways through fiord and sound, past forests and waterfalls, islands and mountains and far azure headlands, it seems as if surely we must at length reach the very paradise of the poets, the abode of the blessed."

- John Muir, *Travels in Alaska*

Top B.C Ferry crossing lower Jervis Inlet, one of many many winding and essentially wilderness inlets on the North Coast. Below: Point Atkinson Lighthouse with Howe Sound behind it. Opposite page: Totems at Stanley Park in Vancouver.

L ook to the right a few miles after you pass under Lion's Gate Bridge, leaving Vancouver, to the Point Atkinson Lighthouse. If you want to get a clear sense of what much of the coast of British Columbia and Alaska is like, look beyond the lighthouse.

This is Howe Sound, the first of the many deep and winding inlets that penetrate far into the interior. For example, there is no road around the head of the inlet —the land is too rough, you have to take a ferry across instead.

And it was here that the first explorers, like British Captain George Vancouver, who explored and named much of the B.C. and Southeast Alaska coasts, had their troubles. At the time, the British were under the impression that there was a passage somewhere across or through North America from the Pacific to the

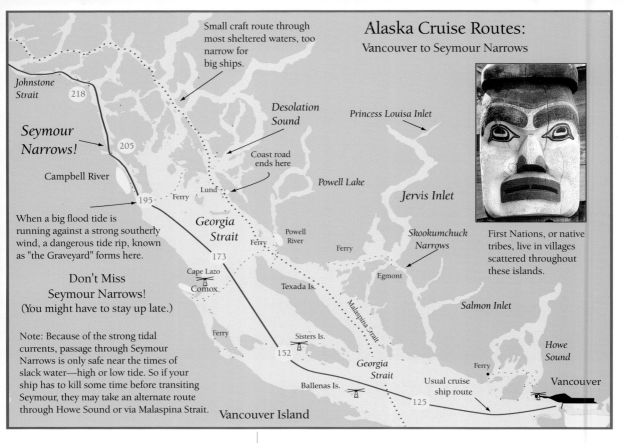

Alaska Cruise Routes:
Vancouver to Seymour Narrows

Small craft route through most sheltered waters, too narrow for big ships.

Johnstone Strait 218

Desolation Sound

Princess Louisa Inlet

Seymour Narrows!

205

Campbell River

Coast road ends here

Powell Lake

Jervis Inlet

195 Ferry

Lund

Georgia Strait

When a big flood tide is running against a strong southerly wind, a dangerous tide rip, known as "the Graveyard" forms here.

Powell River

Skookumchuck Narrows

First Nations, or native tribes, live in villages scattered throughout these islands.

173 Ferry

Cape Lazo
Comox

Ferry

Egmont

Texada Is.

Salmon Inlet

Don't Miss Seymour Narrows!
(You might have to stay up late.)

Malaspina Strait

Ferry

Sisters Is.

Howe Sound

Note: Because of the strong tidal currents, passage through Seymour Narrows is only safe near the times of slack water—high or low tide. So if your ship has to kill some time before transiting Seymour, they may take an alternate route through Howe Sound or via Malaspina Strait.

152

Georgia Strait

Ferry

Usual cruise ship route

Vancouver

Ballenas Is.

125

Vancouver Island

Atlantic—the "Northwest Passage"—and his job was to see if it existed. This meant that each promising inlet or channel had to be explored to make sure it wasn't the legendary channel.

Leaving Vancouver, you enter Georgia Strait, sort of an inland sea that is the home to much of the population and industry of lower British Columbia.

It also has a climate that is often noticeably different from that just a hundred or so miles to the north. This is the rain shadow effect of the mountains of Vancouver Island; the mainland coast north of Vancouver city are nicknamed the sunshine coast for the same reason.

EXPLORING BY BC FERRY

The BC Ferry system offers a very modest priced way to explore here, island hopping by day, and spending the night in bed and breakfasts, camping, etc. One possibility is to take the ferry across Howe Sound from the Horseshoe Bay terminal north of Vancouver, exploring the Sunshine Coast, ferry across Jervis Inlet to the Powell River area, explore, then ferry across to Vancouver Is.

From there you have even more ferry and island choices. Explore at www.bcferries.com

Imagine this: several cubic miles of water must pass through the maze of narrow channels north of Vancouver, every six hours. This is the tide pouring in and out of Georgia Strait to the North Pacific.

Unless you are from the Northwest or from Nova Scotia, the tides here are larger than any you probably have encountered before and can have major effects upon mariners traveling here, even on a ship as big as a large cruise ship.

The main effect is in the narrow channels where the tide can create currents up to almost 20 MPH, as well as whirlpools big enough to capsize 60 foot boats! The prudent mariner transits such areas at slack water—near the time of high and low tide.

Once, when I was an incautious young skipper in a 60 footer, I was towing a disabled 36 fishing boat down from Alaska to Seattle. Eager to get home, but too late for safe slack water, I though I could still get through constricted Dodd Narrows against the current. So I went up onto the flying bridge and shouldered our way into the current.

Instantly I knew it was a bad mistake—the current shoved us violently back and forth and I was desperately afraid that the boat I was towing would hit the shore in one of our wild swings. But finally we got through, and I radioed back to the fellow I was towing, a cool customer, on his 25th season as an Alaska commercial fishermen.

"It wasn't too bad," he answered me, " I had to steer a bit to keep off the rocks. ...and, oh, yeah, I bit my cigar in half..."

Top: Skookumchuck Rapids—the effect of the tide here is to create a standing wave, which a skilled kayaker can 'surf' for minutes on end. Above: Low tide strands boats in Bristol Bay, where the tidal current runs so fast boat propellers spin when your boat is anchored!

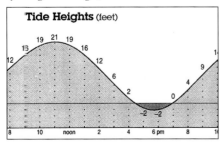

Tide Heights (feet)

19 21 19
13   16
12   12
              6
              2   0
          -2 -2

8   10   noon   2   4   6 pm   8

Fly up here for dinner! The West Coast Wilderness Lodge in Egmont, B.C. has a wonderful package offer—dinner and round trip floatplane flight from Vancouver. Contact www.wcwl.com. Below: At low tide; a dungeness crab and a chiton. ML Upton photo

Looking for a great place to retire? The **Gulf Islands**, directly across Georgia Straits, with dozens of islands large and small, served by several ferries, would truly be a great choice. They are particularly popular with boaters, and noticeably less crowded than the **American San Juan Islands**, just across the border to the south. Many Canadians have second homes here, a short ferry ride away from Victoria or Vancouver.

Things to look for:

- Log and chip barges: British Columbia is a legendary producer of forest products. Wood chips are moved in big high-sided barges so full they seem almost submerged.

- Log booms: The rectangular rafts of logs towed slowly behind tugs are hard to see at night, because frequently they are marked only by dim and flickering kerosene lamps.

- Alaska-bound tugs and barges from Puget Sound, stacked high with container vans with large items, such as boats, strapped on top.

- The big mills: Most noticeable is Powell River, east of Mile 173, one of the largest in the world.

To the mariner, 'inside' basically means protected, away from the ocean waves and swells, and the effect of a strong wind. And when the Pleistocene glaciers carved out the canyons and fjords of the Northwest about a million years ago, they created the Inside Passage and a boaters paradise.

If there were no Inside Passage—if the coast of British Columbia and Alaska were like that of Oregon and California—bold with great beaches but few harbors—there probably wouldn't be any Alaska cruises either. For there would be no glacial fjords to cruise into and no harbors to visit.

The very history of Alaska and British Columbia would have been much different, for it was the existence of all these sheltered passageways that allowed travelers, even in the smallest craft to travel north in safety.

When cruise ships were small, say less than 500', they followed the traditional Inside Passage north of Vancouver Island: Milbanke Sound, Lama Passage, Tolmie Channel, Graham and Fraser Reaches, and dramatic quarter mile wide Grenville Channel, to Alaska.

Unfortunately for you, almost all of today's very large ships find the traditional route a little too narrow. There are alternate, wider, and still scenic routes, via Caamano Sound and Principe Channel. But for some reason, probably a very minor cost savings—you don't need a Canadian pilot—now most large ships just go straight up Hecate Strait from Vancouver Island to the Alaska border. It might be cheaper, but it sure isn't as scenic.

Above: Particularly for smaller vessels—say under 200'—the myriad winding channels of the Inside Passage offer a better route to Alaska. Look carefully in the foreground and you will see tide swirls as immense volumes of water try to squeeze through narrow passages. Right: Would you want to go to Alaska in this? Actually many modest fishing and pleasure craft of this size and even smaller travel the Inside Passage to Alaska each summer.

DESOLATION SOUND

There are few things better than exploring around one of the anchorages here by small boat on a still summer morning. In several places there are rope swings on overhanging trees —perfect for swinging out and dropping into the deep water!

Northbound Passengers: look to the north, or to the right of your ship's course with the last of the daylight. If it is at all clear, you should be able to see the dramatic mountains in the Desolation Sound area, west of about **mile 180** on your map.

Poor Captain Vancouver—he was here on a particularly wet June in 1792, described it as 'gloomy and forlorn.' OK, in reality he had a bit of a melancholy disposition to start with and he was finding what would be a three year search for the Northwest Passage a bit... tedious.

But this is easily the most misnamed place on the entire coast: it is totally spectacular. And the best part is: there are no roads—the steepness of the mountains ends the BC coast road a few miles south—and it is almost all a protected marine park!

And this: the salt water is warm enough for great swim-

The new boardwalk at Lund, where the road ends on the mainland coast. North of here the steep mountains in the Desolation Sound area end any possibility of continuing the road north. Lund is the jumping off point for kayakers and boaters with small craft who have perhaps trailered their boats here for easer access to the wilderness to the north. Below: A classic cruiser in Roscoe Bay, one of Desolation Sound's special places.

ming and oysters grow wild on the shores—for boaters it doesn't get much better than that. The reason is that the tidal currents from the south—coming in Juan de Fuca Strait and the north—coming in from Johnstone Strait - meet here. The effect is that you have the normal high and low tides here, but the water doesn't move very far and just gets warmer and warmer. Plus the effect of the high mountains seems to throw the heat back at the water sometimes. We were here the last week of June in 2004, and it was so warm that we would go up to the flying bridge of our chartered boat in the early evening to have our gin and tonics in the shade! Only when the sun went over the mountain did it get cool enough to cook!

Fortunately it is a long ways from the major Puget Sound yachting centers. But it is definitely a Mecca for boaters, for whom a trip to Desolation is something to yarn about all winter!.

DON'T MISS SEYMOUR

Star Princess in Seymour Narrows, just about to pass over the exact spot where Ripple Rock was blasted out of the middle of the channel. Several cubic miles of water must pass through this channel every few hours as the tide rushes in and out, creating very swift currents. Safe passage through the Narrows is only possible near the times of high or low tide. On Saturday nights when north and southbound cruise ships must all transit the Narrows within a fairly short period, it can get a bit anxious for the Captains and British Columbia pilots!

"Hey, kid, wake up, ya gotta see this..!"

It was June, 1965, I was just 18, just left Seattle on my first Alaska fishing boat job, and the 70 year old mate woke me. I stumbled up into the wheelhouse, amazed at what I was seeing: great, slowly turning whirlpools, through which the skipper struggled, turning the wheel back and forth, trying to find a safe way between them.

"It used to be worse, before they blasted Ripple Rock!"

Along the waterfront, Seymour Narrows, **mile 205**, was a legendary place. A ship killer rock had lurked, right in the middle of the channel, creating whirlpools large enough to suck down good sized boats. Safe passage was only possible at slack water, near the times of low and high tide. For big ships, this was the only sheltered route north, and as they got bigger, "Old Rip" became more and more of a hazard.

First they tried drilling from a barge anchored with four **250 ton anchors**! Didn't work—the violent current meant that the drill bits kept breaking off.

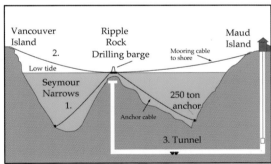

Top: drill barge positioned directly over Ripple Rock with the violent rapids generated by the two pinnacles that lurked just below the surface clearly visible. Because of the currents and whirlpools, drilling from the barge proved infeasible. Left: The tunneling project was only begun after it became clear that the swift currents made it impossible to blast the rock any other way.

Finally a huge drilling project was undertaken—over 3200' of tunnels and vertical shafts—reaching up into the interior of the rock. This was before the sophisticated sort of surveying equipment that we take for granted today was available, and drillers would explore with small diameter drills—until they broke through to the water. Then they'd plug the hole and use the information to create a 3D map of where they were.

Finally tugs pushed **bargeloads of dynamite**—2.8 million pounds to load into the cave they had excavated, and on April 7, 1958: Adios Ripple Rock!

— Passenger Tip —

Ships departing Vancouver usually transit Seymour late at night or early morning. If the time isn't announced, ask; even in the dim twilight it is a dramatic sight. Southbound ships headed for Vancouver usually transit early evening so you'll have a much better chance to view it..

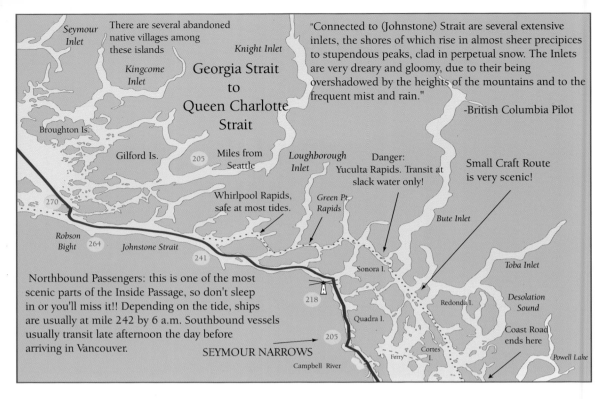

Seymour
Inlet

There are several abandoned native villages among these islands

Knight Inlet

Kingcome
Inlet

Georgia Strait
to
Queen Charlotte
Strait

"Connected to (Johnstone) Strait are several extensive inlets, the shores of which rise in almost sheer precipices to stupendous peaks, clad in perpetual snow. The Inlets are very dreary and gloomy, due to their being overshadowed by the heights of the mountains and to the frequent mist and rain."

-British Columbia Pilot

Broughton Is.

Gilford Is.   205   Miles from
                            Seattle

Loughborough
Inlet

Danger:
Yuculta Rapids. Transit at
slack water only!

Small Craft Route
is very scenic!

270

Whirlpool Rapids,
safe at most tides.

Green Pt.
Rapids

Bute Inlet

Robson
Bight   264   Johnstone Strait

Toba Inlet

241

Sonora I.

218

Redonda I.

Desolation
Sound

Northbound Passengers: this is one of the most scenic parts of the Inside Passage, so don't sleep in or you'll miss it!! Depending on the tide, ships are usually at mile 242 by 6 a.m. Southbound vessels usually transit late afternoon the day before arriving in Vancouver.

Quadra I.

205

Coast Road
ends here

SEYMOUR NARROWS

Campbell River

Cortes
I.

Ferry

Powell Lake

Most large ships take the route marked by the blue line through this area. Smaller ships—say up to 225'— usually take the more winding and scenic route further east via Yuculta Rapids. Below: The old government dock at Shoal Bay is a good place to wait for slack water if you are southbound through Yuculta Rapids.

--- Passenger Tip ---

Vancouver departing passengers: the area between Seymour Narrows, mile 205 and Pine Island, mile 319, are very scenic. If you sleep in, you'll miss it.

MAJOR LANDSCAPE CHANGES

Seymour marks a huge transition in your trip. Literally it is as if there were an invisible line that ran from just south of Seymour to just south of Yuculta Rapids. To the south is civilization—towns, roads, lights on the shore at night, a warmer climate.

But the land to the north is very different—wilder, lonelier, cloudier, and chillier. This is the wild north coast where vast areas are sort of de facto wilderness, with here and there a logging camp, native village, or sportfishing resort. And the further north you go, the wilder it gets. Once you get north of Vancouver Island and into the channels and bays on the east side of Hecate Strait, you may find bays that go months or perhaps even years without seeing a boat or a human.

And the tide runs very swiftly through the Discovery Islands. There are a number of routes: Seymour for the big cruise ships, Yuculta Rapids for small cruise ships, yachts and fish boats (they like the narrow channels,) and the narrowest channels in between, for even smaller craft, with crews willing to pick their ways through the rock piles.

But whatever the route, vessels must wait for slack water or close to it, for safe passage. To do otherwise risks getting capsized or swamped by the powerful whirlpools and rips.

It is almost as if nature set a gate across the route. At the very place where the busy south coast ends, and the wilderness begins. As if to warn the traveler of what lies beyond.

"May 30, 1981, Wellbore Channel, B.C: My crew and my wife and I had worked for weeks to get our fish-buying vessel ready for a long season. We'd left Seattle with a deck load of cargo to stow and a two-page list of jobs still to do. We'd gotten underway early, traveled late, caught slack water at Yuculta Rapids at midnight, tied to the deserted wharf at Shoal Bay an hour later. We just needed to rest, to sleep for a few sweet hours, before going on: to Greene Point Rapids, Whirlpool Rapids, Johnstone Strait, Queen Charlotte Sound, on and on, until we got to our cannery in Alaska, 600 miles north.

In the hour before dawn, I got up quietly, stretched my legs in the starlight, making dark footprints on the frost covered dock, past the abandoned lodge, the rusting farm equipment. As I slipped back aboard, first light was coming to the sky above the dark hills and the wild, lonely land all around.

The big Caterpillar engine rumbled to life. I threw the lines off the empty dock, got a coffee, and took it up to the flying bridge. We moved out into the channel; there was just the whistle of the turbo, the rush of the tide, the green smell of the woods, and the rich smell of the sea."

- Author's journal

"I was tied up to a log raft, up in Teakerne Arm, you know where it is, about 10 miles south of Yucultas, waiting for the tide. There was a big Canadian troller laying there, and the guy was out on the logs, so we visited for a bit. Then there was a sound from his boat, like a woman crying out, and he excused himself and went aboard. A long while passed with more crying, and then it got quiet and he came out again, wiping his hands on a rag. It looked like blood, so I asked him if everything was alright.

'Ah,' he said, 'that was the baby coming out.' He shrugged. 'A little girl. They're both fine.'"

- A B.C salmon troller

"It was thick o'fog, when we were waiting below the Yucultas 'fer slack, and we kept hearing some-thing, like it was blowing, then they came up all around us—this pack o'killer whales—Jesus, there musta' been ten or twelve of them, with them big fins. Well sir, I want to tell ya', they waited and wait-ed just like us, and then when that tide stopped running, they timed it just right and went through along with us, slack water, right on the button."

- A B.C. logger

ORCA ALERT!

The classic orca shot—a trio of big males in Johnstone Strait. If you are a passenger leaving Vancouver in July and August, try to get up early when your ship is transiting this part of the coast, as most ships will transit this area around daybreak. If you're south-bound, you pass here in the after-noon, so you have a better chance to see one. Frans Lanting, Minden Pictures
Below: Orcas are a ubiquitous cultural symbol all throughout the Pacific Northwest.

Johnstone Strait is probably the best known place in North America to see orcas. The good months are July and August, when the orcas are chowing down on migrating salmon as well as seals which also eat the salmon.

British Columbia orcas played a huge part in the worldwide change in human perception and understanding of orcas. In June of 1965, Bill Lechkobit, a B.C. salmon fisherman caught a big bull orca in his net, near **Namu, mile 375**, and decided to try to keep it alive and sell it.

Seattle Aquarium owner Ted Griffin was very aware of the success that the Victoria Aquarium had with its captive orca, Moby Doll, and jumped at the opportunity to get one. He rushed up to Namu with a crew, built a floating underwater cage or pen, hired a tug, crossed his fingers and headed down to Seattle.

For the first day or so, an obviously distressed female orca with two young or calves, followed Namu's cage, squeaking and chirping in communication according to one watcher.

Griffin was very lucky, getting Namu safely to Seattle and installing him in a big tank in his aquarium with big viewing ports for the paying customers. As Moby Doll had in Victoria, Namu thrilled the customers, who quickly had to revise their perception of what an orca was.

Instead of an angry killer, audiences found a creature that was obviously intelligent, gentle, and even funny. Ted Griffin spent huge amounts of time with his new capture, teaching it tricks, and even putting on a neoprene wet suit and getting into the water with him. National Geographic ran a 28 page story on Griffin and Namu that went a long ways to dispel the myths

many had about orcas.

But just 11 months later Namu died from an infection. Griffin, devastated, realized what a money maker Namu had been for his struggling business and set out to capture another one.

Unfortunately all the publicity about Namu and Moby Dall created sort of a wild west gold rush mentality about capturing orcas, and Griffin captured a whole school of orcas on the east side of Whitbey Island, and offered them for sale. Tragically, in the commotion, several of the captured orcas accidentally died.

This was not good publicity for folks who wanted to make a buck capturing orcas. Eventually the Washington state legislature became concerned and involved after an even more spectacular orca capture a few years later. This one occurred in an inlet so close to the actual capitol building in Olympia, Washington, that legislators could hear the helicopters! This was in the era of Earth Day and a swiftly growing awareness of the environment and the natural world, and shortly thereafter Washington, followed by British Columbia banned the capture of orcas. Unfortunately in the decade between Namu's capture and the bans, around 100 orcas were killed or taken from the Puget Sound-lower British Columbia orca population.

Orca awareness probably reached a peak after the release of "Free Willy,' starring an orca whose real name was Keiko. Poorly housed in a Mexican aquarium after the film, Keiko's plight inspired a large number of supporters, and his life became an astonishing saga of high profile fund raising by schoolchildren all over the world up to millionaires like Craig McCaw, an interim home in an custom made Oregon aquarium tank, and eventually a high profile ride in a U.S. Air Force C-17 transport and finally to the fjord in Iceland, near where he had been captured some 25 years earlier. There had always been an element of worry if he could be successfully reintroduced into the wild after so long in captivity. But he was released successfully in the wild, where he survived for about 18 months before dying of pneumonia. At 27, he was old for a captive orca, but young for a wild one, many of whom live for 40 years plus.

Orca: Size: to 30 feet. Range: global, but especially coastal. Distinguishing features: bold black and white markings and dramatic tall dorsal fin on the male. Habits: Travels in extended family groups called pods, feeds on salmon, herring, marine mammals and other fish. Have been known to slide up onto ice floes to eat resting seals! Will also occasionally slide up on a beach with a breaking wave to grab an unwary seal, and try to wriggle off again in the next big wave.

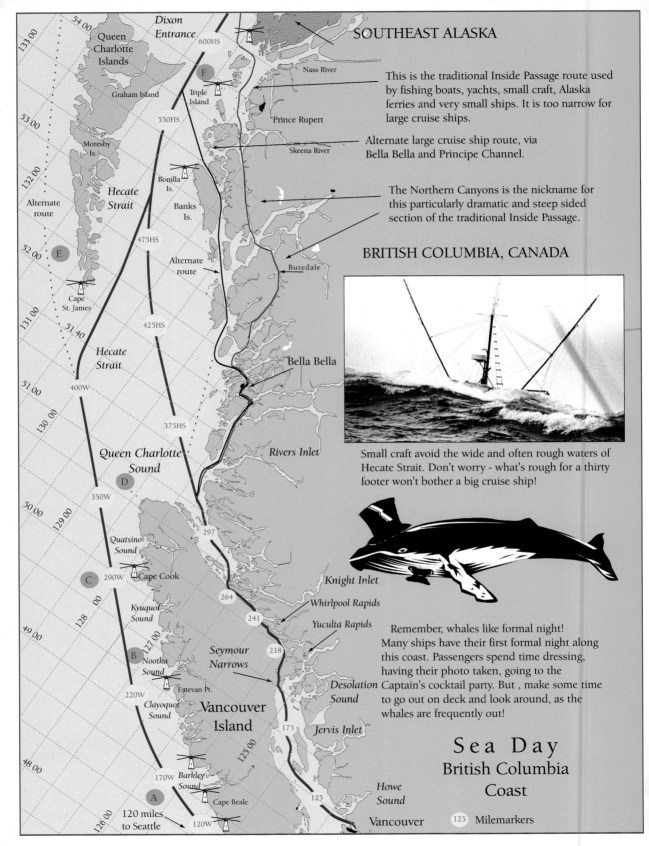

SOUTHEAST ALASKA

Dixon Entrance

Queen Charlotte Islands

Graham Island

Nass River

Prince Rupert

This is the traditional Inside Passage route used by fishing boats, yachts, small craft, Alaska ferries and very small ships. It is too narrow for large cruise ships.

Skeena River

Alternate large cruise ship route, via Bella Bella and Principe Channel.

Moresby Is.

Bonilla Is.

Banks Is.

Triple Island

The Northern Canyons is the nickname for this particularly dramatic and steep sided section of the traditional Inside Passage.

Hecate Strait

Alternate route

BRITISH COLUMBIA, CANADA

Alternate route

Butedale

Cape St. James

Hecate Strait

Alternate route

Bella Bella

Rivers Inlet

Small craft avoid the wide and often rough waters of Hecate Strait. Don't worry - what's rough for a thirty footer won't bother a big cruise ship!

Queen Charlotte Sound

Quatsino Sound

Cape Cook

Knight Inlet

Whirlpool Rapids

Kyuquot Sound

Yuculta Rapids

Nootka Sound

Seymour Narrows

Remember, whales like formal night! Many ships have their first formal night along this coast. Passengers spend time dressing, having their photo taken, going to the Captain's cocktail party. But , make some time to go out on deck and look around, as the whales are frequently out!

Estevan Pt.

Clayoquot Sound

Vancouver Island

Desolation Sound

Jervis Inlet

Barkley Sound

Cape Beale

Howe Sound

Sea Day
British Columbia Coast

120 miles to Seattle

Vancouver

(125) Milemarkers

600HS
550HS
475HS
425HS
400W
375HS
350W
297
290W
264
241
220W
218
173
170W
125
120W

ALONG THE WAY - BRITISH COLUMBIA COAST

A **Barkley Sound-Broken Islands** area: wild and extremely rugged, accessed via settlement of Bamfield on eastern shore. The road to Bamfield itself is also very rugged; many visitors prefer to come by steamer from Port Alberni. Before about 1975, usually only visited by commercial fishermen and loggers. In recent years the Broken Islands, a mini archipelago of over 100 islands, and part of the Pacific Rim National Park, has become a major attraction for sea kayakers from all over the world. For the well-heeled, there are outfitters providing guided expeditions with the guides putting up the tents and cooking up the meals. But many prefer it the old-fashioned way: putting in at Bamfield, loading up with tents and supplies and exploring the islands on their own.

B **Friendly Cove, Nootka Sound:** In March of 1778 came the watershed event that was to change the coast forever: the arrival of the Europeans. British Captain James Cook arrived on his remarkable voyage of Pacific exploration, the very first wave of a tide of exploration and settlement that inadvertently decimated the native population through disease.

C **Cape Cook:** At the very western end of the Brooks Peninsula, this has traditionally been a difficult cape for small craft to round. More than one sailing couple with round-the-world ambitions, trying a trip around Vancouver Island to get their 'sea legs,' has abandoned further ocean sailing after a bad time at Cape Cook!

D **Triangle Island:** The British Columbia government had big plans for the 600' cliff here—the highest and brightest lighthouse on the entire coast, commissioned in 1910. Unfortunately they hadn't planned on the wind. The lightkeeper's dog blew off the cliff, and one storm blew the radio towers away and moved the office off its foundations against the generator building. Another storm blew the roof off the bunkhouse and the crews' clothes and bedding out into space. After just 8 years, the light was abandoned. Today, however, it is a major bird rookery. Each spring some 50,000 pairs of tufted puffins arrives, each to lay and incubate a single egg!

E **Ninstints:** Part of the Gwaii Haanas-South Moresby National Park Reserve, this was the site of a major village of the Haida tribe. Early visitors found a line of large multi-family lodges, fronted by dramatic mortuary totems. Today weather has taken its toll and just a few rotting house frames and tilting and fallen poles remain. Cape St. James, 15 miles south, is usually the windiest place on the British Columbia coast.

F **Tide Rips:** The sea floor rises at the north end of Hecate Strait to within 100' of the surface. In winter, when southerly storms are opposed here by flooding tides from the north, a violent tide rip can form, with seas big enough to threaten vessels as large as 100'.

Top: Alaska bound salmon boat in Grenville Channel. Low on water? Lay alongside the waterfall and fill your tanks! Above: A nasty day In Queen Charlotte Sound. Exposed to the wind from many directions, mariners try to get across quickly and up into the shelter of Fitzhugh Sound.

There are a number of abandoned native village sites among the islands in this vicinity. The larger ones are usually watched over by a caretaker in the summer months. If you are traveling by small craft here, ask at Alert Bay to make arrangements to visit the old village at Mamalilacula.

Most Alaska-bound large cruise ships take a route just east of Hanson Island into Blackfish Sound, then George Passage and thence into the much wider waters of Queen Charlotte Strait. The area around mile 270—between Hanson and Harbledown Islands is particularly scenic, plus you can usually see the current swirls in the water from the tide here. Unfortunately northbound vessels often transit here early—7 a.m. or earlier, so you'll need to be an early riser to see it! Fortunately southbound vessels pass in the late afternoon to early evening.

Occasionally big ships might instead follow Broughton Strait along the Vancouver Island shore a little further, and stop briefly in front of **Alert Bay**. This town, whose economic base is commercial fishing, is also the main center for native culture in the Johnstone Strait area. Your ship will probably get close enough for you to see the classic longhouse style buildings of the **U'mista Cultural Center**, and, if you look above town, you'll see what might look like a cell phone tower, but actually it is the **world's tallest totem pole**, 173' feet tall. At the opposite end of the waterfront from the cultural center is the **Namgis Burial Ground** with another noticeable collection of totem poles.

As you get north and west of here, especially if you take the Blackfish Sound route, you may notice that the trees closest to the shore are bent and twisted, conveying a clear sense of the wilder land and seas that lie ahead. This is because the land is much more exposed to the wind because the high mountain ridge of Vancouver Island no longer provides protection from North Pacific gales.

Look for the **Pine Island Lighthouse at mile 319**. If your route will go up straight up boring Hecate Strait, your ship will slow here to discharge (or receive, southbound) the Canadian pilots, who work with the navigational staff to guide the ship though the tricky channels inside of Vancouver Island.

Lighthouse families, particularly at Pine Island and the next

---

EDITOR'S CHOICE

I Heard the Owl Call My Name, by Margaret Craven, published by Doubleday, is a haunting and powerful tale of a young Catholic priest working with the Kwakiutl people, at the head of **Kingcome Inlet**. Few books describe the mystery and power of native life as well.

(Today the name Kwakiutl is often rendered in English as Kwagiulth).

"The snow lay thick on the shoulders of the Cedar-man; the limbs of the young spruce bent beneath its weight. He saw the lights of the houses go out, one by one, and the lanterns begin to flicker as the tribe came slowly, single file along the path to the church. How many times had they traveled thus through the mountain passes down from the Bering Sea?

"He went to the door and opened it, and he stepped out into the soft white night, the snow whispering now under the footfalls. For the first time he knew them for what they were, the people of his hand and the sheep of his pasture, and he knew how deep was his commitment to them. When the first of the tribe reached the steps, he held out his hand to greet each by name. But first he spoke to himself and he said, 'Yes, my Lord.' "

lighthouse to the north, equally exposed Egg Island, did not have an easy life. A 50' wave from a 1967 winter gale smashed most of the buildings here and the staff with their children huddled by a campfire on higher ground until the storm had passed. Another storm smashed the Egg Island keeper's house into kindling; they were lucky to survive until help arrived.

For all smaller vessels traveling up the BC coast, this section—Queen Charlotte Sound—was almost always the most challenging as it was open waters, exposed to the wind, a 40 mile 'crossing' between the shelter of a cove nicknamed God's Pocket on the south and Safety Cove on the north.

God's Pocket, mile 309: Any afternoon in late May or early June—the boats start arriving and keep coming until well after the northern latitude dusk. They are Canadian fishing boats bound for the northern fisheries and American salmon seiners and gill-netters. Some are friends who perhaps haven't seen each other since the previous season. The anchorage is small so vessels raft up and the crews visit their neighbors as they put their boats in order, tie down loose gear, and get ready for the trip across the sound.

This small harbor, which is on the west side of Hurst Island in Christie Passage, is the traditional jumping-off place for the 40 breezy miles across Queen Charlotte Sound. On fall evenings the scene is apt to be different. Boats get beat up at that time of year, and the ones that slide in as the early dusk falls might have antennas snapped off, perhaps a window broken.

Your route in Hecate Straits usually pretty much runs up the middle of the strait. You may see the snow covered 10-11,000' tops of the coast mountains to the east, and you may see some lower land to the west.

The beauty of traveling by small ship is that they can sneak in close to the shore where a big 900 footer with its many restaurants and all night casinos wouldn't dare! Such cruises are, however, considerably more expensive than traditional big ship cruising.

Tip for Mariners

Get up early to get across this bit of often nasty water. Typically the wind won't make up until mid morning or so. Experienced mariners here will set their alarm for around 3 a.m., get up, 'sniff the weather,' and if it looks like a chance, start up, make sure everything loose is tied down or put away and start across. Also consider an alternate route—along the mainland shore, where there are more place to duck into if the weather gets nasty.

In March of 1971, I was headed up Hecate Strait as crew on a brand new 104' king crab boat, when on my afternoon watch, running before a building gale, I saw a strange target on the radar where none should have been. I woke the skipper.

He quickly scanned the chart and radar, pulled the throttle back to an idle. Sensing something was happening, the rest of the crew filed into the big pilothouse, peering forward into the early and snowy dusk. For a long while there was nothing but the march of the big, grey-bearded seas past in the thickly falling snow. But then there was a lightening in the snow ahead and we all peered forward intently, trying to get a glimpse of whatever it was that the radar was seeing ahead of us. Then, just for the briefest moment we saw it, glimpsed through the gloom and as quickly gone — heavy breakers, covering the entire area ahead of us.

"Damn...hang on, guys." Our skipper swiveled to look behind us, throttled up to a third, and pushed the steering lever all the way to starboard. As we swung into our turn, our boat dropped suddenly, at the same time rolling sickeningly to port for what seemed like a very long moment as a huge sea plowed into us. Time seemed to stand still. I heard dishes crashing, a strident alarm bell ranging, and then only slowly did we come around, and tilt back to an even keel, and finally the alarm stopped ringing.

Our skipper stood at the chart, shaking his head.

"Lookit this...breaking here, in a hundred feet of water...breaking, fer crissake...I heard about it once, but I didn't really believe it until just now..."

The combination of the heavy southerly gale and a flooding tide from the north was producing breaking seas in deep water, seas that we'd be foolish to risk, even in our new and rugged 104-footer.

For an hour, in that wild wasteland of snow and white water, we sought a way through, for the little gully of deeper water that might not be breaking. But if it were there, we couldn't find it. With the coming of the dark, the wind came on stronger still, and it was no place to be.

We headed east, to find a way to the sheltered waterways of the Inside Passage, through a maze of islands. We had no detailed chart, only the hazy memory of the mate, from a trip through several decades earlier. Snow and black enveloped us. Our radar could barely penetrate it. Three false starts led only to dead ends with the sea beating violently on three sided narrowing cul-de-sacs. Once there was not even room to turn around and we had to back out, ever so carefully, and no one spoke and the tension in the pilothouse was very thick.

The fourth channel opened up to another, the sea died away, the water stayed deep, and long after midnight, we found our way into the calm waters of the Inside Passage.

This would be the **Queen Charlotte Islands**, among the most rugged and thinly settled of the B.C. coast. They were originally settled by the Haidas, a First Nation tribe, who suffered the same ravages from disease and alcoholism as their mainland brothers. The islands are becoming favored by kayakers and adventure travelers seeking a true off the beaten path experience. Guides stress the remoteness of the land, and the importance of carrying adequate survival equipment and leaving a travel plan with a friend at home in case you don't return on schedule.

30 miles west of **mile 480W** is **Skedans**, once the side of a large Haida village, now abandoned, but site of many old totems and other artifacts. It is a United Nations World Heritage Site.

> **Passenger Tip**
>
> Don't feel you have to eat dinner in the big formal dining rooms. Explore your ship particularly the buffet areas. Many are up the bow with 180 degree views, some even segregate part for white tablecloth, waiter served dinners. (Sometimes you have to pay extra.) But consider the view: you can go out to an elegant restaurant anytime, but how often do you get a view like this on on the Horizon Court on the Dawn Princess, near mile 1480?

ANOTHER GREAT BOOK

The Curve of Time, by M. Wylie Blanchet, published by Whitecap Books, is an unusually simple but powerful account of travel along the British Columbia coast in the 1920s and '30s. A widow with five children whose summer home was their 26-foot cruiser, Mrs. Blanchet cruised the north coast in the days when yachts were rare. Her account of an age less busy reminds us of the grace in simple lives:

"They waited until they had each caught a shiner [a small fish easily caught by children]. 'Squeeze them,' finally ordered Jan. They squeezed them... From the vent of each shiner came a perfectly formed silver baby. They were slim and narrow, not deep and round like their mothers. The second they were put in the water they darted to the bottom, to the weeds and safety. John kept on squeezing his, and his fish went on borning babies just as he had said. But each next baby was more transparent than the last; and they began to look like vague little ghosts with all their inner workings showing through."

Above: a big oceangoing raft being constructed on the Columbia River, circa 1920. Davis rafts used to transport logs from the Queen Charlotte Islands were similar. The traditional flat style of log raft was not suited for the rough waters of Hecate Strait.
OHS 7863/11436

A distinctive, Haida mortuary style totem, usually carved to honor a deceased chief, whose ashes are sometimes put in a cavity on the back.

From about 1910 to 1941, several whaling stations operated out of the Queen Charlottes, harvesting the schools of humpback, finback, sperm, and even the giant blue whales that migrated up and down the coast. It was hard, hard work with crude navigational equipment on an unforgiving coast:

"The entire area is a sailor's nightmare, offering unexpected, conditional shelter to the knowing, and anxious, if not disastrous moments to the ignorant.

"Those damn willies (williwaws, violent winds that sweep down off the mountains without warning) would spring up in the middle of the night and shake you loose. Then we'd have to heave up the anchor, stow the chain and then steam around in the pitch darkness to find a place out of the wind to try it again."

- William Haglund in *Raincoast Chronicles: Forgotten Villages of the British Columbia Coast.*

Commercial fishing, logging, and a bit of tourism are pretty much the economic base of these islands. Most of the logs cut here are transported to mills at Prince Rupert or on Vancouver Island for processing. In the inlets and passages between Vancouver Island and the mainland, the waters are sheltered enough for the traditional flat log rafts. However, this sort of raft could not stand the rigors of the rough ocean conditions of Hecate Strait, so an alternate raft design was developed, with hundreds of thousands of board feet of logs chained tightly together tightly enough to survive rougher conditions. Eventually big barges were used, complete with cranes to allow them to load themselves in remote inlets. With the addition of ballast tanks that could be flooded or pumped out as needed,

these barges became self dumping as well—they'd get towed to their destination, then the tanks on one side would be emptied and the barge would tip all the logs into the water!

The islands suffered a hard blow in March of 2006, when their regular ferry, the *Queen of The North* hit a rock in the middle of a rainy, windy night and sank. Fortunately a few fishermen at a near-by First Nations village were awake with their radios on and immediately headed out in their boats to rescue the survivors who were shivering in life rafts. Two passengers were lost in the confusion of the sinking.

If you are northbound, this will usually be a formal night. Couples will spend time getting dressed; perhaps the ladies might get their hair done. Then there is the Captain's cocktail party as well as the all important formal portrait.

But don't forget this is whale country as well. Today most ships carry naturalists who have a beeper. If the bridge staff spots a school of whales, they would often page the naturalist to come up to the bridge to do a running commentary. But if it's just one whale, and if an announcement would interrupt an important passenger activity, it might not be announced. Many times in Hecate Strait, I've been walking the deserted outside decks and spotted whales, seeming eager for attention, while almost everyone else was inside, occupied with formal night activities.

So... remember to take time in your busy afternoon to take a stroll on the outer decks—the promenade decks on most ships are sheltered from the wind—and keep a sharp eye peeled for whales.

The Alaska border is at **mile 604**, but it is a lonely windy place, far from any town, usually passed by big cruise ships in the middle of the night with little fanfare.

Passenger Tip

Remember, Hecate Strait is whale country. There is a lot going on board your ship the first day out of Vancouver, but don't forget to keep a eye out for humpbacks. Look for the distinctive puff of what looks like smoke as they surface and exhale.

Humpback Facts

Size: 30 to 50 ', weight to 40 tons. Range: oceanic, cooler waters like British Columbia and Alaska in the summer, and warmer, like Hawaii, in the winter. Distinguishing features: black with white throat or belly, long flipper with irregular edges. Knobs and bumps on head and flippers. Likes to breach or jump dramatically. Most common big whale along the northwest coast.

Salmon troller near Work Island, Mile 438, in Fraser Reach. A boat this size, traveling daylight hours, will take about a week to travel from Seattle to Ketchikan. Below: Two floating fishing lodges being towed to their summer locations. Because of the challenges of maintaining lodges in remote locations, lodges on barges are becoming popular, as after the season they can be towed to a town for the winter. Opposite top: Grenville Channel, near Mile 515—the narrowest part of the Inside Passage.

When cruise ships were small, say 300' feet and smaller, everyone pretty much took the traditional Inside Passage route, also nicknamed The Northern Canyons, instead of traveling up wide and sometimes windy Hecate Strait. See map on page 88. The Northern Canyons begin at **Boat Bluff Lighthouse, Mile 439**. The next hundred miles or so are among the most spectacular of the whole Inside Passage. The walls of the channels seem to rise vertically in places and waterfalls tumble down their flanks. In places there is not enough room for two ships to pass.

This region was especially popular with hand loggers because of the steepness of the slopes which made it easier for the men who worked alone or with a single partner, to slide the huge trees down into the water.

If you take this route, look for **Butedale Cannery**, on the west side of Fraser Reach at **Mile 473**, a traditional stopping spot for fishing boats. Once a complete little town all by itself, with neat rows of houses for administrators and their families, and bunkhouses for hundreds of workers, it was all powered by water from the lake in the hills behind it. Sadly, after the canning operations were transferred to Prince Rupert, the large cannery fell into disrepair and, now, like many old North Coast canneries, lies abandoned.

AT THE BISHOP BAY HOT SPRINGS

In the windy fall of 1982, my crew and I were headed down the Inside Passage after a long and tiring four months of buying salmon all over Southeast Alaska and delivering them to the Icicle Seafoods cannery in Petersburg. The summer had been cold and rainy and the seas rough. Seeking a little R&R in that lonely stretch of coast, we steamed 15 miles up a narrowing side channel and   tied to the roughly made ramp at the Bishop Bay Hot Springs. The only man-made structure in thousands of square miles of wilderness, it was a simple cinder block building over a pool in the rocks filled with hot water and a washing pool outside.

As we sat up to our necks in the steaming water, the aches and cares of a long season in The North seemed to fade away. Many miles from the nearest settlement, it was a favorite with yachtsmen and weary southbound Alaska fishermen.

But we were lucky; that mid-October afternoon we were totally alone and we savored it.

Then there was a sound, and we looked out the windows to see a single humpback whale lifting his tail high in the air and then it was gone.

It was magic.

PRINCE RUPERT, B.C.

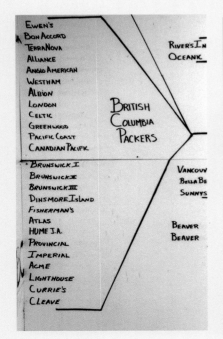

Before the Grand Trunk Pacific Railway punched a line down the through the coast mountains to connect interior Canada to the sea at Prince Rupert, Port Essington, a cannery town on the Skeena River, 8 miles south, was the business center of northern British Columbia,

The railroad totally changed things. It was the first place north of Vancouver where a direct line from interior Canada reached the sea, and almost immediately exports, particularly grain and timber poured out, and imports from Asia came in. Having the railroad made "Rupert" (as it is known locally) a cheaper place to process fish as well. And as fish runs declined, and refrigerated tenders—fish buying & transport vessels—made it possible to bring fish from remote areas in to Rupert, the outlying canneries eventually closed—see the cannery consolidation chart on the left—and most salmon came here. Today, Port Essington, once a booming town with several canneries, is a ghost town and Rupert is the regional center.

Sadly, Charles Hays, manager of the GTPRR, whose vision of Prince Rupert as a major port, never got to see his dream fulfilled. Returning from England where he had raised capital for the rail line through the mountains, he unfortunately chose to travel on the *RMS Titanic*. He was lost along with many, many others when it grazed an iceberg that sliced the magnificent

ship open and sent it to the bottom.

Today Prince Rupert's economy is like much of Southeast Alaska's was a few decades earlier: essentially dependent on commercial fishing and pulp mill employment, although port operations are a major employer as well.

Sensing the crowding of Southeast Alaska ports, and wanting to further diversify its economy, a modest cruise ship dock and terminal was completed in 2006, and a few ships began to schedule stops there.

A few blocks west of the new dock is the **Museum of Northern B.C.** with excellent displays on local First Nations culture and local history. A short walk away in downtown, behind the courthouse are the **Sunken Gardens**.

Today, almost all of all the hundreds of remote outlying canneries up and down the B.C. and Alaska coast are gone, abandoned or burned, most just pilings on a beach and buildings rotting in the forest. Fortunately at Prince Rupert, a group of concerned local citizens have preserved one, the old **North Pacific Cannery** on the Skeena River as a National Historic Site. Offered as an excursion to most visiting passengers, a visit is a remarkable glimpse into the past and a time when it seemed as if the salmon resource was, like the forest, endless.

There's also a great local cafe—Smiles Seafood Cafe—with wonderful seafood if you are looking for a colorful eatery.

Opposite top: Loading logs aboard an Asian log ship; a good way to export jobs as well. Top: Interior, Museum of Northern B.C. Below: Inside the North Pacific Cannery, a National Historic Site, an aide explains the canning process.

Native Culture

"When the tide is out, the table is set."

- old Pacific Northwest saying

In the last ice age, around 30,000 years ago, so much water was contained in the vast glaciers, that the sea level was low enough that what is now the shallow Bering Strait was a land bridge between Asia and Alaska. Historians and archeologists believe that migratory hunters from Siberia crossed to Alaska, following game, eventually becoming the Aleuts and Eskimos of Western Alaska and the coastal tribes that settled much of Southeast Alaska, British Columbia, and Washington.

This latter group found an environment that allowed them to live thousands of years in a culture that, compared to other Native Americans, could only be described as idyllic. The sea and the forest provided.

Top: The quintessential native community was this: big lodge houses set behind a protected beach where their canoes could be safely drawn up. Each house was home to several extended families. This was on Hope Island, west of Mile 320, around 1910. Note the sawn house planks, indication that it was built after the white man and his sawmills had come to the coast. AMNH Dossetter 42298 Left: Yup'ik Salmon Mask Author's collection

71

Abandoned house and rotting totem, Saxman Village, Ketchikan. Today up and down the coast, native tribes, whose economy primarily depends on harvesting timber and fish are seeing the impact of low prices, and, particularly in Canada, small harvests. Below: Small First Nations community in British Columbia. There are many small villages up and down the coast, each in a preserve—waterfront native lands with 'Crown Land—essentially National Forest around it.

There was cedar for houses, and halibut, salmon, herring, whales, candlefish (a herring-like fish harvested for its oil), clams, and berries for food. They had no agriculture; they didn't need it. They were hunter-gatherers but they could gather food without the nomadic life of their plains brothers. And to those nomadic plains indians, they were simply known as "Those who live in big houses." (They might, however, move each spring to summer villages of more modest homes, near the mouths of salmon streams.)

Their numbers were modest, but they settled in the most protected locations, traveled and traded in their long, carved canoes, fought occasionally, but in general lived in harmony with the land and enjoyed a rich culture.

THE COMING OF THE WHITE MAN

The arrival of the first Europeans brought something worse than the loss of their lands; it brought a plague like that which swept Europe in the Middle Ages. Who first brought smallpox, syphilis, gonorrhea, and tuberculosis to the Northwest Indians? Was it a Spaniard, a "Boston man" from Gray's ship? Captain Cook's sailmaker or Vancouver's gunner?

It mattered little; when the first sail appeared over the horizon in the 1770s, the curtain was about to be drawn on a powerful culture that had endured for centuries:

"We lifted the long bar from the great door of a community house, and stood, hesitating to enter. In the old days a chief would have greeted us when we stepped inside—a sea otter over his shoulder, his head sprinkled with white bird down, the peace sign. He would have led us across the upper platform between the house posts, down the steps into the center well of the house. Then he would have sung us a little song to let us know we were welcome.

"Sunlight and darkness; heat and cold; in and out we wandered. All the houses were the same size, the same plan, only the house posts distinguished them. Some were without wallboards, some were without roof boards—all were slowly rotting, the remains of a stone age slowly dying."

- M. Wylie Blanchet, *The Curve of Time*

"There was not a soul here today. The large totem that I took a photo of a year or two ago is now lying on the ground and the Hoh hoh totem that I photographed last year has now only one wing. So it goes, til at last they rot."

- Beth Hill, *Upcoast Summers*

These travelers, exploring abandoned village sites in the 1920s, 30s, and 40s were seeing the effects of disease and alcohol among the previously stable homes of coastal tribes in British Columbia.

Before the white man, although there was some trading between tribes, many lived more or less in isolation. With the

By the beginning of the 20th century, many of the old villages that had been the center of First Nations culture were beginning to show signs of dramatic population decline. Top: The Haida village of Skiddegate, in the remote Queen Charlotte Islands. Today all that is left of these once grand village sites are a few rotting totems and decaying house beams. AMNH Dossetter 42264 Bottom: Gifts displayed at a major potlatch celebration at Alert Bay, 1908. Hudson's Bay blankets were also a popular gift item. The stacked boxes appear to be cases of pilot bread. RCBM 1889

Top: Using low technology and the products of the forest and the sea, Northwest coast natives were able to produce remarkable products. Some of their baskets were so tightly woven as to be almost waterproof. UW NA2126
Opposite: George Hunt and his wife, Francine, at Fort Rupert, mile 300, around 1930. Hunt, brought up surrounded by Kwakiutl culture, was responsible for the collection of much of the Kwakiutl art found in museums all around the world. AMNH Scott 32734

whites came the first of the cash economy as Hudson's Bay Trading Company stores were established at a number of coastal locations. Natives, their tribes today known as First Nations in British Columbia, worked in the sawmills and the early fish plants that began to be constructed. Natives from the most remote villages would travel long distances to work in the new cash economy. When they returned to their homes after a season of work, bringing the new store bought goods, they also often brought disease as well which could spread quickly.

The long established tradition of Potlatching also did not set well with BC provincial authorities. Essentially parties given to celebrate important events, they became, after the establishment of the new stores, major transfers of wealth as chiefs strove to show their stature by giving away blankets, mirrors, bags of flour, even furniture and boats.

Worried that such celebrations only served to impoverish the the tribes, Potlatches were banned in 1884, though the natives responded by having them in more remote locations. By the time the ban was lifted in 1951, many traditional elements of native culture had disappeared.

THE COLLECTORS

In a sense, it was fortuitous that collectors such as Franz Boas from the American Museum of Natural History and Johan Jacobsen from the Royal Berlin Ethnological Museum happened along in the late 1800s when the quality and availability of Northwest Indian art were at their peaks. After about 1920, many of the villages experienced the sort of decline witnessed by Blanchet and others, and it is possible much of the art would have been lost.

They were also very fortunate George Hunt, son of a Hudson's Bay Company store manager and a First Nations princess was around. He was intimate with native culture and a huge help.

They also got *a lot* of art. So much disappeared to collectors and museums that decades later, when the Kwakiutls and other tribes wished to set up their own museums, many of the artifacts available to them were inferior to those on display elsewhere. Museums have become aware only recently that pieces in their collections are valuable parts of the tribes' cultural heritage, and some pieces are being returned.

Kwakiutl mask of Born-To-Be-Head-Of-The-World. Collected by George Hunt at Hopetown, B.C., in 1901. This mask opened to reveal another human face, with hands painted on the inside of the opening sections. AMNH 16/8410

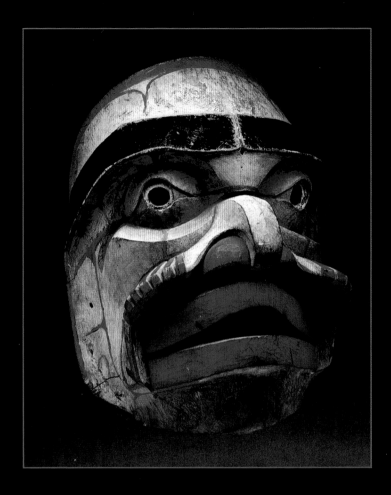

THE MASK TRADITIONS

With their food and shelter needs generally taken care of easily, Northwest coastal tribes had the time and the resources to create intricately worked ceremonial art. The most obvious to European visitors were the totem poles that dominated native village landscapes. But less obvious and usually only brought out for ceremonial occasions were the impressively colored and carved masks.

These were generally used by performers as part of dance ceremonies, often celebrating an important ritual like the naming of a new chief or occasion, like the beginning of end of the fishing season. AMNH 16/771

Totems

One fair July day in 1981, when I was a young fish buyer waiting for our boats to come in, my wife and I rowed ashore to the long-abandoned site of a Tsimshian village near the southern border of Alaska. Mary Lou searched the fine white sand for glass trading beads, and I poked through the nearly impenetrable undergrowth for the remains of the village.

The beach yielded a dozen exquisite glass beads, some little larger than the grains of sand that hid them, yet all of bright color, hardly faded with the passing of centuries. In the forest was a single totem base, decayed from decades of rain and wind.

A century earlier, there would have been high-bowed canoes drawn up below the simple cedar plank-and-beam houses. In front would be art: carved cedar in its many forms, the most dramatic of which were the totems.

Totems were a highly visible sign of the success and wealth of the native cultures that evolved along the coast, whether Haida, Kwakiutl, Tlingit, or Tsimshian. Sheltered by a benevolent forest, blessed with a food-filled sea, the tribes could afford the luxury of permanent village sites and ornamental art. Their art celebrated legends, events, or simply the wealth and crest of the family for whom it was carved. The poles had no religious significance, but were records of the past in a society where there was no written language.

At first, the coming of the whites was the catalyst for a burst of creative energy among northwest tribes. Steel tools, and the cash from the fur trade and native employment, led to an affluence celebrated in larger potlatches, with more carved masks and totems.

By the 1860s, the situation had changed radically. Epidemics had ravaged the coast, and missionaries and government worked to reform a way of life they viewed as pagan and against the spirit of modern commerce.

At the beginning of the 20th century, travelers remarked on the curious combination of the presence of sophisticated carved art and its apparent abandonment. The reason was simple: so many natives had died that whole villages were abandoned.

The result was that much native art disappeared—either rotted into the forest, was purchased by individuals, or, fortunately for us, was collected by museums. But in many villages, where the people struggled with poverty and alcoholism, the tradition of art, as it was practiced in the 19th century, essentially disappeared.

Fortunately the 1960s and '70s brought a rekindling of the flame of carved art among northwest coastal tribes. Today, intricate newly-carved totems fetch high prices and are in demand—from Disney World to corporate offices.

Totems have become cultural icons for the northwest coast. We shouldn't forget what they were carved to celebrate: the centuries-old success of a native culture that suffered badly with the coming of the whites.

SOME ALASKA HISTORY

Around 30,000 years ago, enough water was frozen all over the earth that the sea level was much lower than today, and a land bridge formed across what is today the Bering Strait between Alaska and Russia.

And across it, anthropologists suppose, Siberians, perhaps following game, wandered, and eventually settled Alaska, becoming, over many centuries, the three separate cultures in the state: Aleuts, Eskimos, and Indians.

Each group developed a unique and rich culture based on their particular climactic circumstances: harsh in the north and west, gentler in what is today Southeast Alaska.

But despite the climate, in most areas, the wildlife, and particularly marine life, was sufficient for these tribes to develop substantial cultures rich with with art and tradition.

In the perspective of their times, these were prosperous and successful tribes. Yet, all was to change dramatically for the worse with the arrival of the first European explorers in Alaska, starting with the Russian Vitus Bering in 1741. Bering's men brought home sea otter and other pelts, and left smallpox and other diseases, which devastated native populations throughout Alaska.

But when they got back (Bering's ship wrecked on the Siberian coast and he and 20 of his men died. The survivors built a boat from the wreck and eventually reached home) they discovered that the sea otter pelts were so highly prized in China that a single pelt could be worth three times more than the average sailor earned in a year!

White men started coming to exploit the natural resources of Alaska late in the 1700s. This is the American whaling fleet anchored in Port Clarence, near the Arctic Circle, around 1898. On the shore are Inupiat Eskimo tents, of canvas stretched over whalebone and driftwood frames. If you look carefully at the right hand tent, you can see several carved ivory figures above it. UW NA2125 Below: Alaska Natives made remarkable adaptations to their environment. These goggles to prevent snow blindness are made from a walrus tusk.
Opposite: Tlingit dancers at Hoonah, courtesy Icy Strait Point.

Eskimo in bidarka, made of sealskin stretched over a frame of whalebone or driftwood and made waterproof by coating with whale fat. UW NA 1995
Below: The Russian influence lingers in the villages of Western Alaska.

And the brutal exploitation began. Spreading eastward along the Alaska coast, the Russians sometimes murdered whole villages if the hunters wouldn't bring in enough sea otter pelts.

Establishing villages with their distinctive Russian Orthodox churches, the Russians moved their colony capital to Sitka and and pursued the sea otter almost to extinction all the way down to California.

With the sea otters basically gone, humiliated by France and Britain in the 1853-5 Crimean War, Tsar Alexander II was looking to save a few dollars and found a buyer, the US, and a great price–7.2 million dollars (about two cents an acre) in 1867.

Decried as "Seward's Folly" (the US Secretary of State) the purchase of Alaska hardly excited most Americans.

Fur seals were the next little mini-boom, and millions were quickly slaughtered by Canadian and American sealers.

But the thing that really put Alaska on the map was the arrival of the steamer *Portland* in Seattle in June of 1897 with its legendary ton of gold, and the frenzy that was the Yukon Gold Rush began. While the actual diggings were in Canada's Yukon Territory, almost everyone who went traveled and left through Alaska, primarily along the mighty Yukon River.

Sadly, almost all of the almost hundred thousand that set off for the Yukon with such high hopes arrived to find all the good claims taken long before they had even left home. Most found some work in the diggings, made enough money to move on,

perhaps to the next smaller gold rush in Nome, and eventually made it home, rich with Alaska tales more than with gold.

About this same time, the canning process for preserving food was being perfected and canneries for salmon, the most prolific west coast food fish were springing up along the upper California coast and the shores of the Columbia River. These processors began to hear stories about the supposedly vast schools of Alaska salmon, and the stage was set for the business that essentially originally created all the settlements in coastal Alaska: salmon fishing.

The challenge was simply getting all that... stuff: lumber, boats, tools, canning equipment, and supplies: essentially enough for a whole little town, up to some remote bay in Alaska in the spring in time to build the cannery and have it all ready for the expected run of fish.

The solution was big square riggers, being nudged out of the ocean freight business by coal fired steamers. Purchased cheap, the big ships were loaded and sent to Alaska with boats, fishermen, construction materials, cannery equipment and supplies, as well as cannery and construction workers. What an organizational challenge! Then at the end of the season, the ship would be loaded with tens of thousands of cases of canned salmon, fishermen and workers, and head south, leaving just a caretaker, hopefully with his family, to watch over the cannery for the long lonely months before it all started over again. Whew!

As the salmon fishery grew into the biggest business in Alaska

Sukoi Islands and the mainland mountains north of Petersburg. Shortly after John Muir described the scenic wonders of Alaska, the first steamers began to make excursion trips to Alaska. Below: Skagway graveyard. Disease and the rigors of the trail up and over the high mountain passes into the Yukon Territories took a heavy toll.

83

For almost 100 years, commercial fishing has been one of the most important parts of the Alaskan economy. This is a salmon purse seiner in Chatham Strait, near mile 825. Below: The 800 mile long Alaska Oil Pipeline carried hot crude oil from the remote oil fields on the Arctic coast to the tanker port at Valdez in Prince William Sound. When the North Slope oil fields were at full capacity, 2 million barrels of oil a day flowed, loading a steady series of tankers out of Valdez to California and Puget Sound ports. Thousands of eager workers spent all their savings to rush to Alaska, hoping to get hired for the high paying jobs.

for the first half of the 20th century, two issues rankled Alaskans: the fact that the fishery–season openings and closings, etc.–was all managed from Washington, D.C., too distant to be quickly responsive to fast changing local conditions, and that most of the Alaska canneries were owned and operated by Seattle or California based companies.

World War II (the Japanese occupied some of the Aleutians) was good to Alaska with over a billion dollars in projects and tens of thousands of sailors and soldiers stationed there. It got the state to sort of a critical mass in terms of population and industry. Finally, despite a last minute fight against it by the salmon magnates, Alaska became a state in 1959.

The next big thing was oil. Atlantic Richfield's Prudhoe Bay strike in 1968 transformed the Alaskan economy. After a five year delay to sort out Native land claims and environmental issues, thousands rushed north to construct the 800 mile Alaska oil pipeline and work in the oil fields. The revenue from the oil royalties allowed the state to begin providing unheard of services and facilities as well as establishing the Alaska Permanent Fund, which annually distributes a dividend of around $1,000 to every Alaska resident.

In a larger sense, many old timers might say that it was the also the end of the 'Old Alaska.' where you could homestead in the bush and no one would say too much if you happened to be on federal land. Most of the land in Alaska is owned by the federal government in some fashion or another—National Wildlife Refuges, National Parks, National Forests, National Monuments, etc. But with the influx of new settlers, squatting on federal land was pretty much out.

About this time another fisheries boom—this time in the previously little fished (at least by the US) Bering Sea—got rolling. First for king crab—as in the Discovery channel TV series, "The Deadliest Catch," then for finfish, primarily cod and the huge resource of pollock, primarily for Asian markets. As in most Alaska booms, it burned red hot for a while, fortunes were made - and lost - before settling down to a more sustainable pace.

And then, starting in the early 1980s and continuing today, a boom of a very different sort—the cruise ship boom. Of course cruises to Alaska were nothing new - John Muir's 1879 trip to Alaska and discovery of Glacier Bay had the first steamers cruising regularly to Alaska and the big ice starting in the 1890s. But few people in Southeast Alaska in the 1970s, when a few small ships were nosing around the town and the glaciers, could have imagined how large and fast the industry would grow. Today 26 large ships, and a dozen smaller ships take a million passengers plus to Alaska each season. The impact of a '5 ship day' (that's around 12,000 people) in a town like Ketchikan with a total population of 15,000 is huge. Yet, usually by evening the ships are gone, and the industry provides employment at a time when timber and fishing are in a mild downturn.

Today, the greatest threat to Alaska comes from a totally unexpected source: global warming. Will there be polar bears or tidewater glaciers to even see in fifty years? Given the present pace of change, it seems unlikely. As one travel agency marketed cruises to its clients, "See Alaska before it melts."

Ketchikan transformed—30 years ago the economy rested on two strong legs: commercial fishing, a busy pulp mill, and a weak third: tourism. Today the little homegrown gift shops have largely been taken over by outfits like Little Switzerland and Columbian Emeralds, and serving the needs of almost a million cruise passengers is the main game in town. Below: A happy Bering Sea king crab crewman with some big crab aboard the crabber Flood Tide in 1971.

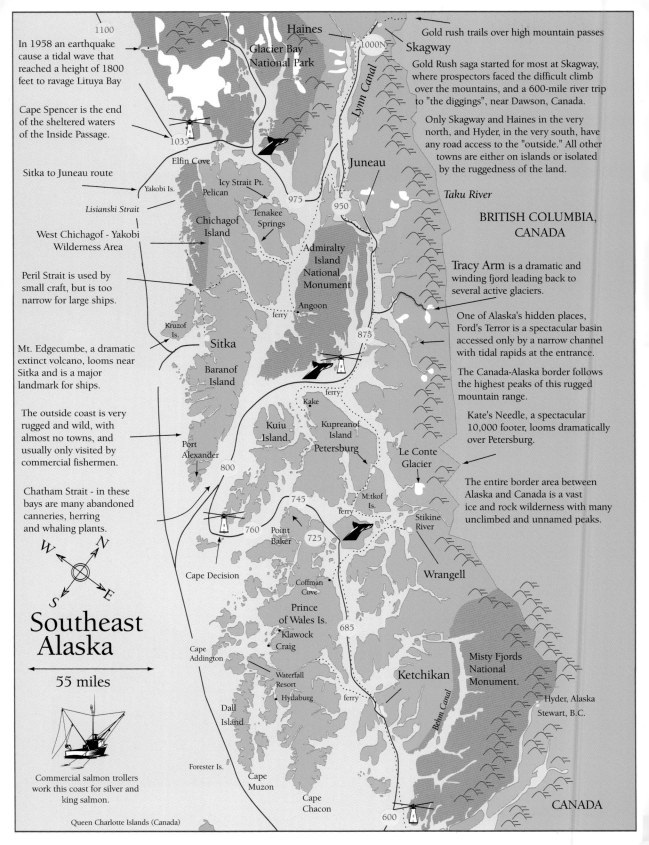

Southeast Alaska

55 miles

In 1958 an earthquake cause a tidal wave that reached a height of 1800 feet to ravage Lituya Bay

Cape Spencer is the end of the sheltered waters of the Inside Passage.

Sitka to Juneau route

Lisianski Strait

West Chichagof - Yakobi Wilderness Area

Peril Strait is used by small craft, but is too narrow for large ships.

Mt. Edgecumbe, a dramatic extinct volcano, looms near Sitka and is a major landmark for ships.

The outside coast is very rugged and wild, with almost no towns, and usually only visited by commercial fishermen.

Chatham Strait - in these bays are many abandoned canneries, herring and whaling plants.

Commercial salmon trollers work this coast for silver and king salmon.

Gold rush trails over high mountain passes

Gold Rush saga started for most at Skagway, where prospectors faced the difficult climb over the mountains, and a 600-mile river trip to "the diggings", near Dawson, Canada.

Only Skagway and Haines in the very north, and Hyder, in the very south, have any road access to the "outside." All other towns are either on islands or isolated by the ruggedness of the land.

Taku River

BRITISH COLUMBIA, CANADA

Tracy Arm is a dramatic and winding fjord leading back to several active glaciers.

One of Alaska's hidden places, Ford's Terror is a spectacular basin accessed only by a narrow channel with tidal rapids at the entrance.

The Canada-Alaska border follows the highest peaks of this rugged mountain range.

Kate's Needle, a spectacular 10,000 footer, looms dramatically over Petersburg.

The entire border area between Alaska and Canada is a vast ice and rock wilderness with many unclimbed and unnamed peaks.

Haines
Glacier Bay National Park
Skagway
1100
1000N
Elfin Cove
1035
Yakobi Is.
Icy Strait Pt.
Pelican
Lynn Canal
Juneau
975
950
Chichagof Island
Tenakee Springs
Admiralty Island National Monument
Kruzof Is.
Sitka
Baranof Island
Angoon
ferry
875
Le Conte Glacier
Kake
Kuiu Island.
Kupreanof Island
Petersburg
ferry
Port Alexander
800
Mitkof Is.
ferry
Stikine River
Point Baker
760
725
745
Cape Decision
Coffman Cove
Prince of Wales Is.
685
Wrangell
Klawock
Craig
Cape Addington
Waterfall Resort
Ketchikan
Misty Fjords National Monument.
Hydaburg
ferry
Dall Island
Behm Canal
Hyder, Alaska
Stewart, B.C.
Forester Is.
Cape Muzon
Cape Chacon
600
CANADA
Queen Charlotte Islands (Canada)

N W E S

CHAPTER 3

Islands Without Number

Southeast Alaska: Canadian Border to Juneau

"Gazing from the deck of the steamer, one is borne smoothly over calm blue waters, through the midst of countless forest-clad islands. The ordinary discomforts of a sea voyage are not felt, for nearly all the whole long way is on inland waters that are about as waveless as rivers and lakes. So numerous are the islands that they seem to be sown broadcast; long tapering views between the largest of them open in every direction."

- John Muir, *Travels in Alaska*

A man and a boat could travel for weeks here and never find a town. In Southeast Alaska, the size of some small states, thousands of islands are divided by tide swept channels. To the east the border runs along the highest peaks of the coastal range; to the west the North Pacific Ocean beats on a rugged coast with just a single town: Sitka.

The land is not friendly. The forest starts right at the water's edge and is almost impenetrable. In the roadless communities residents often find it easier to take an outboard skiff over to a neighbors just a hundred yards away rather than brave the spiny

Homesteaders at Port Protection, 1972. 'Port P' was one of the few places in Southeast Alaska in the 1970s where inexpensive waterfront lots were available. Below: Salmon boats anchored in Sumner Strait, near Point Barrie, Mile 745. The US-Canada border runs along the tops of the peaks in the distance. The actual mainland coast of SE Alaska here is only about 30 miles wide from the border to the salt water, but just offshore are thousands of islands.

A Hercules air freighter unloading Yukon River dogs (chum salmon) at Petersburg to be processed, July, 1975. In the 1970s and 1980s, the Japanese demand for Alaskan seafood was booming, and fish buyers set up operations in the most remote areas, in some cases like this one, flying their fish out to distant processing plants. Below: Interior, fish buying vessel.

devils club and thick undergrowth in the forest.

In summer, the days are long, sunlight often until ten or eleven at night near the June summer solstice. People stay up, working or fishing, 16,18, 20 hours a day. But then comes the long winter with the sun over the mountain at 3 in the afternoon, not to reappear until 9 or so the following morning. And those are the hard days.

But even from the earliest days, it was a land that drew hardy people: fishermen, trappers, loggers, cannery workers, sawmillers, tugboaters, card sharks. And drinkers.

In the early days, most everyone made their living with their hands. As much as anything perhaps, this is what appealed to a certain type of people from 'down south,' or the 'lower 48.' That here was a land where if you were strong, and you worked hard, you could make your place. Single men, with perhaps not much to recommend them except for maybe a certain bullheaded strength would say goodbye to friends and family and 'head up North.' Then maybe a few years later they'd stop back home again, obviously a modest success from their labors 'up North,' and maybe looking for a bride, for as The North had many things in abundance that might attract a man, like fish, and trees, and land, women were not among them.

For much of the 20th century, the economy of Southeast Alaska had three elements - fishing, logging, and tourism. It was a good mix, with the sawmills providing a good base of employment in

the wintertime when fishing was pretty much over until spring. Then in summer all the towns would boom as seasonal workers for the canneries and fish boats would roll in for the fishing season. Starting in the 1970s, when the Japanese economy entered the high growth mode, prices paid to Alaska fishermen seemed to rise, sometimes even weekly. Fishermen had new boats built and shiny new pickups rolled around town.

Then the 1980s and early 1990s brought sort of a double whammy. After many years of allowing logging practices that were damaging salmon streams and fish production, the Forest Service drew up stricter rules and the big mills at Sitka and Ketchikan closed. Then the Japanese economy took a big tumble, taking fish prices down with them, and fishermen and processors quickly reigned in their spending.

Today in most of the coastal towns that a cruise passenger might see, tourism is pretty much the biggest game in town, (except for the capital, Juneau, with its many government jobs) and many residents hope for the return of the days when their economy was more balanced.

A retired fisherman, living on his boat at the dock at Point Baker, one of the roadless fishing communities scattered among the islands of coastal Alaska.

Herring skiff at Kah Shakes Cove, mile 625. "Hurry up and wait" is the motto in the herring business—often the fleet will arrive in late March and wait for several weeks while the herring roe or eggs ripens or matures. Then, with spotter planes buzzing around the 'fishing period'—often as short as 12 hours—starts and hundreds of these strange craft set their gillnets for the wily herring. The area just north of the border is a salmon gillnet area—look for the 30-40 footers setting and hauling their nets, generally Sunday through Wednesday (Alaska fisheries are tightly regulated to maintain the health of the resource.)

B.C. BORDER TO KETCHIKAN

There aren't any duty free shops clustered around this border: it's a lonely, windy spot, exposed to the wind, wracked by tidal currents. The prudent mariner hurries across. Consider this entry from my 1973 journal:

"So we came to Alaska, on a wild and lost afternoon, caught in a tide race off a nameless point, in failing light, far from any help. The heavy westerly swell, the dirty southwest chop, and the push of the tide on top made it all I could do just to keep the boat moving forward, throttling over the big ones and then diving deep into the troughs. The seas came from all directions, and even at dead slow, waves slapped at the windows, sagging-in the thick glass".

Look for the high ridge of snow-covered peaks to the east. They effectively seal off Southeast Alaska from any land connection, except in the very north at Haines and Skagway, and tiny Hyder, pop. 100, far up **Portland Canal**. Fortunately the larger (population 500) town of Stewart, B.C. is just two miles away and residents can share shops and services. The 2001 movie, Insomnia, was filmed near here.

Study the map carefully here. This entire area, with many winding inlets that all had to be explored, was very difficult for Vancouver and his men.

In the 1920 and 30s, there were several canneries in this area, at Hidden Inlet and Nakat Inlet. Today the old canneries have pretty much disappeared into the forest, just leaving old pilings and rusty machinery on the shore, and the whole area is essentially wilderness, all part of the

Misty Fjords National Monument.

Look for salmon gill-netters, typically fishing Sunday noon through Wednesday noon. If the weather is calm, you may also see fish packers (they're larger) making their rounds among the fleet, buying fish. Many vessels remain the summer here, remote from any town or cannery, getting water, groceries, fuel, and supplies from the tenders, or fish packers, that service the fleet. The nets they use here are 1,800 feet long by 30 feet deep; a good day might be 2,000 pounds (400 fish) of red salmon or 5,000 pounds of pink salmon.

Just a decade or so ago, fishermen would just throw their fish into their dry fish hold and deliver them at the end of the day. Today all Alaska salmon processors are working hard to improve the quality of their fish, and encourage their fishermen to ice their fish. To this end, a barge with a generator and an ice-making machine is usually anchored in **Foggy Bay, Mile 622**, to serve the fishermen in this area.

The salmon fishery in Alaska is huge - each season more than 3,000 salmon fishing boats work the vast Alaska coast. Many come up from the Puget Sound area as there actually aren't enough fishermen in Alaska to catch all the salmon. Some of these fishermen leave home with cases of jars of fruit and vegetables that their families have put up for them from the garden at home. With a typical fishing period of just three or four days a week, there's plenty of time on the weekends. Crab and salmon are so abundant here, that some fishermen will set up little processing

Secrets of the Old Time Fish Buyers: When the guys aren't catching much, you end up with a lot of time on your hands. If you're on the "Garnet Point Run," jump in the skiff and head ashore to pick a coffee can full out of the rocks. But make sure you bring your radio with you in case one of your boats needs something!

ORCA TALES: AT LORD ISLANDS

One summer when my wife and I were running a fish buying boat on the Garnet Point run, we had an afternoon to explore and anchored our big 70 footer just east of the **Lord Islands, mile 602**, and motored ashore in the skiff.

Possibly we were the only human visitors in decades - the islands were remote and tiny and there were far more sheltered anchorages just a few miles away.

And so wild! The trees were bent and sculpted by the winter storms, the underbrush thick as a wall, but with exquisite tiny beaches on the west side, hemmed in on both sides by rock bluffs. My wife and I could tell at once that it might be a good place to look for the highly sought after glass balls - old Japanese net floats. We started onto the beach then stopped, not wanting to disturb the two obviously very young seal pups sunning just above the surf line.

Then as we watched, stunned, a big orca surfed in on a wave, headed like an arrow for the pups. He snatched one up with a single snap of his big jaws, as the other quickly wriggled further up the beach. Then, when the next big sea washed around him, the orca wriggled back into the water and disappeared. And all probably in less than 30 seconds. Our mouths hung open; we were amazed.

A classic Alaska cannery at Loring, near Ketchikan, circa 1920, complete with square rigger waiting for her load of canned salmon. Tongass Historical Society Below: The old boat ramp at the Tree Point Lighthouse in 1982.. The lighthouse was automated in 1969.

operations aboard their boats and refill the same jars with crab and salmon to be consumed all winter!

Tree Point Light at **mile 607** is the first in Alaskan waters. Before it was automated in the 1969, the crews lived in three beautifully crafted houses set in the woods near the cove south of the light. The fourth was originally a school for the families of the isolated staff. One house was barged to Ketchikan after the families left.

East of **Mile 628** is the **Boca de Quadra**, 50 miles of steep-sided fjords and side channels, whose sides quickly rise to two- and three- thousand-foot peaks. Aside from the ubiquitous cannery ruins and a lodge on the shore of Mink Bay, the land is wilderness, visited mostly in summer by people seeking its natural beauty by floatplane, kayaks, and excursion boats, and in winter by shrimp and crab fishermen.

The two-mile-wide channel extending to the northeast at around **mile 630** is **Behm Canal**, which leads to Rudyerd Bay and Punchbowl Cove, which is the most visited part of Misty Fjords.

Twelve miles farther north is **Yes Bay**, where a hand-logger in 1925 almost knocked an airplane out of the sky with a tree. The huge cliff-top spruce W.H. Jackson had just cut was toppling toward the water far below when he spotted a Fish and Wildlife floatplane almost directly beneath the falling tree, flying low along the beach looking for fish pirates. It was a close call.

So... National Monument (the Boca de Quadra is part of the Misty Fjords National Monument,) naturally you'd think that something like a huge strip mine would definitely not be allowed there. In the early 1980s we (I was a herring and salmon buyer in those years) were stunned to learn that an English mining consortium, Rio Tinto Zinc, was planning the largest molybdenum strip mine in the world in the hills north of the Boca. And the mine tailings, millions of tons of them, were to be dumped into the deep and pristine waters of the Boca.

"No way" was the collective reaction to the proposal from the region's commercial fishermen. But Ketchikan's big employer, the pulp mill, was about to close, so there was a lot of pressure to open the mine, as it was close enough so that Ketchikan workers could commute by fast ferry to the mine.

At one of the critical hearings, to determine the environmental impact of dumping millions of tons of possibly toxic tailings into the Boca, a biologist hired by the mining company testified that there was nothing of economic value on the bottom of the Boca.

A well respected Ketchikan fishermen who spent his winters fishing crab and shrimp in the Boca, freezing them on board and shipping his excellent products down to Seattle restaurants, spoke up in a dry monotone:

"Well, if there's nothing on the bottom, then there's a hell of a lot of shrimp and crab that crawl into my pots on the way up from the bottom..."

Of course the fishermen's concerns were ignored and the plans for the mine went full speed ahead. That spring, when I was killing some time, waiting for the herring fishery to open, I was back in the Boca and saw a friend anchored up, and went alongside him for a visit. Naturally the mine was one of the first things to come up.

Mink Bay, Boca de Quadra, 1982

"I coulda' stopped it." my friend said, point blank.

"How the hell," I answered, "could you have stopped it when the whole Southeast Alaska fishing and environmental community and the Sierra Club and all those high priced lawyers couldn't?" What he was saying didn't make any sense, but if there was anyone who knew the Boca's secrets it was him.

"I met the guy. I could have stopped it. Back then when I first met him."

"Which guy?" I asked, still not getting where he was going.

"The prospector, the geologist, the guy who found the moly."

I leaned forward. This I definitely didn't have a clue about.

"Four winters ago. I kept seeing this funky old cruiser anchored up, back in the Boca and up the head of Smeaton Bay. No one else's ever there in the winter, so one night I anchored up next to him and rowed the skiff over for a visit."

"It was him, the guy, the geologist. He was all excited about it, he showed me some of his ore samples. He said he'd been all over Alaska, hadn't ever seen as rich a strike. He hadn't told anyone. He was flying out the next week with his samples and his report." He paused, looking out the window at the lonely country across the bay. "I could have taken care of it."

I didn't get. I think I was naive then. My friend must have seen the puzzlement on my face.

"I should have sank the dammed boat, maybe him with it. No one would have ever known. None of this," he waved out at the Boca, but meaning the whole controversy, "would have happened. None"

But the unexpected happened. The Cold War ended. The demand for moly—used in jet fighter engines –plunged. The mine was never built.

KETCHIKAN
Salmon and Totem Pole Capital of Alaska

Don't be fooled by the restaurants and jewelry boutiques along the waterfront here; until relatively recently, this was a full on rough and tumble logging and commercial fishing town. Right where the cruise ships now tie up used to be a big sawmill and a three story smoky sawdust burner, and canneries, cold storages, and fish processors lined the waterfront. Fishing boats, headed up to Alaska from the lower 48, and bound for other parts of the remote Alaska coast would always stop here to let the crew wet their whistles. And the next morning the skipper would just hope that they all made it back aboard.

Saturday nights in those days were particularly rough. Out in the channel floatplanes would start to land, big twin-engine Grumman Geese, and the slow, lumbering Stinsons, bringing in loggers from Prince of Wales Island and Tsimshian Indians from the village of Metlakatla. Then the fishing boats - big seiners and tenders - would start to arrive from the outer districts, the crews with a few bucks in their ass pockets, ready for a big night, drinking and carousing at Dolly Arthur's and the other brothels along the boardwalk at Creek Street, known as the only place in Alaska where the fish and the fishermen both came to spawn.

The first whites arrived in the 1870 to salt salmon, Next, as the technology to put fish in cans was developed, the first of many canneries were established. In the early days of the salmon fishery, almost all fish were caught by floating fish traps—elaborate mazes of logs and netting, either anchored to the bottom or hung from thick pilings, and placed along the routes of migrating salmon. The

Top photo: Cannery worker feeding salmon into fish processing machinery. Asians provided a major part of the seasonal workforce; many canneries had separate kitchens, mess halls and bunkhouses for them. MOHAI 16233 Lower photo: The old Sunny Point Cannery in Ketchikan was owned by A&P, a major east coast grocery chain.

canneries and the fish traps were mostly owned by big fish companies from Seattle. This out of state ownership caused deep resentment among many Alaskans and was one of the key factors in the push for Alaska statehood that was finally achieved in 1958.

Of course, the entrepreneurial spirit flows strongly in Alaskans, and so Alaskan fishermen made it a point of honor to steal as many fish from the traps as they could. When one new cannery, that eventually grew into one of the largest salmon companies in Alaska with many canneries, started up, observers at the time noted that they had neither seine boats—another way of catching salmon—nor owned any fish traps, but somehow had plenty of fish to can: all reportedly stolen from the fish traps of the Seattle owned companies.

The history of Ketchikan is deeply intertwined with the three major native tribes of the region, the Tlingits, Haidas, and Tsimshians. Natives traditionally fished commercially and worked in the canneries as well as the sawmills.

When the whites arrived, there were numerous native villages throughout the area, but over time some of these settlements were depopulated primarily because of the diseases that the first whites brought to the area. In an effort to preserve the totem poles they were brought from these outlying settlements into Ketchikan as monuments.

Over time, even the rot-resistant cedar of the totems deteriorated in SE Alaska's notoriously moist climate, and new ones or "recarves," were carved by native carvers to replace the old. Today, almost all the poles on display in Ketchikan are recarves.

Master carver Nathan Jackson has been carving totem poles for 40 years. His work is on display at the National Museum of Native American Art in Washington, D.C. He works regularly at the carving shed at Saxman, three miles south of downtown Ketchikan.

Top: fishing is still a big part of the local economy here. Have a look at the fleet moored just south of the cruise ship docks. Bottom: A sad commentary on the Ketchikan economy—the pulp mill log sorting area in the foreground, mostly empty, and the old Wards Cove Packing Company cannery on the far shore, closed and sold to non-fishing interests in 2004.

Big industry came to town around 1950, in the shape of the big pulpmill out at Wards Cove, eight miles north of downtown. Ketchikan had been a lumber producer for years; in World War I, Ketchikan mills shipped light, strong, Sitka Spruce dimensional lumber to Boeing and other aircraft manufacturers in the days when aircraft structural members were made of wood.

Conceived as a way to utilize some of the vast spruce and hemlock forests of the region, and generate good paying, year round jobs (most fish and fish processing jobs were seasonal) the mill got a sweet deal from the U.S. Forest Service, and quickly became the largest employer in town.

But by the 1960s and 70s, salmon fishermen began to complain that logging practices like driving bulldozers down the middle of salmon streams and indiscriminate clear cutting was reducing the salmon runs on which they depended. The mill operators wanted to cut when and how they pleased, were backed up by the Forest Service, and for years there was ill feeling between these two factions in town.

Eventually more responsible logging practices reduced the timber available to harvest and much to the surprise of its employees, the mill closed its doors in 1986. Today, a smaller plywood mill operates on Gravina Island, but employs just a fraction of what the big Louisiana Pacific owned mill did.

THE NEW ECONOMY

A few years after the mill closed, salmon prices took a big tumble as well when the economy of Japan, our largest seafood customer, hit the skids. This hit the coastal communities, where there was little work except for fishing and processing, very hard.

About the same time, the cruise industry was beginning a major expansion, building much larger ships, and building lodges and infrastructure to transport, entertain, and house their passengers after they left the ships. Within a few years major changes came to Ketchikan, Skagway, and Juneau, the major cruise ports, as entrepreneurs created new excursions to offer the many new visitors off the ships, as well as new shops. The rapid growth was not without its blemishes as Caribbean based chain jewelry stores began to drive smaller, local stores out of business. Additionally, the downtown shopping areas on the main streets that used to be primarily focused on services and products for locals became primarily oriented to visitors. These stores would close up quickly after the last ships of the season, leaving deserted streets with window after window, covered over with plywood for the winter.

Over time, many residents hope that economy that is more balanced between tourism, fishing, and timber will return to the region.

Ketchikan visitor to child:
"How long has it been raining?
Child:
"I don't know; I'm only five"

WALKING AROUND TOWN

The good thing about all the major towns in Southeast Alaska is that they're small and the ships usually tie up or lighter passengers ashore right in downtown.

In Ketchikan, there's plenty to see on foot within a few blocks of the ship, and lots of variety if you want to walk a little further, as well as regular city buses if your feet get too tired to walk back!

The big **Southeast Alaska Discovery Center** downtown has excellent historical exhibits, a bookstore, coffee shop, and theatre showing a free regular feature on native culture. Adjacent is **The Great Alaska Lumberjack Show**, highlighting loggers competing in axe work, tree climbing, etc.

Another block or so of walking takes you to **Creek St.**, the old red light district, today transformed into one of the more unique and eclectic shopping and eating areas of Alaska. The creek was handy - in prohibition days, bootleggers would slink up in the black of the night at high tide, paddle under the establishments, give the secret knock, and trapdoors would open and eager hands change cash for booze. A short walk to

Top: Totem at Saxman. Opposite: Ray Troll is Southeast Alaska's most eclectic artist. His shop, on Creek Street should not be missed. His T-shirts have become Northwest icons, but there is a lot more in there as well.

the north is the Tongass Historical Society, and to the east the Totem Heritage Center.

A really nice two mile walk, one way, is along the waterfront to the south past cannery row and the Coast Guard Station to Saxman, a native village with an excellent collection of totem poles, a clan lodge with the Cape Fox Dancers performing when the ships are in, as well as a carving shed. Of the three totem pole collections around Ketchikan, I like Saxman the best, because it is in an actual native village, and one gets a true sense of the struggle to make it in a fishing and logging economy.

Also the walk along the shore is a great place to look for bald eagles and see how many of the waterfront places have a plane in their backyard. There is a city bus that stops at the bottom of the hill - schedule and fare posted inside the little tribal museum on the right just up the hill - if you want to rest your feet on the way back. If you are up for a longer walk, consider the trip up to Deer Mountain Trail, entrance near Creek St.

Back in town a good place to catch some lunch is the Westmark Cape Fox Lodge - take the tramway that operates from Creek Street. On a bluff just south of downtown, the dining room offers a dramatic vista of the busy waterways and islands in front of town. At sea level just south of Creek St, is the unpretentious New York Hotel and Cafe, looking out on the boat harbor and the cruise ships beyond.

Most of the galleries and gift shops are located between the tunnel on Front Street, and Creek St. If you walk along the waterfront to the north past the tunnel, you'll find plenty of authentic Alaska to look at, especially along the water side.

Take some time to look around at the boats in the small boat harbors on both sides of the downtown docks where the cruise ships tie up. On most of the US coasts, boats this size - 40' and under - would be mostly be used for day fishing, the crews returning home at night to sleep in their own beds. But in Alaska with the fishing grounds often many hours from the nearest town, these boats are homes for their crews - often couples, sometimes with young children, for months at a time.

IN MISTY FJORDS

Actually, all of the lower southeast mainland and islands of Southeast Alaska are part of the Misty Fjords National Monument, essentially a vast wilderness, with few visitors except in the summer.

Excursions to Misty are available both by boat and plane or a combination of both. The most frequently visited spots, like Rudyerd Bay to the right, are about three hours away by boat, so if you travel both ways by boat, you'll spend a lot of your day going back and forth. One option is to take the boat in and then fly out in a seaplane. In my view, this is a wise choice, allowing you to see the dramatic marine seascape in one direction and then getting up up for a higher vista on the other leg. When the visibility is good, the view from a seaplane above Misty can be truly spectacular. It's busy in the summer with planes, kayakers, and cruise boats, but in the winter, it's pretty much deserted except for two or three boats that fish the deep inlets and fjords for crab, shrimp, and halibut. Imagine what a week's trip in that awesome country would be like for them, probably without seeing another boat the whole time.

Opposite top: Homestead along the channel south of town, near Saxman. Opposite bottom: If you have a telephoto lens, bring it; there are a lot of eagles hanging around in the trees all around town, but especially along the waterfront.

CATCHING THOSE LEGENDARY ALASKA FISH

Will I catch a fish? At each cruise port excursions offer opportunities to go out into the salt water after the wily salmon. Typically the boats are modern, comfortable cruisers with heated cabins, toilets, and able to take parties of up to six. Depending on the season and where the "bite" is, vessels may run an hour or more to get to the fish.

Most sports fishermen here like to target on king and silver salmon. Kings, running up to 60 pounds and larger, (if you catch a king over 50 pounds, it is a big event...) are generally caught from May through August with the best fishing generally in the first half of the season. Silvers run smaller, typically 6 to 12 pounds, and are available mid-June through September. Pink salmon, much smaller and less desirable to the sportsman are primarily caught by net and canned.

If you're not experienced, don't worry, there are a lot of fish in Alaska, and charter skippers are quick teachers.

But remember, it's not all about the fish—as much as anything else, going out on a charter boat for a day is an opportunity to get out close and see, up close and personal, some of the most abundant marine life and most dramatic scenery you will find anywhere. Whales, dolphins and eagles are all common sights for the charter fishermen so bring your camera.

What to do with your fish? In all towns, services are available to freeze, smoke, store, and ship your fish.

THE TWO MOOSE AIRPLANE

The floatplane arrived at the remote lake, where two hunters had each bagged a big moose. The pilot looked at the big moose racks, the bags of heavy meat, and all the hunters' gear.

"I'll have to make two trips for all this stuff," the pilot said to the men, "it'll be extra. You didn't tell me you had two moose."

"Two?" the hunters asked, annoyed. "We had two moose in here at this same lake, five years ago, and Pete just made one trip. He had the same kind of plane you had..."

"Who's Pete?" the pilot asked, "I don't know any Peter flying around here..."

"Ah, he retired," one of the hunters, said, "but he got two moose in his plane and all our gear..."

"O.K." said the pilot doubtfully, "we'll try 'er..."

The men brought all their gear down to the beach and the pilot managed to stuff it all in. Twice he had to move the plane out into deeper water so that the floats wouldn't rest too heavily on the bottom. When everything was aboard, he pushed the plane gingerly out into the lake and stepped aboard. He looked doubtfully down at the floats. They were almost underwater.

"You're sure Pete had this kind of a load?" asked the pilot again, shaking his head at how deep the floats were.

"Yep, same plane, same load," a hunter said, "plus Pete, he was a big heavy guy."

Only slightly relieved, the pilot settled into his seat, did his preflight checklist, picked the angle that would give him the longest take off run on the irregularly shaped lake and gave the engine full throttle. The plane moved very slowly at first, finally staggered into the air at the very end of the lake, but failed to clear the trees, crashing into the upper branches, which slowly lowered the plane, minus its wings, to earth.

After a long silence while the men all made sure there was no fire or broken bones, one of the men spoke up,

"Yep," he said, "this is about as far as Pete got..."

FLOATPLANE EXCURSIONS

Alaska is a bush pilot's dream. Rugged, with extensive remote and roadless areas, the floatplane pulled up behind a modest house is a common sight all throughout the state. And as any cruise ship passenger with a cabin on channel side of the ship learns in Ketchikan, there are a lot of floatplanes around. And it's not just flightseeing; these planes regularly ferry supplies as well as passengers to the many, many remote lodges and roadless settlements scattered throughout this part of Alaska

There are flightseeing excursions offered at all the places where your ship stops. Each area offers its own unique landscape. If you want to see glaciers and icefields, Juneau and Skagway are your best bets, but the scenery around Ketchikan and especially the Misty Fjords area are extremely dramatic. Don't be discouraged if the flightseeing excursions on your ship are sold out. Generally in each port of call, there are flightseeing trips offered by vendors on or close to the docks, so feel free to make your own arrangements. In recent years flying services delivering freight to remote communities and logging camps offered space available room for passengers as well. Such flights offer a chance to see the dramatic scenery of Southeast Alaska as well as the tiny out of the way scattered communities with only boat or plane access.

You might see some drama as well. On one recent freight flight with a few passengers aboard, the plane circled a small broken off bit of ice flow—sort of a flat iceberg—near LeConte Glacier, northeast of Petersburg. A mother seal was there with her two very cute and recently calved pups. As the plane circled and passengers and pilot looked on in horror, an orca (killer whale) zoomed out of the water, sliding across the ice, jaws snapping and leaving only bloody pieces of seal behind him as he slid into the water on the other side.

"That's not something you see every day..." said the pilot.

Ketchikan artist Ray Troll's legendary Humpalope sculpture. Ray's art is a cultural icon of Southeast Alaska. Don't miss his gallery on Creek Street. Below: A coil of rope in a warehouse at the Waterfall Cannery waits for workers that will never return. Once the showpiece of Southeast Alaska salmon canneries, Waterfall closed in 1970. Today it is reincarnated as Waterfall Resort, a popular high end fishing lodge.

KETCHIKAN TO JUNEAU

North of Ketchikan you'll pass out into Clarence Strait. To the west the big land mass is **Prince of Wales Island**, actually the third largest in the US. POW, as it is called locally, was pretty much ground zero for a huge logging effort starting in the 1950s. Actually, it was logging practices on POW, damaging salmon streams that essentially were the cause of the new regulations that led to the closing of the Ketchikan pulp mill in the 1980s.

Today, some logging still continues, but to a much lesser degree with some of the logs being shipped to Puget Sound, and others to small local sawmills.

In a sense Prince of Wales is making the transition to the new Alaska economy—more based on recreation than commercial fishing and logging. 25 years ago Craig, on the west coast of the island, was a rough Native town where commercial fishing was pretty much the main economic activity. Today Craig features a number of sportfishing lodges and has a surprising amount of second home construction. Much of this has been spurred by the paving of old logging roads and daily ferry service from Ketchikan to Hollis, on the east coast of Prince of Wales Island.

If you seem some small fishing skiffs around **Mile 686**, they'll be from **Meyers Chuck**, one of a handful of roadless fishing communities scattered throughout the region. In the late 1930s, the crew of the *Maggie Murphy* stopped here, still looking for the fishing bonanza they had come so far for:

> "We found a feud raging in the harbor that was as ancient and fierce as that waged between picnickers and ants. The most tedious chore the cabin dweller knows is keeping up a supply of firewood. In Alaska, stoves burn continuously for nine months of the year, and they consume prodigious

amounts of fuel. All this fuel must be obtained by felling trees and chopping them into cordwood.

"Where fishermen are living on boats, the problem is even more acute. While most boats have oil stoves, many still have old fashioned wood burners, and the owners must make frequent trips ashore in search of fuel. In Meyers Chuck, the fishermen who lived in boats piled their stove wood on the float alongside the point where they habitually docked at night.

"Once Ed and I watched a fisherman creep out of his boat and approach a nearby woodpile. He gazed furtively about to see if anyone was watching, then lifted the canvas, deftly grabbed a slab of wood, and dashed back to his boat. A few minutes later we heard him chopping, and it wasn't long before clouds of smoke were bellowing from his stove pipe.

"When the owner of the firewood came to dock, he took inventory of his woodpile and promptly missed one piece.

"'Gathering firewood is the god-awfulest job in this country!' he roared, 'A man that'll steal it ought to be strung up like a cattle rustler.'"

—John Joseph Ryan, *The Maggie Murphy*

With no road connection between most towns, tugs and barges are an essential part of transport here. Below: Deadheads: half-sunk logs, weighing several tons and sometimes extending only a few inches above the surface, are a constant treat to boaters here. Because of them, prudent mariners are very reluctant to travel after dark n small craft.

WHERE THERE ARE NO PHONES

While the roads were being paved on Prince of Wales, one of the flaggers was Ethel Hamar, who at the time lived on a floating home–on a log raft–in Coffman Cove. One of her sons worked at a log sorting yard at Craig, on the other side of the island. With no phone connection, and not having a vehicle - Ethel took a skiff ashore and walked to work - she missed keeping up with the progress of her grandchildren in Craig. Finally her son found a novel way to communicate.

So every now and then one of the big logging trucks carrying logs from the sorting yard at Craig to a log dump on Clarence Strait would honk and slow down as it passed Ethel and call down: "Got a message from yer boy, Ethel."

And on the side of one of the big logs in big spray painted red letters would be a message like:
"HEY MOM, WE'RE OK, BILLY GOT HIS FIRST TOOTH THIS WEEK"

FLOATHOME TALES

Land to buy is so scarce in this region that some enterprising folks build their houses on floating log rafts. Of course, living like this entails a few wrinkles that wouldn't occur to land dwellers. For one family with growing kids, sometimes the house just didn't seem big enough. So when the kids had cabin fever, this mother just sent them out to fish in the outhouse!

Another time, the husband noticed one of his big hundred pound propane bottles was leaking, and he was unable to fix it. Concerned that the leaking gas would be ignited by the nearby fish smoker, he disconnected and rolled it into the cove, thinking he'd let it drift out a bit with the tide, and shoot a hole in it so as to let it sink harmlessly to the bottom. But, by accident, his first shot instead knocked the valve off, and, propelled by the escaping gas, the propane bottle began moving rapidly like a torpedo in a circle back toward the float home.

Now the man really had a problem—as his horrified wife and children watched, the propane bottle gathered speed and straightened its course into a beeline right for them.

Letting his rifle rest on the porthole opening in the door to steady his aim, he tried to get a bead on the speeding bottle, but each time he was ready to shoot, the propane bottle would submerge and travel along just under the surface, impossible to hit with the rifle! Finally, when it was about 20 yards away, it surfaced just long enough for him to get a clear shot, blowing a hole in its side and it quickly sank!

When they built their home, the foundation was two huge cedar logs, with their ends cut at an angle, so that if land ever became available nearby, they could drag the cabin off the raft and onto the new land.

Top: The new house—note the floating outhouse—popular fishing spot for the kids on those long rainy days. Middle: In accordance with their native heritage—the mother was a Haida Native—the family built a dugout canoe in the traditional manner for the kids. But it looks like the boys would prefer a nice fast aluminum skiff like everyone else... Bottom: Land at last—the house moved to the new lot overlooking the cove where it used to float! Ethel Hamar photos

At **Mile 720**, about three hours after leaving Ketchikan, your ship will transit narrow **Snow Passage**. The constricted channel often creates tide rips that will bunch herring together and often attract humpback whales. Get your binoculars and go out on deck, preferably up near the bow where you can see both sides of the channel. Most ships carry a naturalist and in addition most captains are alerted to the possibility of whales here, so the presence of whales is likely to be announced. But different ships have different protocols. If there are passenger activities, and there's just a single whale blowing occasionally, it might not be announced.

If you're really fortunate and have strong binoculars, you may be able to observe bubble net feeding, a method used by humpback whales to herd fish into compact, easy-to-eat schools. The whales circle beneath the herring, exhaling slowly. The circle of bubbles serves to contain or herd the fish, and the humpbacks then surface in the middle, with their mouths open.

This area is also open to salmon gillnetting, usually fishing Sunday - Wednesday. If the fish are running the gillnetters will often work the shore near Pt. Macnamara, five miles north of the pass, off the east or right side of the ship if you are traveling northbound. The trick at this spot is <u>get close to the beach</u>. If there are boats there, glass them with your binoculars; you'll be surprised how close they get.

> ┌─── Passenger Tip ───┐
> Northbound travelers: don't miss Snow Pass, about two hours or so after leaving Ketchikan.

Four humpbacks! Below: Put your binoculars on the buoy on the east side of the channel. Often there will be sea lions on it!

PETERSBURG: 'LITTLE NORWAY'

A classic net shed along the Petersburg waterfront. In a big tide a fishing boat can come alongside to load right from the building. Bottom: In the can loft, Icicle Seafoods cannery. Cans are shipped flat and most canneries have an upper floor where the pieces go through a re-forming machine before having the end put on and being filled with salmon on the main cannery floor.

If you are on an Alaska ferry or a small cruise ship, chances are you'll travel through **Wrangell Narrows** to Petersburg. Set in one of the most dramatic landscapes in the region with 10,000' Kates Needle rising spectacularly behind, the town is known as Little Norway for its original descendants, who settled here after coming from the old country.

With strong shrimp, salmon, crab, and halibut resources close at hand and icebergs very conveniently drifting right into the boat harbor from nearby Le Conte Glacier, it was a commercial fisherman's dream. Eventually, three salmon canneries, a shrimp processor, and a cold storage plant served the needs of its fishermen.

Until about 1985, the Petersburg fishermen mostly worked the waters of Southeast Alaska. With markets for Alaska seafood expanding with the robust Japanese economy, Petersburg fishermen and a locally owned cannery, Icicle Seafoods, made a major expansion into fisheries in the remote areas of western Alaska, particularly the Bering Sea and Bristol Bay.

When many seafood markets weakened in the 1990s with the major slump in the Japanese economy, Petersburg fishing companies were mostly able to survive, while some others in Wrangell, Ketchikan, and Juneau had to close their doors.

Today, while tourism plays a huge part in the economy of most towns in the region, here it is conspicuously absent. The harbor

isn't big enough for the big ships, and candidly, the town fathers prefer to concentrate on what they know best: fishing. Nevertheless, small cruise ships—100 passengers and less—often stop here, as does the Alaska ferry.

If you do visit, stop by the harbormaster's office, just off main street, with canneries on either side. There you can pick up a town map, etc.

Two big events are the **Little Norway Festival** celebrating Norwegian Independence Day in mid May, where traditional costumes and crafts are in evidence, and Fourth of July, a bit more raucous, as the fishing fleet is usually in town.

Hammer Slough is close by with the **Sons of Norway Hall** and **Sing Yee Alley**, an excellent place for local crafts, and the **Clausen Museum** celebrating local commercial fishing.

A nice stroll is just along the watefront, north out of town. On the right you'll see the homes fishermen and processors built overlooking Frederick Sound and the entrance to Wrangell Narrows. From their view homes it was a short walk down to either the boat harbor or 'cannery row.' Not a bad life.

Stop at the Eagle's Roost Park—just north of the Icicle Seafoods cannery. With all the fish coming and going to town, not every one makes it onto the docks, and the park is a good place to observe the bald eagles who are waiting for something tasty to float by...

Just off cannery row the tide swirls into Wrangell Narrows. In a big spring tide, the level of the water is almost up to the very top of this marker! Bottom: high fish prices in the 1970s made everyone smile.

A TALE OF WRANGELL NARROWS

Once a twisting, shallow slough, Wrangell Narrows was in such an convenient place as as shortcut—saving 70 miles off the trip between Ketchikan and Juneau—that eventually the US Corps of Engineers dredged, widened, and marked the channel with 60 markers and buoys.

Even so, it is still a considerable challenge at night or in fog. The problem is that the region's big tides—the water level rising or falling as much as 23 feet in six hours—create very strong currents. It wouldn't be so bad if the channel was straight, but not only is it a real corkscrew in places, but the current can sweep obliquely across it!

In the fog and in the black the prudent mariner is best served by anchoring up off the south entrance, or tieing up to the docks in Petersburg to wait better conditions. But canneries want their fish and ferries have schedules, and sometimes they meet in the middle of the narrows:

"I hate to go through them narrows in the black and the fog, but the cannery wanted the fish, so we had to go. Then right in the narrowest place, the radio blasts in my ear: 'This is the Alaska ferry *Matanuska,* southbound at marker 16. Northbound traffic please advise.' The *Matanuska?* Just a mile ahead, and him with the tide pushing him on? I called him right back, and mister, I could hear the tension in that man's voice. '*Matanuska* back. Yeah... I see you on my radar... but you'd better pull over and let us by... it's pretty damn tight here.' We were right below Burnt Island Reef, and I could see his target on the radar getting bigger and bigger all the time. So I just slowed down and pulled over into the shallows. I'd rather put 'er ashore on a mud bank than get T-boned by a 400-foot ferry!

"I slowed right down until I was just idling into the current, and looked out into the black, trying to see him. You know how it is with that radar: when something gets really close, it just disappears into the sea clutter in the middle of the screen and you can't really tell exactly where it is. Well, the ferry did that and I was just bracing myself to hit either the shore or him, when I saw him—just a glimpse of a row of portholes rushing by fast in the night, the big tide pushing him on, and then he was gone. Man, I don't know how them fellows do it, but I know I wouldn't have liked to been him that night."

—An Alaskan tender skipper

WRANGELL AND THE STIKINE RIVER

Off the beaten path, about 25 miles southwest of Petersburg, Wrangell's history stems from its position at the mouth of the Stikine River.

This small town was the busiest spot in Alaska when the hordes bound for the Stikine and Cassiar gold rushes poured through in 1861 and 1873, bound up the Stikine, the natural route into the interior. But when the rushes were over, Wrangell settled back down into a small fishing and logging community, with many Chinese coming to work in the canneries and the first sawmill constructed in 1888.

Compared to the bigger towns where crowds overflow the sidewalks when the big ships are in, visitors here find a welcome slower pace, perhaps encountering schoolchildren selling garnets they've dug from the riverbank, and small locally owned shops instead of the big chains.

But it is still the river that is the biggest draw. It is on the main migratory route north for many species. April is especially dramatic, when 1500 plus bald eagles congregate to feed on the hooligan (a small oily fish) run, and 8-10,000 snow geese pass through on their way north to nest in the grassy tundra of western Alaska. The 160 miles between Wrangell and Telegraph Creek, in Canada, are especially dramatic, and raft or floatplane or jetboats are a great way to explore. Another visitor option is a boat trip to the Anan Creek Bear Observatory, about 30 miles south. When the fish are running, the bear are waiting for them and it's an impressive sight. Short on time? Consider a floatplane trip and ask the pilot to swing over Petersburg, Wrangell narrows, and LeConte Glacier.

Wrangell, around 1880. John Muir passed through here a few years earlier and called it "a lawless draggle of wooded huts and houses." Today's visitors will find it to be a welcome change from the crowds of the main cruise ports when the big ships are in town. ASL PCA-87 Winter& Pond Below: Totem on Shakes Island, where there is an excellent Tlingit lodge house.

Homesteader's barn at Point Baker, south of mile 745. Both the sides and the roof are covered with hand split cedar shakes, probably from driftwood logs, pulled off a Sumner Strait beach.

Salmon gillnetters usually work the Sumner Strait area, mile 740-745, typically fishing from Sunday noon to Thursday noon. The fish come from the west here, and the trick is to set your net back from the district boundary at Point Baker, so that the ebbing current carries you to the line, then stops, just as the tide turns. This gives you a front row seat, with no room for another boat to set legally between you and the incoming fish. There is also a nasty tide rip, nick-named 'the big meanie,' which blasts around the corner from the west on the bigger tides, which has given an ugly surprise to many an unsuspecting gillnetter.

It was this strongly flowing tidal current that caused Captain Johnny O'Brien's luck to run out in the black of a November night in 1917. The *Mariposa* was one of the finest steamers on the Alaska run, but while Dynamite Johnny caught a nap in his stateroom as a pilot steered, the strong current set her off course and onto Mariposa Reef, **mile 745,** where parts of her still remain.

Watch for humpback whales at Point Baker, mile 745, usually in close to the shore, west of the point. Typically a pair remains here for most of the summer, feeding on herring in the tide rips. In the 1960s, a particular whale got to be known as Ma Baker. Local lore has it that she once surfaced under one of the puddle jumpers, or small fishing skiffs, lifting the surprised fishermen and his boat completely clear of the water for a moment Point Baker and the nearby community of Port Protection are two roadless fishing communities. It was here that we built our little island homestead in 1973.

Port Protection was the occasion of one of Vancouver's closest calls. Late on the afternoon of September 8, 1793, while exploring and charting Sumner Strait, a storm was seen approaching the area. It was at last light that Lieutenant Broughton in the *Chatham* saw the entrance to what looked like a cove and signalled Vancouver to follow him into the bay, south of **mile 745**. It was just in time:

> "We had scarcely furled the sails, when the wind shifting to the S.E., the threatened storm from that quarter began to blow, and continued with increasing violence during the whole night; we had, however, very providentially reached an anchorage that completely sheltered us from its fury, and most probably from imminent danger, if not from total destruction. Grateful for such an asylum, I named it Port Protection."
>
> —Captain George Vancouver, *A Voyage of Discovery*

Look north as you pass Port Protection; the land seems to knit together at the head of the distant bay. Actually there are two separate major islands, Kuiu Island on the west and Kupreanof Island to the east. Between them is **Keku Strait**, known locally as **Rocky Pass**, a popular short-cut for small craft before the Coast Guard removed the navigational markers in the late 1970s as not cost-effective.

Hole in the Wall, east of **mile 751**, is one of Southeast Alaska's special places. From my 1973 fishing journal:

> "Of all the places we visit each year, this is one of my favorites. It's like a lake in the woods, with grassy

Beachlogging: over the years, huge logs that have broken loose from log rafts have accumulated on the shores here. In 1972, needing to build a raft for a place to work on our fishing nets, we scavenged or beachlogged these huge spruce logs off the rocky shore. Each log required almost a day's work to get it off the beach and floating again. Below: Net colors are critical to salmon gillnetters. The net on the left is a Sumner Strats net, while the bluer one on the right is a Lynn Canal net, where the ground up dust from the many glaciers make the water a bluer color.

Above: Troller entering the very narrow entrance to Hole-in-the-Wall. It's quite an experience to pick your way in here on a day when it's stormy on the outside, and enter the unruffled lake-like basin on the inside.

The lonely Cape Decision Lighthouse, Mile 773. Today, like most Southeast Alaska lighthouses, it is automated. It's a bit of a blind turn, so your bridge staff will be calling out on the radio to make sure no other big ship is coming from the other direction.

flats and steep hills above. The dusk came with muted colors, and a deer slipped out of the woods to drink in a stream. We did the dishes after supper and sat up for a bit. I don't suppose this bay sees 20 visitors a year. But within a few years the loggers will be here; they're just over the mountains now. And when they come, I don't believe I'll be back."

Near Rocky Pass in August, 1794, Lieutenant Johnstone, exploring in Vancouver's small boats, was approached by several canoes, with natives who apparently wanted to trade:

"One of the canoes now advanced before the rest, in which a chief stood in the middle of it, plucking the white feathers from the rump of an eagle and blowing them into the air, accompanied by songs and other expressions, which were received as tokens of peace and friendship."
—Capt. George Vancouver, *A Voyage of Discovery*

However, ever since the near-disastrous struggle with natives at Traitors Cove the previous summer, Vancouver's men were wary of situations in which they were outnumbered. So they wisely declined the invitation to stop and kept on rowing.

An hour or so past Point Baker, the vessel track turns sharply northward again at **Cape Decision Light, mile 773** and into **Chatham Strait.**

On some itineraries, like Seattle or Vancouver to Juneau, you'll come up the outside of Prince of Wales and Dall Islands. Look for dramatic **Helm Point**, at **Mile 730W**, a conspicuous headland on Coronation Island, 10 miles south. Rising sheer from the sea to a thousand feet, it is the nesting place for thousands of sea birds.

The bays of Coronation Island have a bad reputation among fishermen for williwaws: violent, unpredictable gusts of wind.

"Fishermen are not certain what causes the williwaws. They only know that on peaceful summer evenings, when the sea is calm and boats are resting at anchor, a dull roaring noise is sometimes heard in the harbors of Coronation Island. The noise gains steadily in volume, and suddenly, with terrifying force and swiftness, a blast of wind sweeps down off the rocky hills, scattering boats like bowling pins."
—John Joseph Ryan, *The Maggie Murphy*

LIFE IN A ROADLESS COMMUNITY
Point Baker, Mile 745

Imagine, cheap waterfront land and good fishing close at hand. This was the situation at the remote and road-less communities of Point Baker and nearby Port Protection (south of **mile 745**) in the early 1970s. A person could get an acre-sized waterfront lot on a sheltered cove, with the right to harvest a substantial amount of timber each year from the adjacent forest to use for lumber. So if you couldn't afford store-bought lumber, you could build your house from the nearby trees and make enough cash fishing salmon from an outboard skiff to support a family.

A floating store/bar/fish-buyer at Point Baker served the needs of the hundred or so souls settled around these two coves on the edge of the vast woods. The mail and freight boat came once a week, supplemented by the occasional floatplane. Families with gill-netters or trollers tried to make a trip to town—Wrangell or Petersburg, each about 40 miles away, a long day's round trip—every few months to stock up on supplies a little cheaper.

Top: Skiff fishermen at sunset, Point Baker. The fishing grounds were close enough that a person could make a living salmon fishing in in small craft. Bottom: Herring for bait was abundant and could be had by just setting a small gillnet overnight.

Top: With dock space in town for working on nets scarce, my friends and I scavenged big float logs off the beach, ordered lumber from the sawmill in Wrangell and built our own float. Bottom: A gillnet comes in. A foot pedal controls the drum that pulls the net in. This is a 'dead man's' control; getting pulled off your feet by the net stops the drum! Right: My neighbor, "Flea," a skiff fisherman who taught newcomers the trade.

Behind the shore was the forest—thick, almost impenetrable. For the most part walking was so difficult everyone traveled by outboard. At Point Baker, especially, one's traveling decisions were dictated by the tide. Have a whiskey warmup some snowy winter afternoon with your groceries at the store? Stay too late and the trip home might be a nightmare: wading along the shallow channel, towing your skiff behind you, lifting, scraping it over the thin places, picking your way with the flashlight through the snow, and hoping your batteries last until you make it home.

When I arrived here with my former wife on our 32-foot gill-netter in the spring of 1972, the flavor of the place was compelling. The older residents welcomed younger blood, and the salmon fishing in Sumner Strait was great. We found part of an island, on a private cove, with a gorgeous western exposure and view, for $17,000. After the season, in our houseboat on Seattle's Lake Union, made plans for a cabin on our newly- purchased land in Point Baker. As our money dwindled, so did the size of our new-home-to-be until whatever roof we could get over our heads for fifteen hundred bucks would have to be it. We settled on a 16-by-20-foot box with a half loft, 480-square-feet, total, tiny, but it would have all that we needed.

With tight-fisted determination, we scoured garage sales and discount building suppliers. At a second-hand store we found a big diesel oil range for $35; at another, all our windows and doors for $175. In my tiny floating shop I pre-

AT THE POINT BAKER FLOATING BAR

Conveniently located on a raft of big logs, tying up at the Point Baker Bar allowed you to avoid having to make your way down a steep ramp to your boat at low tide after hoisting a few with your fishing buddies after a hard day 'on the grounds.'

On a busy Saturday night with all the fleet in, you'd better be wearing your boots as well, as when it got crowded, water would begin to seep through the floor as the log raft settled with the load!

And being a bit of a rough and tumble place, it offered less of a drink selection than some visitors are used to in other places. Once, a couple arrived on their nice new gillnetter, fresh in from the run up from Seattle and went in to toast the upcoming salmon season.

"What'll it be?" said the burly bartender who was also the fish buyer in town.

"What d'ya want, honey?" said the newcomer to his nicely coiffed wife.

"Hmmm," said she, "How about a Manhatten? That'd go down pretty smooth..."

"Look guys," said the bartender, "We got whiskey and water, whiskey and coke, and whiskey and tang. And we save the ice for the fish. So what'll it be?"

Top: View out our front window in 1975. If you are a commercial fisherman and can look out your front window and see your boat moored peacefully below your house, you are living your dream! Below: Fuel delivery! Romey Kaleski, a local homesteader, prepares to tow a drum of gas, delivered by a fish buying boat, back to his waterfront home. Gas is lighter than water so a drum floats!

fabbed a Formica kitchen counter top, complete with sink and drawers. We got plywood, nails, and shingles, all on deep discount, and purchased a 16-foot cedar skiff with a 10-horsepower 1958 Evinrude outboard. Tool by tool, fitting by fitting, we packed all the supplies and extras aboard my 32-foot gill-net vessel and skiff to tow north.

Shortly after arriving in Point Baker, the mail boat arrived with our pickup truck sized bundle of lumber, The plan had been to tow the tightly strapped bundle of lumber through the narrow back channel to our secluded cove and house site. But it was so green and dense, it wouldn't even float. It was what was locally called, "pond dried."

So we had to set it temporarily on the dock and then haul it in our skiff, load by load, to our cove.

In the two weeks before the salmon season began we struggled: the wood was so wet it splashed when your hammer missed the nail. My one and only hand saw bent on the first beam we cut. It rained every day; every night we would take the skiff back to our boat at the Point Baker dock, heat up something quick, and fall, exhausted, shivering, into our sleeping bags.

And we created something exquisite: out of every window was the water. As we ate at the driftwood table, we could see eagles swooping low over the cove. There were curious seals, and most marvelous of all, a pair of hump-

backs that hung out in the tide rips by West Rock, off the mouth of our cove. On still nights, we could hear the sigh-like breathing of the whales as they surfaced and exchanged fresh air for stale. When the first snow came one November evening, the fire in the wood stove crackled cheerily, our kerosene lamp shone out on the vast and wild world beyond the windows, and it was magic.

In summer, with daylight that lasted from four in the morning until after eleven at night, the focus was fishing: making enough to make it through the long winter. But when the season was over, there was time for the kind of relaxed visiting that is a highlight of life in such places.

Seeking greener pastures, I sold my cabin at Point Baker in the mid-1980s and built a new boat for the remote salmon fishery in Bristol Bay, Alaska, 1,000 miles west. Bleak, austere, remote, with violent tidal currents and few good harbors, Bristol Bay was the opposite of Southeast Alaska. The fishing was a competitive frenzy I'd never experienced before, but many of my friends from Point Baker and Southeast Alaska were there and the shorter season allowed us more time at home with our families and children.

Yet to a man (Alaska law allows salmon fishermen to fish only a single region), we all missed the wooded waterways and secluded harbors we'd left behind.

Working on your net is an integral part of salmon fishing! Below: A salmon fishing family enjoys a little free time between the weekly fishing periods.

AROUND TOWN

Right: The Point Baker floating post office. The post mistress's husband also had a tiny store in here as well with some canned goods, paper towels, etc. It was definitely just the basics!

Left: Retired fisherman living on his boat at the Point Baker dock, right in the middle of all the action. Bottom: Troller's homestead, Port Protection. Bottom left: A hand troller pulls in to the fish buyer to unload. The bartender at the Point Baker floating bar was also a fish buyer and you could sell your fish for bar credit!

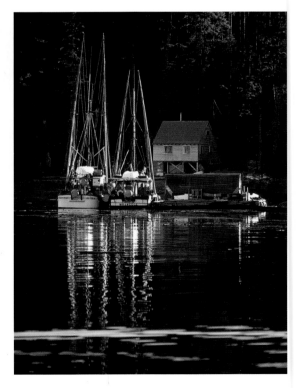

LEVIATHAN OF THE DEEP
SPERM WHALE 65 FEET LONG

CHATHAM STRAIT: THE LONELY CANYON

"June 4, 1974 - The day came cloudless and still. To pull the anchor in the pale predawn off another lifeless cannery, slip out into the empty strait, put our gear in the water before the sun comes over the mountain, just our two boats in maybe a hundred miles of shoreline - this is my bell, ringing."

- Author's journal

If you're a northbound passenger on the Ketchikan - Juneau itinerary, try and go up to the forward lounge or any place where you have a good view ahead the evening of the day you leave Ketchikan. If you left at 2, like many ships, you'll probably be at Cape Decision lighthouse at around 10 PM. Have a look around as your ship makes almost a right angle turn around the lighthouse and north into wide and lonely Chatham Strait.

For much of this century, **Chatham Strait** was a beehive of activity. Between the salmon plants, the herring plants, and the whaling stations, almost every bay in this canyon-like region was home to some sort of commercial activity, frenzied during the summer fishing season, and sleepier in winter, with usually just a caretaker and his family keeping a watch on things. Then the herring and the whales disappeared, and refrigerated tenders allowed consolidation of the salmon canneries into towns like Petersburg and Ketchikan.

Sperm whale at Port Armstrong, Chatham Strait, Mile 800, circa 1900 Many of the bays on both sides of this strait once held some sort of fish processing facility. MOHAI 15329
Below: Fishing buddies. On this particular boat, the child was also tied to the middle of the boat with a tether, allowing him to get to the rail but no further...

The old store at Killisnoo near the Native village of Angoon, in 1974. Today the building is almost gone, and the island is the location of the Whaler's Cove Lodge for sport fishermen. Below: An old timer at Port Alexander remembers the old days when hand trollers set up their tents all around the harbor to fish the run of big king and sliver salmon running at Cape Ommaney.

For the small craft traveler today, it is almost spooky to travel in Chatham Strait, to anchor and go ashore and wander in the ruins, rarely encountering another traveler.

One of the few settlements along here is **Port Alexander, Mile 792.** With a good harbor, a settlement, a fish buyer and a store, and good fishing at Cape Ommaney (west of mile 786), it's a popular spot in summer. In its heyday, the 1920s and 1930s, it was Alaska with a capital A, as the *Maggie Murphy* boys noted:

"It became the number one trolling port in the territory, a wide-open, carefree, money-kissed little place that old-timers still recall with nostalgia."
—John Joseph Ryan, *The Maggie Murphy*

When they walked into town, they were halted by an elderly man who told them, "Boys, it's illegal to walk on the streets of Port Alexander sober."

In those days, many trollers worked out of open boats, some without motors, rowing as they towed their lines through the water. A little tent city sprang up south of the dock each summer. By the late 1940s the party was over, the great runs rapidly diminishing as the newly-built dams on the Columbia River, 1,200 miles south, prevented the big kings from reaching their spawning grounds.

At **Port Conclusion**, three miles north of Port Alexander, Vancouver anxiously awaited the four overdue cutters and yawl boats that were filling in the last blank places on his chart in August, 1794. Finally the boats hove safely into sight during a rainstorm on the 19th.

Then with grog for all hands, and cheers ringing from ship to ship in a remote cove halfway around the world from England, there ended one of the most remarkable feats of navigation and exploration in modern times. In three summers of exploring and charting this unknown coast, through persistent fogs, swift currents and occasional thick ice— losing just one man to bad shellfish— Vancouver had disproved the ages-old notion of a Northwest Passage back to the Atlantic. In doing so, he charted, explored, described and named much of the Northwest coast. It was nothing less than a stunning achievement. He was 38 years old.

Look southeast from around **mile 845** to the head of the island-choked bay and to Rocky Pass, the narrow back channel to Sumner Strait. It was this narrow channel ("we paddled on through the midst of the innumerable islands") from which John Muir, an evangelist companion, and a group of native paddlers emerged on the morning of October 19, 1879. The natives dreaded the crossing of Frederick Sound to Point Gardner at the southern tip of Admiralty Island:

> "Toyatte said he had not slept a single night thinking of it, and after we rounded Cape Gardner and the comparatively smooth Chatham Strait, they all rejoiced, laughing and chatting like frolicsome children."
> — John Muir, *Travels in Alaska*

Baranof Island looms in early morning light across Chatham Straits from the Native village of Kake, southeast of Mile 845. Below: The forest slowly reclaims the old salmon cannery at Washington Bay, east of Mile 820.

When salmon prices were particularly high in the 1970s and 1980s, folks in small open boats like this could make a pretty good paycheck, and old abandoned canneries offered a place to live for the summer months as well. When I was a fish buyer, I met a couple fishing out an open skiff like this one, and the fellow shared this story with me:

"My wife was 7 months pregnant, so I pretty much fished alone except when it was really calm We didn't have money for rent anywhere, so were just squatting in the old abandoned cannery at Pillar Bay. There was a fish buyer down at Tebenkof that summer, so we could sell our fish without having to run across the strait. But still, when I needed supplies or medicine, I'd have to take my boat over to PA, (Port Alexander) all the way across the strait.

"It can get really nasty out there. Once I was crossing, and a big northerly came up, blowing against a big tide running hard from the south, and all of a sudden I was in the worst tide rip I'd even seen. A big sea came out of nowhere and filled my boat just like that. The engine stopped, and I couldn't start it, and I threw everything heavy over the side. I figured I was toast, and wondered if anyone would even know to check in on Judy...

"Then out of nowhere this big troller appeared, and threw me a line–I tied it off on my bow and he just put it on the slow bell, towing me slow ahead. Just that was enough to keep my bow up and the boat floating long enough for me to bail the boat out and get the engine going again.

"But the weird thing was I'd looked around just before the wave hit me and I hadn't seen another boat <u>anywhere</u>! He just came out of nowhere and saved me. It was a miracle."

The next year I bumped into him again in Port Alexander. They had a nice rented cabin then, a fat baby, a full woodshed and a big garden out back. Life was good.

Gaff hook and ADF&G placard aboard hand trolling skiff. All fishing vessels must be licensed by the Alaska Department of Fish and Game.

The village visible to the southeast from **mile 845** is **Kake**, a Tlingit village supported by a cannery and logging on native land. Locals use narrow Rocky Pass frequently as a short cut to Sumner Strait. According to one story they were astounded a few years back, to see a tug towing a big barge emerging from the constricted passage. No one could remember such a big vessel or barge coming through the pass before. The skipper stepped out and hailed some locals fishing from a skiff:

"Say," the rough-looking man said, waving a hand back toward Rocky Pass, "that Wrangell Narrows ain't nothing like the chart." He stopped and looked over at the village on the shore, "And I thought Petersburg was larger than this." He was 40 miles west of where he thought he was!

As recently as the early 1980s, icebergs could be seen near Turnabout Island, Mile 856. This is the southern limit of drift ice from the glaciers in Tracy and Endicott Arms, east of **mile 900**, and Le Conte Glacier, east of Petersburg. But today the ice has receded so substantially that it is rare to see

ice out into Stephens Passage.

It doesn't take much of an iceberg to puncture the hull of a fiberglass or wooden fishing boat. Plus ice is not very buoyant so an iceberg the size of a dump truck would hardly show above the surface of the water, and be almost impossible to see on radar if there was any kind of a choppy sea running or a swell driving up from the Gulf of Alaska. So boats would travel very cautiously in these waters if visibility was poor.

The icebergs did have benefits though. When I was a fish buyer, trying to save time and fuel on the long run up to Chilkat Inlet in Lynn Canal, **Mile 1000N**, we'd pull up as close as we could to the biggest iceberg we could find - tie right to it if it was calm - and turn on our pumps and suck the cold water right around the iceberg into our big insulated fish hold and thus save hours of running the noisy refrigeration system!

On the shore of **Harbor Island**, which guards the entrance to Tracy Arm, west of **mile 900**, is an abandoned homestead and fox farm These were common on small Southeastern Alaska islands in the 1940s and 1950s. Typically fed salmon in season, the foxes were a problem to feed when the fish weren't running.

"When we were low on fox food, Dad would send my brother and me over to Point Astley, where there were lots of seals and sea lions. We'd shoot those big sea lions, and then we had to cut the carcasses into pieces with a two-man saw to load into the skiff. God, it was a mess."

— A fox farmer's son

Top: Iceberg in Stephens Passage in 1975. The glaciers that produce icebergs have receded so much in recent years that icebergs are quite rare here. Below: Old wind up record player or victrola, at abandoned fox farm on Harbor Island, at the entrance to Tracy Arm. See story on left.

Tracy Arm, 1972. Don't let your dog off on an iceberg; they don't like it... Below: If you look carefully at the walls, you can see the striations—long gouges or scratches made by the glacier as it moved down the canyon.

TRACY ARM. TIP: GET UP EARLY.

Many ships enter Tracy Arm around 6 a.m. so they can get to Juneau for a port call in time for passengers to go on their shore excursions

If yours does: get up early! The entrance, particularly that first right angle turn is truly spectacular, as the light can be exquisite at that time of day.

Traveling up Tracy Arm (the entrance is five miles northeast of **mile 900**) is like going back through geologic history. The fjord's dramatic walls lose their vegetation until they become bare shining rock, shaped and ground smooth by the ice. In many places the mountains plunge vertically into the water, which is more than a thousand feet deep.

Muir was genuinely moved by the power and the beauty of the glaciers, and he was able to communicate some of this enthusiasm to his companions. Once, when they had paddled most of an afternoon up Tracy Arm, frustrated with the narrow and ice-choked channel, they turned yet another corner and found what he had come to seek, the glacier itself. While Muir stood in the canoe, sketching the glacier, several huge icebergs calved off, thundering into the water of the narrow fjord. "The ice mountain is well disposed toward you," one of the native paddlers said to Muir, "He is firing his big guns to welcome you."

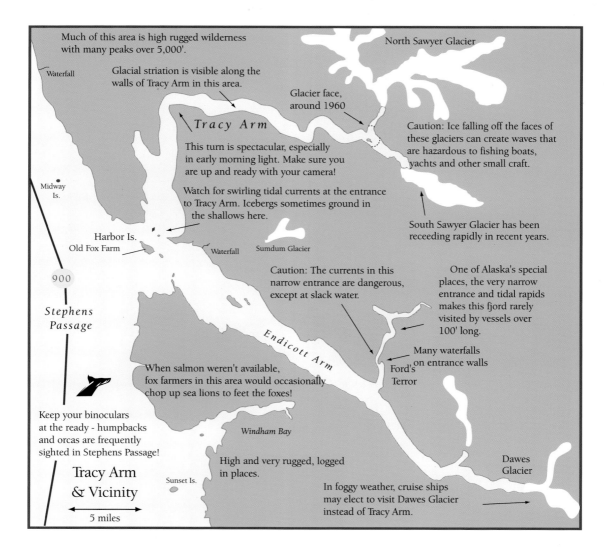

Much of this area is high rugged wilderness with many peaks over 5,000'.

North Sawyer Glacier

Waterfall

Glacial striation is visible along the walls of Tracy Arm in this area.

Glacier face, around 1960

Caution: Ice falling off the faces of these glaciers can create waves that are hazardous to fishing boats, yachts and other small craft.

Tracy Arm

This turn is spectacular, especially in early morning light. Make sure you are up and ready with your camera!

Midway Is.

Watch for swirling tidal currents at the entrance to Tracy Arm. Icebergs sometimes ground in the shallows here.

South Sawyer Glacier has been receeding rapidly in recent years.

Harbor Is.
Old Fox Farm

Waterfall

Sumdum Glacier

Caution: The currents in this narrow entrance are dangerous, except at slack water.

One of Alaska's special places, the very narrow entrance and tidal rapids makes this fjord rarely visited by vessels over 100' long.

900

Stephens Passage

Endicott Arm

Many waterfalls on entrance walls

Ford's Terror

When salmon weren't available, fox farmers in this area would occasionally chop up sea lions to feet the foxes!

Keep your binoculars at the ready - humpbacks and orcas are frequently sighted in Stephens Passage!

Windham Bay

Dawes Glacier

Tracy Arm & Vicinity

Sunset Is.

High and very rugged, logged in places.

In foggy weather, cruise ships may elect to visit Dawes Glacier instead of Tracy Arm.

5 miles

"Tracy Arm, the north arm of Holkam Bay, takes a general northerly direction for 9 miles, then turns eastward 13 miles to its head, where two large glaciers, North and South Sawyer discharge into salt water. The arm is often clogged by small icebergs for several miles and great care is needed in navigating the ice field. At times South Sawyer Glacier is very active, huge blocks of ice falling off its face into very deep water."
– U. S. Coast Pilot, Volume 8, 1969

Entering Tracy Arm aboard the 110 passenger ship, Spirit of Oceanus. Be sure to set your alarm and get up early—the entrance is a dramatic twisting canyon.

Tracy is especially suited for small ships, that can get up close to the ice. Many, like the Spirit of Oceanus group here, use inflatable boats or Zodiacs to explore the shore. The area close to the glacier is narrow and can be congested with ice; large ships might not be able to get as close to the ice as their passengers might like.

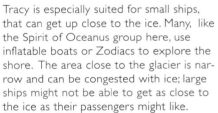

Fords Terror, 1973: one of Alaska's Special Places, little visited, very wild, and very lonely.

VOICES FROM FORDS TERROR

Ford's Terror is a wilderness basin about 15 miles south of Tracy Arm, named for a naval lieutenant who was sucked in by the current in 1899 and had a terrifying few hours while the ice and the violent current in the entrance swirled around his boat. A few yachts visit each year and float planes fly in kayak groups. Its challenging entrance keeps the visitors away, but it truly is one of the most spectacular places in Southeast Alaska.

"...we found ourselves on a smooth mirror reach between granite walls of the very wildest and most exciting description, surpassing in some ways those of the far-famed Yosemite Valley."
- John Muir, *Travels in Alaska*

"Sept 5, 1973: Just at one, traveling dead slow, with little water under us, we passed the rapids in the creek-like entrance to Fords Terror. Hardly spoke a word for the next mile, so overpowering was the scenery. The sun went over the mountain at 4:30, and the evening came early and chill. At dusk, flight after flight of ducks came in low and fast, to settle on the water near the shore with a rush of many wings and soft callings.

"The night was chilly, with northern lights again. Stood out on deck and watched, until the cold drove us in. Yesterday and today, the places we visited make us feel tiny indeed.

"September 6, 1973: First frost! The stove went out in the night, and we woke to find the dog nestled in between us. To go out onto the frosty deck on such a morning, with the still glassy basin around, and the dark forests and frozen hills above— words can't tell it, pictures can't show it.

"Our cup seems pretty full just now."
- my fishing journal

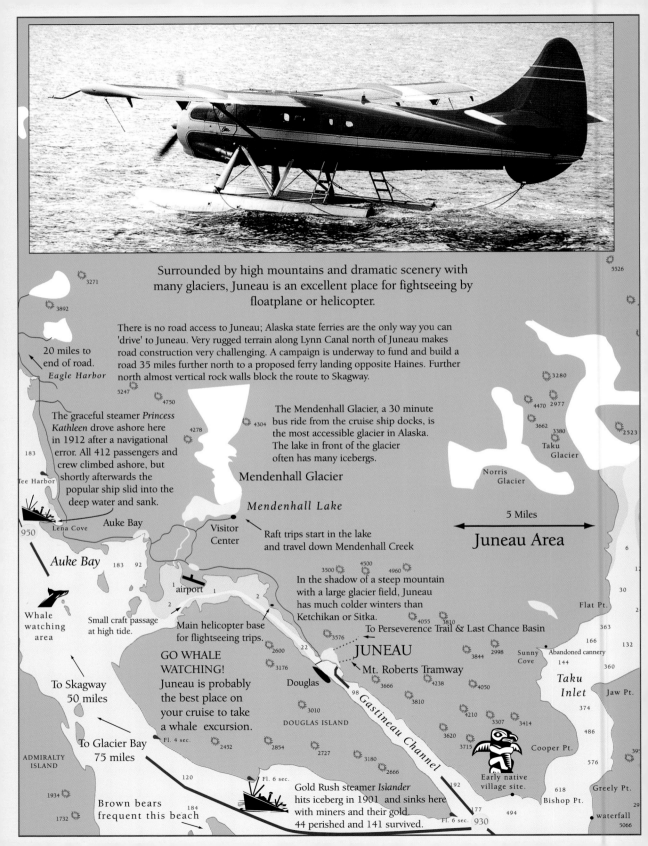

Surrounded by high mountains and dramatic scenery with many glaciers, Juneau is an excellent place for fightseeing by floatplane or helicopter.

There is no road access to Juneau; Alaska state ferries are the only way you can 'drive' to Juneau. Very rugged terrain along Lynn Canal north of Juneau makes road construction very challenging. A campaign is underway to fund and build a road 35 miles further north to a proposed ferry landing opposite Haines. Further north almost vertical rock walls block the route to Skagway.

20 miles to end of road.
Eagle Harbor

The graceful steamer *Princess Kathleen* drove ashore here in 1912 after a navigational error. All 412 passengers and crew climbed ashore, but shortly afterwards the popular ship slid into the deep water and sank.

Tee Harbor

Lena Cove   Auke Bay

Auke Bay

Whale watching area

Small craft passage at high tide.

To Skagway 50 miles

To Glacier Bay 75 miles

ADMIRALTY ISLAND

Brown bears frequent this beach

The Mendenhall Glacier, a 30 minute bus ride from the cruise ship docks, is the most accessible glacier in Alaska. The lake in front of the glacier often has many icebergs.

Mendenhall Glacier

Mendenhall Lake

Visitor Center

Raft trips start in the lake and travel down Mendenhall Creek

airport

In the shadow of a steep mountain with a large glacier field, Juneau has much colder winters than Ketchikan or Sitka.

To Perseverance Trail & Last Chance Basin

JUNEAU

Mt. Roberts Tramway

Main helicopter base for flightseeing trips.

GO WHALE WATCHING! Juneau is probably the best place on your cruise to take a whale excursion.

Douglas

DOUGLAS ISLAND

Gastineau Channel

Norris Glacier

Taku Glacier

5 Miles

Juneau Area

Flat Pt.

Sunny Cove   Abandoned cannery

Taku Inlet

Jaw Pt.

Cooper Pt.

Early native village site.

Bishop Pt.

Greely Pt.

waterfall

Gold Rush steamer *Islander* hits iceberg in 1901 and sinks here with miners and their gold. 44 perished and 141 survived.

Fl. 4 sec.
Fl. 6 sec.
Fl. 6 sec.

JUNEAU AND VICINITY

A bear? Behind the espresso stand? No roads in or out? (you have to come by boat or plane...) What kind of a state capital is this? Probably different from what you're used to...

Almost surrounded by high mountains and with a vast ice field—larger than Rhode Island—to the north, Juneau winters are substantially colder than Ketchikan or Sitka. Tlingit natives had fish camps near today's downtown, but wintered in a more temperate and sheltered area near Auke Bay.

In 1880 Kowee, the local Tlingit chief, led two prospectors, Joe Juneau and Richard Harris, up Gold Creek, which runs through today's downtown, to what is now Silver Bow Basin. The men found ample nuggets and quartz laced with gold, and Alaska's first gold rush was on.

However, the easy to find streambed gold was quickly gathered up, and a new kind of enterprise was formed to follow the gold underground. This industrial scale deep tunnel hard rock mining was very different from other Alaska gold rushes where individuals or small groups of men worked creeks and beaches with essentially hand tools.

At Juneau, high grade ore was quickly exhausted and massive stamp mills were built to extract gold; it wasn't uncommon for 20 or more tons of ore to be dug and processed to yield a single ounce of fine gold. The tailings—the crushed rock that was left, was dumped along the shore, creating the flat land on which today's downtown Juneau was built on. At peak capacity, the big stamp mills of the Alaska-Juneau mine, still visible above the

See it before it melts—kayakers at Mendenhall Lake. This glacier has receded dramatically in recent years. Below: Tulips and totem at the Governor's Mansion overlooking the harbor.

135

Treadwell mine, on Douglas Island, across from Juneau, around 1905. UW La Roche 10021 The area on the far shore, above the island is the location of downtown and the Mt. Roberts Tramway. Below: Sculpture commemorating the hard rock miners who toiled far underground in Juneau area gold mines. Opposite page: downtown waterfront, tramway station in center of photo.

cruise ship docks, could crush 12,000 tons of ore a day. Working conditions were dangerous and - the entrance to the big Treadwell mine was nicknamed the "glory Hole," for all the miners—sometimes one a week—that went to glory there. Eventually the gold played out, the tunnels—by then deep under the channel—filled with water, and today all that's left is ruins of the old stamp mill on the hill above the cruise ship dock.

But the gold is still there and a 21st century style mine—designed with minimal visual and environmental impact—is being built on a slope above Lynn Canal, above 45 miles north of Juneau.

The gold made Juneau the economic capital, so the legislative capital was moved there as well from Sitka in 1906. As the gold played out, government jobs, both state and federal, assumed a dominant role in Juneau's economy.

Because of these government jobs, economic life in Juneau is much less seasonal than in other Alaska coastal towns which are more dependent on tourism and sport and commercial fishing. For this reason, the impact of the growing cruise ship industry sets a little less easy with Juneau residents. Cruise ship captains have learned that if they want to avoid an angry call from the harbormaster, they need to keep their deck public address systems off as they pass Douglas (across the channel from Juneau) as they approach and leave town. Another source of annoyance to locals is the noise created by the flightseeing helicopters and float planes, which echo up off the steep rock walls behind town. In order to avoid the air pollution that occurs when four or five big thousand footers are running their generators in the harbor, cruise operators have installed dock wiring to allow their ships to operate off local hydroelectrical power while in port.

Like most cruise ports, the shops and galleries are concentrated right near the docks, and passengers will be pleasantly surprised at the peaceful pace of life on the streets if they take the time to walk up and out of the downtown commercial district.

The **Mt. Roberts Tramway** operates from right by the main cruise ship docks, and takes visitors about 1,800 feet up to a visitors center with dramatic views, restaurant and gift shop. The facility is owned by a Tlingit native corporation and shows a well crafted free documentary film.

There is a winding trail back down to the end of 6th St. from the top of Mt. Roberts, but it is narrow, steep, and usually slippery, so have good footware and be limber if you give it a try!

Another good stop close to the docks is the **Taku Fisheries Ice House,** at the south end of the main downto dock complex. This is an active fish processing facility with ice being delivered, boats unloading, as well as a great seafood restaurant and retail shop with some excellent smoked seafood products.

Shopping: North Franklin Street, which runs right past the cruise ship docks, is the main passenger shopping venue. If you are at all interested in Native Alaskan Art, I recommend taking some time in the art galleries here. Sometimes you have to look a bit for the best buys; I

WALKING AROUND JUNEAU

A quick loop—an hour or so—offers a glimpse of the contrasts in this town. Start by walking up North Franklin Street (the main shopping street that starts at the cruise ship docks), jog right one block on 7th. to Gold St, turn left and follow Gold uphill and onto Basin Road, which parallels Gold Creek back into Silver Bow Basin. It will be noticeably cooler up here and you will have dramatic vistas both of town below and the harbor beyond, as well as the dramatic hills above Gold Creek.

At the first bridge on Basin Road there will be a trail off to the left to The Flume, a mile long boxed water trough with a boardwalk on top, that leads back down to the end over Evergreen Street above downtown again. From there you can work your way down, staying left and avoiding the dead end streets until you cross Gold Creek and the road becomes Calhoun St. You'll pass the **Governor's Mansion** with its totem pole, then the **Juneau Douglas Museum**, before two blocks later, turning onto North Franklin again.

A longer alternative is to continue on Basin Rd. up to the **Last Chance Mining Museum and Historical Park**. The museum is in the restored

compressor building of the old Alaska-Juneau mine. If you go this way, give yourself two hours for the walk and the museum visit.

On either route, take some time to explore the steep streets to the east or right off North Franklin as you walk uphill. As you will quickly discover, these houses are built on steep hills and in some cases are only reached by boardwalks and stairs. Imagine lugging your groceries with a child in a backpack up these steep stairs after dark on an icy winter evening.

Over on Douglas Island is the two mile long **Treadwell Historical Trail**. Take the bridge from downtown, turn left, and walk about 3 miles to the trailhead at Sandy Beach. The woodsy trail meanders through what was once the Treadwell Mile complex. It was here, across from Juneau that the tunnels were bored, eventually several thousand feet beneath Gastineau Channel. This was a productive mine until April of 1917, when a tunnel wall collapsed, quickly filling the tunnel and shaft complex with sea water. Fortunately it gave enough warning for all the miners to escape, but that was it for the Treadwell.

found a wonderful carving of an Eskimo lodge on the dusty bottom shelf of one of these galleries for $500, both an unusual item and an excellent value. There's a photo of it on P. 235.

Mendenhall Glacier: If there ever were a reason for the "See it before it melts," motto used by some travel agents, it is this glacier. Very accessible - just 12 miles from downtown and included on many excursions, it has dramatically sped up its retreat back towards the Juneau Ice Field. Between 1980 and 1999, Mendenhall retreated an average of 90 feet a year, then startled biologists by dramatically speeding up - losing 300 feet in 2000, and more than 600 feet in 2004. What's particularly scenic is that it regularly calves small blue icebergs - the size of trucks and houses into Mendenhall Lake, creating a spectacular foreground.

Getting There: If you are taking an excursion in Juneau, and Mendenhall isn't included consider the inexpensive bus - $6 one way - that operates from kiosks near the base of the Mt. Roberts Tramway. It's about a 25 minute ride. If you are taking a whale watching excursion, you can arrange to take an inexpensive shuttle to Mendenhall on the way back - it is almost on the way.

Whale Watching: A special mention should be made of the whale watching excursions operating out of Auke Bay. There are usually resident populations of both killer and humpback whales in nearby Lynn Canal, and this tour has an excellent record of finding them and many passengers have reported seeing humpbacks bubble feeding or breaching on these tour boats.

Red Dog Saloon: If you're looking for a colorful spot for a modestly priced pub food style meal, stop in at the Red Dog Saloon, right on North Franklin, about two blocks from the tramway station. With sawdust on the floor, banjo playing and rustic decor, it's full of local flavor.

SOME JUNEAU EXCURSIONS

Mendenhall Glacier Explorer
Mendenhall Glacier & Salmon Hatchery Tour
Original Alaska Salmon Bake
Underground Juneau
Rainforest Garden
A Taste Of Juneau
Guide's Choice Adventure Hike
Dog Sled Summer Camp
Gold Panning & History Tour
Glacier View Bike & Brew
Rainforest Canopy & Zipline Expedition
Mountain Zip & Rainforest Bike Ride
Juneau Sportfishing Adventure
Juneau Fly-Out Fly Fishing
Juneau Steamboat Cruise
Photo Safari By Land & Sea

Alaska's Whales & Rainforest Trails
Whale Watching & Wildlife Quest
Mendenhall Glacier & Whale Quest
Whale Watching & Orca Point Lodge
Mendenhall Glacier Float Trip
Glacier View Sea Kayaking
Mendenhall Glacier Canoe Adventure
Taku Glacier Lodge Flight & Feast
Pilot's Choice Ice Age Exploration
Mendenhall Glacier Helicopter Tour
Four Glacier Adventure By Helicopter
Extended Helicopter Glacier Trek
Glacier & Dog Sled Adventure By Helicopter
Dog Sledding On The Mendenhall
Custom Hummer Adventure

S I T K A

Mt. Edgecumbe looms over Sitka. On a recent April Fool's Day, a group of pranksters landed a helicopter in the crater and set a smoky fire of old tires to simulate volcanic activity! Below: Fast waterjet powered boats allow sightseeing and whalewatching access to the intricate waterways around Sitka.

Consider yourself lucky if your ship stops here. The lack of a cruise ship dock (all but very small cruise ships anchor and use lighters to send passengers ashore) and a slightly off the beaten path location make for a much more mellow downtown environment than you will find in other major Alaska cruise ports. Additionally, Sitka is easily your most historic port.

When Juneau was woods and snow and Ketchikan was a summer village of the Tlingit people, Sitka residents enjoyed theater, fine wines, and all the riches that the sea otter trade provided her Russian residents.

It was a trade based on the sometimes unwilling participation of the native people. In the Aleutian Islands, for example, the promyshlenniki, as the Russian fur traders were called, had no qualms about destroying whole villages if the Aleut residents didn't quickly obey them.

At Sitka, the proud Tlingit people cared little for the Russians, and in 1802 they destroyed the first Russian outpost, north of the present town site. Two years later the Russians returned with three ships and many Aleut mercenaries in kayak-like bidarka boats. Finally routing the Tlingits, the Russians reestablished Sitka on the site of the Tlingit village, Shee Atika.

For much of its Russian history, Sitka's leader was Aleksandr Baranov, who established schools for the Tlingits and made Sitka the trading capital of the northwest coast. These were prosperous years when Sitka was the busiest port on the entire west coast of North and South America.

Fortunately for the Americans, the Russians' enlightenment didn't extend to conserving the valuable fur resource, for once the sea otter had been slaughtered almost to extinction, financial reverses made the Russians willing to sell Alaska to the United States for $7.2 million, about 2 cents an acre, which they did in 1867.

After the Americans took over, Sitka slowly evolved into a sleepy fishing and logging town until World War II when the Japanese invasion of the Aleutians triggered a massive navy operation near where the site of the present airport, with a huge influx of sailors.

In more modern times, Sitka's economy pretty much depended on the big plywood mill out in Sawmill Cove, and commercial fishing. The closure of the mill in 1992 was a substantial financial blow. But instead of languishing, Sitka experienced sort of a slow renaissance based on the arts, and to a lesser degree, tourism.

Today, having missed the booms and busts of the gold rush, Sitka, way out on the ocean side of Baranof Island, is the cultural center of Southeastern Alaska. Yet Sitka offers more than museums and vistas:

Go fishing; If you have any inclination to try for a salmon or halibut, Sitka is an excellent place to go out on one of the charter vessels. The city's unique position on the outside coast and the strong runs of king and silver salmon make the chances of getting a fish here very high. Such a trip is also an opportunity to see close-up the dramatic coast of Alaska and its sea life and wildlife.

Jet boats: Advances in vessel design and propulsion have made an unusual experience available at Sitka: the high-speed jet boats. Propelled by water jets (essentially large pumps) rather than conventional propellers, these

Close to the ocean, sport and commercial fishing are an essential part of Sitka's economy. Bottom left: the Alaska Pioneer's Home, many of whose members were commercial fishermen, overlooks the busy waterfront. Below: Unusual totem at Sitka National Historic Park.

The domes of St. Michael's Cathedral part of Sitka's rich Russian heritage. Sadly the original structure was completely destroyed by fire in 1966, so what you see is a reconstruction.
Below: Most cruise ships here anchor a mile or more from the docks, and send passengers ashore by lighter.

impressive craft allow passengers to travel quickly to places such as Salisbury Sound, 25 miles north of town. The abundant wildlife populations make it likely you'll see a whale, bear, or sea otter (today protected by federal law).

The Sheldon Jackson Museum: In his travels through the state as education agent, Dr. Jackson acquired a remarkable collection of native art and historical artifacts. Even if you have seen other such displays, you will find this collection unusually complete and worth seeing. The Aleut and Eskimo exhibits are particularly fascinating, with material such as rain gear made of walrus intestines.

Alaska Raptor Rehabilitation Center: A place where injured hawks, falcons, owls, and eagles (mostly eagles) are cared for, this volunteer-run facility lets visitors view the dramatic birds close-up.

Sitka National Historical Park: If you didn't get to Totem Bight or Saxman at Ketchikan and want to get a good view of totem poles, this is a close-to-downtown opportunity to do so. Set among trees in a dramatic walk along the shore, the 15 totems are "recarves" of poles collected from Prince of Wales Island at the turn of the century. Cedar totems have a life of about 100 years outside exposed to the elements.

The Russian Bishop's House and St. Michael's Cathedral: Both downtown, these are culturally rich elements of Sitka's Russian period. The Bishop's House is the original 1842 structure; the cathedral is a replica of the one destroyed by fire in 1966 (much of the artwork was saved).

Sitka is known as the arts and cultural center of Southeast Alaska. This young woman plays her fiddle at the dock to welcome visitors.

A TOTEM WALK

Here's a great walk along the shore and through one of SE Alaska's major totem sites.

There are two places where cruise ship lighters bring passengers ashore here. From either place you turn to the right, and keep staying right until you pass a major small boat harbor - Crescent Harbor - on your right and then continue along the shore to the entrance to the **Sitka National Historical Park**.

Here you will find the **Southeast Alaska Indian Cultural Center**, with a museum as well as active native craftspeople at work. Out the back is a really pleasant path, through an open spruce forest, with totems spaced along the way, and eventually opening to a beach facing out to where your cruise ship is usually anchored. It's about a half mile to the center and the path itself is about a mile.

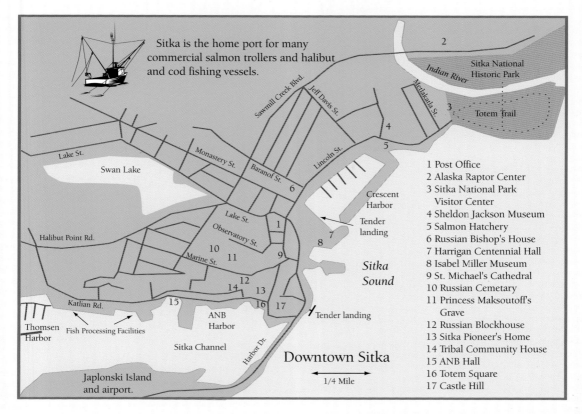

Sitka is the home port for many commercial salmon trollers and halibut and cod fishing vessels.

Map labels:

Indian River
Sitka National Historic Park
Sawmill Creek Blvd.
Jeff Davis St.
Metlakatla St.
Totem Trail
Lake St.
Monastery St.
Baranof St.
Lincoln St.
Swan Lake
Crescent Harbor
Tender landing
Lake St.
Observatory St.
Halibut Point Rd.
Marine St.
Sitka Sound
Katlian Rd.
Thomsen Harbor
Fish Processing Facilities
ANB Harbor
Tender landing
Sitka Channel
Harbor Dr.
Downtown Sitka
1/4 Mile
Japlonski Island and airport.

1 Post Office
2 Alaska Raptor Center
3 Sitka National Park Visitor Center
4 Sheldon Jackson Museum
5 Salmon Hatchery
6 Russian Bishop's House
7 Harrigan Centennial Hall
8 Isabel Miller Museum
9 St. Michael's Cathedral
10 Russian Cemetary
11 Princess Maksoutoff's Grave
12 Russian Blockhouse
13 Sitka Pioneer's Home
14 Tribal Community House
15 ANB Hall
16 Totem Square
17 Castle Hill

Peril Strait: If you are on a small cruise ship, or Alaska ferry that transits Peril Strait on your way to Sitka, make sure you get up early (arriving vessels will often go through around dawn.) The tide runs so strongly here - actually sucking the big Coast Guard buoys underwater at times - that safe passage is only possible at slack water, around the time of high or low tide. It is particularly scenic, as it winds between many islands, both in Peril Strait, but also in Neva and Olga Straits, closer to Sitka. The narrowest part of the channel is called Sergius Rapids for the powerful whirlpools.

Even modern navigational equipment can't always keep vessels out of trouble: the Alaska ferry *Le Conte* hit a rock here in 2004 and almost sank.

Opposite page: A watchman on the bow of the Alaska State Ferry Le Conte stands by ready to call the bridge should any dangers appear. Even such caution doesn't always work in these waters—this same ferry almost sank after hitting a rock near here in 2004.

SOME SITKA EXCURSIONS

Russian America History Tour	Wilderness Sea Kayaking Adventure
Historic Russian America & Raptor Center Tour	Dry Suit Snorkel Adventure
Sitka Nature & History Walk	Sea Life Discovery Semi-Submersible
Sitka Bike & Hike Tour	Sea Otter & Wildlife Quest
Advanced Bike Adventure	Sea Otter Quest & Alaska Raptor Center
Tongass Rainforest Hike	Silver Bay Nature Cruise & Hatchery Tour
4x4 Wilderness Adventure	Captain's Choice Wildlife Quest & Beach Trek
Sitka Sportfishing	Alaska Up-Close Exclusive Cruise Adventure

Building the boats: After making it over the passes, the next step for the Klondikers was to cut down trees, saw them into boards, and build crude boats. Then when the lake ice melted, they had to float and paddle down 500 miles of the Yukon River to Dawson and the Klondike Country. The first part included several violent rapids where boats and men were lost.

CANADA

Carcross

Water route to the Klondike

Lake Bennett

CANADA

ALASKA

Gold Rush Trails

Klondike Highway to Alaska Highway

Chilkoot Pass

Haines Highway connects with Alaska Highway

Skagway

White Pass & Yukon Route RR

Dyea (abandoned)

White Pass

Haines

The Passes - Canada required that all those headed for the Klondike carry a year's food (about a ton) with them. For most prospectors, this meant many backbreaking trips up over the pass, shuttling their supplies to the border checkpoint.

1014N

High rugged mountains

Proposed ferry dock

The Road - Many Juneau residents yearn for a road to somewhere. (The only road connection is by ferry.) However the proposed road only runs up Lynn Canal to another ferry dock, as the last miles to Skagway is blocked by almost vertical rock walls.

Muir Inlet

Glacier Bay National Park

Eldred Rock Lighthouse

990N

Passenger Tip - The landscape of upper Lynn Canal is very dramatic. When you leave Skagway in the evening, spend some time with your camera on an upper deck; the views can be spectacular!

High and rugged with many glaciers.

Glacier Bay

Proposed road

Lynn Canal

Salmon Cannery

Berners Bay

Excursion Inlet

960N

Present road ends here

Pt. Retreat Lighthouse

JUNEAU TO SKAGWAY

<— —>

1" = 12 miles

975

950

Auke Bay

Icy Strait

Mendenhall Glacier

Juneau

Douglas

Taku River

Admiralty Island

ALASKA

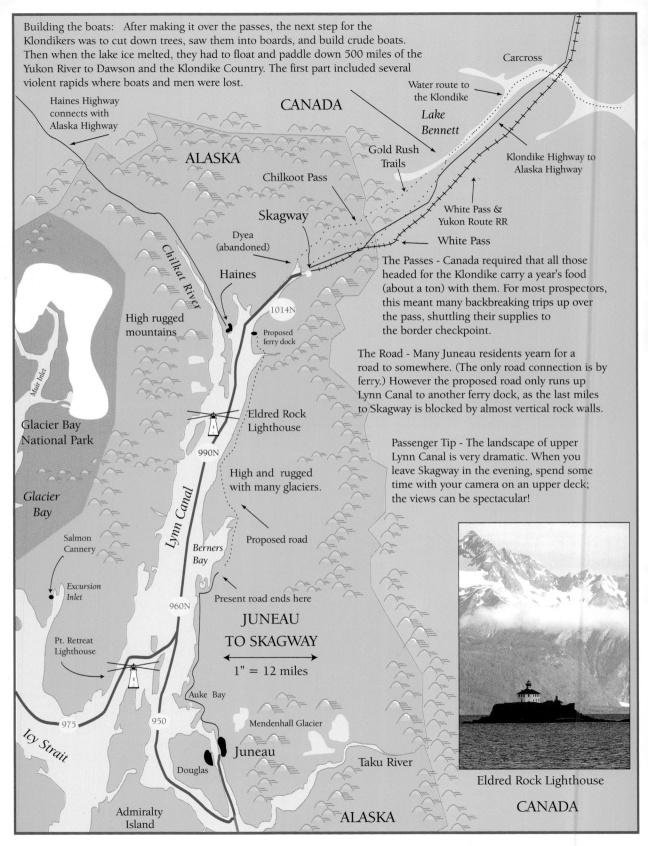

Eldred Rock Lighthouse

CANADA

CHAPTER 4

Where History Lurks

Lynn Canal to Skagway Area, Mile 900 to Mile 1000N

"That country up there didn't look cordial. It made you feel like cutting out the horseplay and saying a prayer for the fellows who wasn't there no more and for the rest of us who didn't know what was ahead, neither."

- Mckeown, *The Trail Led North*

Passenger Tip:

Get up early and stay up late here and go on the upper decks to get a good vista. The landscape is especially dramatic.

There's a dramatic change in the landscape as your ship enters Lynn Canal north of Juneau. The mountains are higher, the vistas starker, glaciers seem to overhang the water in little cirque valleys.

Commercial salmon fishermen in their 30 and 40 footers, coming out of Auke Bay and and making the turn north at **Pt. Lena, Mile 952**, had an expression for it, "Looking up at the Big Lynn."

And it wasn't just the landscape, but the weather as well; Lynn Canal and Chatham Strait, to the south, form a 200 mile long wind tunnel for the wet North Pacific lows sweeping up from the ocean and the cold Arctic highs pushing down from Siberia and the Alaska interior. Sometimes, especially in the fall, there would hardly even be a break between systems, and weatherbound fishermen in Auke Bay would catch a ride out to the shore by Pt. Lena to get their grim weather forecast: row after row of nasty looking grey bearded seas rolling down the canal.

Top: looking southwest toward Haines from about Mile 1000N. This is probably around 5:30 a.m. Early, but see how dramatic the light is? Bottom: Looking west across Lynn Canal from Brigit Cove, Mile 965

The bottom here is littered here with the pieces of two of the finest steamers to travel north, both belonging to the Canadian Pacific Railroad. First was the *Princess Sophia*. At around 1 a.m. on October 24, 1918, the gold miners and the crews from the 10 Yukon River paddle-wheelers aboard the *Sophia* were probably still celebrating. They'd left Skagway a few hours earlier, the rivers freezing up, their season over, the bright lights ahead.

Upstairs in the pilothouse, the atmosphere was anxious. The captain had seen Eldred Rock Light, **mile 994**, at midnight through the snow but navigation on such a night relied on something called "time and compass." The skipper would calculate from the engine revolutions how fast his vessel was traveling. Taking his course line from the chart and making allowances for the wind and the tidal currents, he would steer until his time ran out, that is, when he should be at the next point of reference.

On that bitter night in 1918, with blowing snow and limited visibility, the next checkpoint after Eldred Rock was Sentinel Island Light, 28 miles away. Over such a distance, a steering error of one degree would put the vessel a half-mile off course.

Sometime around 2 a.m., as her skipper was groping through the snow and trying to see the Sentinel Island Light, the *Sophia* drove her whole length ashore on Vanderbilt Reef. Fortunately the rocks cradled her, and there was no need to try and launch lifeboats on such a rotten night.

By first light a rescue fleet was standing by: the *Cedar, King and Winge, Estebeth, Elsinore*, and others. But as the *Sophia* seemed to be resting securely on the rock, it was decided to wait until better weather to evacuate the passengers and crew.

It proved to be a tragic mistake. In the late afternoon, the northerly began to blow with renewed fury, and the rescue fleet was forced to seek shelter in a nearby harbor. Darkness came with driving snow and bitter wind, and the

vessels had to set anchor watches to make sure they weren't dragging.

Roaring down the canal, the wind caught the *Sophia*'s high exposed stern, driving her off the reef, ripping open her bottom, and sending her into the deep water beyond. There was time for one desperate radio call: "For God's sake come! We are sinking." In the morning only her masts were above water, her 343 passengers and crew drowned in the northwest coast's worst maritime disaster.

Thirty-four years later, miscalculation of a course change drove the graceful *Princess Kathleen* ashore at Lena Point, **mile 956**. Her passengers were more fortunate. They climbed down ladders to the rocky beach and watched the favorite of all the Alaska-run steamers slide off the rocks and disappear into deep water.

On the east side of Lynn Canal, at around **Mile 980N** look for what remains of the old mining settlement of Comet. Behind it, in the vicinity of Lion's Head Mountain is a highly mineralised area, with several old abandoned mines. With the price of gold rising, a project at the old Kensington Mine, is being developed, due to start production in 2007. The mining company promised a low environmental impact operation; however part of the tailings will be dumped into a nearby lake, angering local commercial fishermen and environmentalists. Whether or not the mine can successfully operated without any adverse environmental impact will be a critical test of the idea of balancing development and natural resource protection.

Each fall hundreds of chum or dog salmon spawn in flats like these on the Chilkat River, attracting thousands of Bald Eagles and hundreds of commercial fishermen. Bottom: Pacific salmon die after spawning and attract many scavengers!

HAINES AND PORT CHILKOOT

Top: A native totem carver explains the process inside one of the old barracks buildings at Port Chilkoot. Below: Chilkat Dancers lodge front. Below right: walking around Port Chilkoot.

The spot that looks like a New England village at **mile 1012N** is Fort William H. Seward, sometimes known as Port Chilkoot. Decommissioned after World War II, it is now part of the city of Haines, just to the north, and offers a variety of cultural activities.

Haines, until a highway was recently completed out of Skagway, was the only place in southeastern Alaska with a road that went anywhere (it connected to the Alaska Highway). Today it is rich with Tlingit culture and is especially known for the dramatic fall migration of bald eagles that feed on Chilkat River salmon.

Few large cruise ships stop here, but if you want a refreshing change from the congestion of Skagway when the big ships are in town, there is a foot ferry over to Haines.

"Sixty-Eight Rich Men on the Steamer Portland"
"Not a man has less than $5,000. Some of them have over $100,000"
"Big strikes made by tenderfeet"
"Fortune seemed to smile on the inexperienced."
"Strikes in the Yukon the greatest ever known."

Such were the headlines in the July 17, 1897 Seattle Post-Intelligencer that spread across a depression ravaged country like wildfire. In those days, to a family struggling to keep food on the table and coal in the stove, $5,000 was a fortune, $100,000 riches beyond imagination. And in mysterious Alaska and Yukon, the dimensions of which had just began to enter American consciousness, primarily through John Muir's exciting discovery of Glacier Bay just 20 years before.

But the part that electrified struggling men all across America and Canada was that most of the rich men coming out to tell their stories had gone in as inexperienced 'tenderfeet,' with no more knowledge of Alaska, the Klondike, or gold mining than the average midwest sodbuster or eastern factory worker.

Desperate people see what they want to see; most didn't read the small print, at the end of the article that started with

Above: the frenzy that the Gold Rush started—steamer Excelsior leaving San Francisco for the 'El Dorado of the Yuklon,' , with thousands of jealous well wishers looking on. UW Partridge 7964 Bottom: Display in Gold Rush museum in Seattle, just a few blocks from where these scenes occurred: merchants eagerly selling supplies, some of dubious value or quality, to the gold frenzied crowds.

Thwaites. 1286. Mushers. Alaska.

UW Thwaites 10-

Look at these faces: Klondikers aboard a Yukon River paddlewheeler, circa 1898. UW Thwaites 0394-1286 Below: Getting there could be nasty—steamer at Skagway after a rough trip up Lynn Canal, bucking a 'norther.' UW 15549

"GOLD! GOLD! GOLD! GOLD! splashed across the front page. But it was there: "They atribute their success to "lucky strikes," and aver that thousands of people will rush to the Yukon valley in the next year or two, and after undergoing great privations and hardships, will probably return broke in health and finances."

And so they came, from all parts of the country, from all walks of life, fixated on finding the gold that would transform their lives. First to Seattle, where the waterfront was a frenzied marketplace of merchants hawking their supplies to eager men with their family's savings in their pockets.

A Gold Rush fleet was rushed into service. Some were older, tired ships, operated by unscrupulous owners wanting to get in on the Gold Rush frenzy. Overloaded and pushed into dangerous weather, several didn't make it and were lost. For the tens of thousands who came north during the Gold Rush years, upper Lynn Canal represented the last easy miles of their journey to the diggings.

As you enter Taiya Inlet at **Mile 1,014N** from Seattle, imagine yourself at the crowded rail of a ship like the *Queen* or the *Victoria* in the fall of '97, jostling for your place with hundreds of other Klondikers, looking out through a snow squall, trying to get a glimpse of what lay ahead. There is but an hour or two before you must put on your pack, get the boxes and sacks of your "outfit" (a year's worth of supplies) ready to unload, and step out into the wind and the cold and whatever fate had in store for you.

> "Them days it was every man for hisself. The faster a boat could get out of there, the sooner it could get back to Seattle or Vancouver and pick up another load of suckers. A man shipped his gear at his own risk. If he didn't get his stuff off the beach before the next tide, it was just his hard luck. No one else done no worrying about it."
>
> - Monte Hawthorn, in *The Trail Led North*

The snow clears, and a cold and cheerless sun shines on as bleak and unfriendly a landscape as you've probably ever seen. The mountains rise vertically out of the water; there doesn't even seem to be a beach. The chatter of the crowd fades as all look at the mountains and what lies ahead.

For those in the first wave in 1897, there were no wharves. Most gold seekers unloaded their outfits from steamers onto

Fall, 1897: the first wave of Klondikers start to arrive in Skagway. There were no docks; you and your 1,000 pounds of supplies get landed on the beach. If it was low tide, you'd better lug all that gear all the way up to the high tide mark. The ships didn't wait for high tide to make it easier. As one Klondiker put it, "They had to get back and pick up another load of suckers..." UW La Roche 380 Below: At the Skagway graveyard. Disease, cold, and lawlessness took its toll.

153

"HO" FOR KLONDIKE.
Lake Bennet.

Ready for the next phase of their journey: freshly built boats and Klondikers on Lake Bennett, spring, 1898. These boats were built from planks hand sawn from trees around the lake. AMRC b64-1-43 Below: The 'Golden Staircase'—if you stepped out of line to rest, you might have to wait for15 minutes before another spot opened up in the line.
UW Hegg 100

lighters—shallow-draft barges. If the tide was up, the lighters took you right in to shore. If it wasn't, the lighter got as far as the flats and you had to cross 200 or 300 yards of sand and mud to get to shore. Many had brought animals and staked them out with their piles of boxes and gear while they made the first trips across the flats to shore.

Some weren't familiar with the big tides in the northern fjords of Alaska. They rested, perhaps, after lugging their first load up the beach, and visited with others about what they might expect in the rough-hewn town, visible through the snow, and hiked back to find their outfit underwater, their animals drowned. Few were really prepared for the rigors of that journey, or the true nature of the gold country.

For most of the hundred thousand or so who came north in 1897 and 1898, their Gold Rush experience had three phases. The first was often the hardest: the passes. The mountain wall that lay between the salt water of upper Lynn Canal and the edge of the Yukon had but two routes over it: Chilkoot Pass and White Pass.

The most powerful image from '97 and '98 is the long line of climbers, each bent with his load, on the steps cut into the ice on Chilkoot Pass. At the top lay the Canadian border and the North West Mounted Police. No one could pass without a year's supplies, about 1,000 lbs.

Wealthy men hired porters, but most just carried it all up themselves, load by backbreaking load, caching it at the top

and hoping no one would rob them before they got back. A solid stream of upward-bound men filled the steps. If you wanted to rest, you stepped off to the side, but when you wanted to get back in, you had to wait for a gap in the line; it was that crowded. By 1898 cable tramways could carry your gear over the pass for a fee, but the men in the first wave had only their feet.

Down the other side from the summit was Lake Bennett, and after that it was the boats and the rivers. They were 50 miles from salt water, but there were another 500 to the gold country. Arriving in winter, the men camped on the shore, cut down trees, whipsawed them into planks and built boats, and waited for the ice to melt to launch their boats and begin the journey:

> "Some leaked, some didn't steer. They had lots of things wrong with them. But a lot of the boats, made of whipsawed lumber, had beautiful lines and sailed as pretty as anything I ever did see on the Columbia. Yes, sir, that was an expedition, that fleet of boats getting ready to set out from Lake Bennett, come spring of '98."
> —Martha Ferguson McKeown, *The Trail Led North*

For some, the challenge of the north—the cold, the difficult conditions, was simply too much: (See drawing on right)

> "It was a real cold night. We walked along in the snow and we come to a fellow setting on the back of a Yukon sled. Yep, he was setting there in the middle of the road talking to hisself. His head was down on his

How the wealthy traveled to the Klondike: a paddlewheeler winching itself through Five Finger Rapids on Yukon River. UW Hegg 501 Below: Drawing by Christine Cox. See text to left.

The epic of the Gold Rush - how many men would have kept going if they knew what awaited them once they left the comfort of the ships and headed up over the trail? And the sad part was this: few struck it rich; almost all the good claims were staked even before the first wave arrived in the summer of 1898.

hands. He looked plumb played out. He never seen us; he just went on talking to hisself. Over and over he'd say: "It's hell. Yes; multiply it by ten and then multiply that by ten, and that ain't half as bad as this is. Yes, it's hell..."

—Martha Ferguson McKeown, *The Trail Led North*

The trip became a journey of true epic proportions. Down the canyons and through the rapids they came, some capsizing or breaking up, the survivors trying to hitch a ride with the next boat that had room. The wealthier switched to Yukon steamers as soon as the river got wide enough, but all were heading for Dawson Creek and the last phase of their epic sagas: the diggings.

But for most, only disappointment awaited them. The best claims were staked before most of the gold seekers arrived. Many who started north gave up before they got to the Yukon. Only half who made it staked a claim. Just a very few struck it rich. Most found some kind of work in Dawson City or in the diggings, made a little money, and moved on.

Yet their adventure transcends time. All experienced the powerful drama of **The North**. Those who returned to the lower 48, even penniless, brought back stories and memories to entertain generations of breathless children and grandchildren.

THE LUCKY FEW

With no convenient banks, many miners simply brought their gold south with them. One woman, hearing that her husband might be coming home to Seattle on the steamer, brought their children to meet it, hoping he'd have enough money to buy them groceries (he'd been gone six months and they were out of money). He staggered down the gangplank under the weight of his duffel and its 116 *pounds* of gold. MOHAI 404

SKAGWAY

Occasionally in the early 1970s my commercial salmon fishing buddies and I would travel up to Skagway for the weekend, when fishing was closed around Haines, around 15 miles south. The merchants were thrilled to welcome our group, kept their shops and restaurants open late for our business. Dust blew in the empty streets, or if the Alaska state ferry was in, perhaps a few dozen visitors wandered around. It was definately sleepy.

This isn't what you'll find today. If you come by cruise ship, you'll probably arrive with eight or ten thousand other visitors to a town with perhaps 825 permanent residents.

Yet surprisingly, this town still retains its charm and the ghosts of the men who passed through in the epic Gold Rush that essentially put Alaska on the map still walk these streets.

As much as anything that kept the turn of the 20th century buildings intact–Skagway essentially was built between 1897 and 1900–was the weather. Buildings that would have rotted away without maintenance in rainy Ketchikan, simply lasted longer in this much drier, sunnier climate.

But it is the drama of '97 and '98 that fills this town. Skagway blossomed for but a few years, lawless and rough, then almost disappeared.

A classic coach waits for a group of visitors at the Gold Rush Cemetary, just outside of town. Below: The White Pass and Yukon Route Railroad has spurs to both docks that serve cruise ships to make it easier for visitors to board.

The gaunt-faced men have passed through to whatever fate The North had in store for them. But the town the boom built at the jumping-off place for the Klondike remains, looking much as it did in 1897 and 1898, when some 80 saloons and many professional women were anxious to serve the lonely men on the trail north.

Today, Skagway offers a unique experience to visitors. Even the vegetation is different from the rest of Southeast Alaska, as the town is under the influence of the harsher temperature extremes of the interior instead of the milder, cloudier maritime climate elsewhere in the region. Some of the native craftwork available here, especially of ivory, is truly excellent.

Note: Only ivory harvested by Native carvers in accordance with federal regulations may be sold legally. Make sure to get a export/transit permit if you buy ivory and plan to transit Canada on your way home. You'll need it to bring the ivory into the United States.

If Skagway's your last stop and you've saved your shopping until the end, you're in luck, the density of shops, particularly jewelry shops (their website, Skagway.com lists 17...) equals that of any other town on your cruise.

Shopping's great, but make sure you take some time between your excursion if you take one, and shopping, to just walk around town, get a sense of the place and of the drama that took place here.

A good place to start is the Gold Rush **National Historical Park Visitor Center**, on the water side of downtown in the White Pass and Yukon Route Railroad station. It gives a great

Merchants wasted no time - this classic Alaska gift shop started with the Gold Rush in 1897, and was recently acquired by a jewelry chain, who thought better of the totems... Opposite: Dennis Corrington and an exquisite Yup'ik mask from Corrington's Ivory Museum. Dennis was a trader on the Yukon River and an Ididarod musher before opening up several shops in Skagway. Don't miss his museum. Below: Before the big chain gift shops came to town, Skagway had some wonderful locally owned small stores.

TAKE THE TRAIN!

After struggling for years after the end of the Gold Rush, hauling ore from Yukon Territitory mines to the ore terminal at Skagway Harbor allowed the railroad to modernise and operate for over 8 decades. But when mineral prices slumped in the early 1980s, the railroad had to suspend operations and Skagway lost an important source of revenue and outlet to interior Canada.

Fortunately by 1988, enough visitors were coming by cruise ship that the railroad could reopen, focused on providing rides aboard classic restored railroad cars for visiting passengers.

After carrying just 37,000 travelers in 1988, the railroad has become the most popular visitor attraction in Alaska, carrying 431,000 passengers in 2006!

It operates daily on a number of schedules - train up, bus down, train to summit and back, train to Lake Bennett and back (longer.) In my view, as long as you just get on the train and up the mountain, it doesn't make much difference which itinerary you take. But take the train!

Top: And this is in May! When the Klondikers got to Skagway, the snow in the passes was way deeper than this! Opposite top: Up near White Pass on the WP&YR RR. But remember, the railroad wasn't built until most of the Klondikers had passed through. David Hooks Photos. Opposite lower right: On the railroad dock, cruise ship crews used to commemorate their visits on the walls.

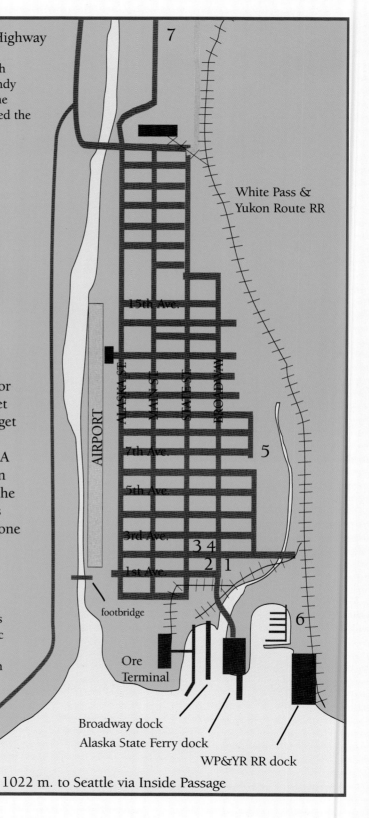

Klondike Highway

Skagway, surrounded by high
mountains, at the end of a narrow windy
fjord, was where the Klondikers left the
(relative) comfort of the ships and faced the
difficulties of the trail.

..."Them days it was every man for
hisself. The faster a boat could get
out of there, the sooner it could get
back to Seattle or Vancouver and
pick up another load of suckers. A
man shipped his outfit at his own
risk. If he didn't get his stuff off the
beach before the next tide, it was
just his hard luck. No one else done
no worrying about it."

- Monte Hawthorne, in Martha McKeown,
The Trail Led North

1. Railroad depot, 2. "Soapy" Smith's
Parlor, 3. Red Onion Saloon, 4. Arctic
Brotherhood Hall, 5. Town Hall and
Trail of '98 Museum. 6. Skagway Fish
Co.
7. Gold Rush Cemetary

9 Miles to abandoned
townsite of Dyea and
start of Chilkoot Trail

White Pass &
Yukon Route RR

15th Ave.

AIRPORT

ALASKA ST.

STATE ST.

BROADWAY

7th Ave.

5

5th Ave.

3rd Ave.

3 4

2 1

1st Ave.

footbridge

6

Ore
Terminal

Broadway dock

Alaska State Ferry dock

WP&YR RR dock

1022 m. to Seattle via Inside Passage

overview of the Gold Rush saga, as well as being in the train station for the WP&YR RR, which is fascinating just by itself. The town of Skagway also operates its own visitor's center, in the restored and very dramatic **Arctic Brotherhood Hall,** with its 10,000 or so nailed on pieces of driftwood, probably the most distinctive building in all of Alaska. The Fraternal Order of the Arctic Brotherhood constructed this hall and at least another in the Yukon Territories as a social and cultural organization to further the interests of the miners. It grew to have substantial political muscle as well. being an early advocate for more political power for Alaskans to manage their own affairs locally rather than through Washington, DC.

Pick up a copy of the walking tour map at the **AB Hall,** it's got directions up to the Gold Rush Cemetary, the **Trail of '98 Museum,** and other points of interest. It's definately worthwhile to walk around with the map as your guide. The hike to Lower Dewey Lake (3 hrs. RT) has a steep stretch at the beginning, but then flattens out for a very pleasant walk.

Of course, Skagway's signature hike is up the old **Chilkoot Trail,** followed by so many of the men of '98. This is way, way more than a pleasant stroll; more like a grueling 4-5 day epic, and that's in summer, not in the depth of winter with the poorly insulated clothing of the day and 1000 pounds of gear to pack over the summit. If you start up the trail, think about this: many

A ranger explains the history of old Dyea, which has largely disappeared into the forest. Because of the railroad and a better harbor, Skagway boomed and Dyea died. Below: There's a lot of ways to get around this town...

163

of the men who took it took a dozen or more trips back and forth to ferry their loads if they couldn't afford to hire a native porter to help them.

One good way to see the old trail is an excursion combining a hike up the first few miles with a raft trip back down the river to Dyea. (Not much left, see picture, on P. 163.) Skagway and Dyea boomed together, but today only Skagway remains, primarily because of the railroad and the docks quickly constructed there. (The tide flats at Dyea were almost a half mile wide on a big low tide, a long, long, way to carry your gear in multiple trips.)

What's interesting about Dyea is this–today the ruins seem really far from the water even at high tide. As it turns out, the land used to be much lower, and hence the water much closer. But as the glaciers that used to cover this whole area thousands of feet deep had only receded recently (well, maybe 10,000 years earlier) the land was experiencing 'glacial rebound' to the tune of about a half to three quarters of an inch a year–enough to lift the land 6-7 feet since the Gold Rush and push the waterline back considerably in that flat river delta.

Just renting a bike downtown for a few hours is also a pretty mellow way just to explore the town and surrounds. The 10 miles out to Dyea is a pretty nice ride, but at least in 2005 much of the road was unpaved and though we loved the free tour by a ranger around the old townsite, we were really glad when a kind driver offered to run us up to "the top of the hill." (Which was most of the way back to Skagway.)

The helicopter excursions that operate out of near the waterfront are a good way to see the dramatic landscape as well as the Chilkoot Trail. There are a number of different variations most of which include a landing on top of one of the nearby glaciers and a chance to walk around. If you're ready to dig deep and have never been around dog teams, there is an excursion that includes a dog sled ride. The dogs get really excited then the choppers land and they know that they will be on the trail soon!

Save some time at the end of the day to drop in to one of the local watering holes like the Red Onion

Saloon, where a lot of the Klondikers tipped a few before they hit the rugged trail. If you want a bit more local color, try Moe's Frontier Bar, between 4th and 5th. Another highly reccomended spot is The Skagway Fish Company, located by the small boat harbor out near the Railroad docks.

But most of all, try and take a few moments to think about the men who came, in the fall of 1897, and walked these streets and prepared for the obviously difficult challenges ahead. And the Skagway of those days was very very different from the cheerful busy place you'll encounter. By all accounts it was a grim place full of hard men.

Above: it gets pretty busy when the big ships are in. Opposite bottom: the Arctic Brotherhood Hall with its intricate driftwood front was a Gold Rush gathering place.

SOME SKAGWAY EXCURSIONS

Skagway & The Dangerous Days Of '98
Klondike Summit & Liarsville Experience
Klondike Summit, Bridge, & Salmon Bake
Historical Tour & Liarsville Salmon Bake
Skagway's Original Street Car
To The Summit
Experience The Yukon
White Pass Scenic Railway
Best Of Skagway
Klondike Scenic Highlights
Delectable Jewell Gardens
Deluxe Klondike Experience & Rail Adventure
Alaska Garden & Gourmet Tour
Yukon Jeep Adventure
Horseback Riding Adventure
Klondike Bicycle Tour
Rainforest Bicycle Tour

Klondike Rock Climbing & Rappelling
Alaska Sled Dog & Musher's Camp
Chilkoot Trail Hike & Float Adventure
Glacier Point Wilderness Safari
Glacier Lake Kayak & Scenic Railway
Dog Sledding & Glacier Flightseeing
Glacier Discovery By Helicopter
Heli-Hike & Rail Adventure
Alaska Nature & Wildlife Expedition
Remote Coastal Nature Hike
Takshanuk Mountain Trail By 4x4
Eagle Preserve Wildlife River Adventure
Chilkoot Lake Freshwater Fishing
Wilderness Kayak Experience
Skagway's Custom Classic Cars
Glacier Country Flightseeing

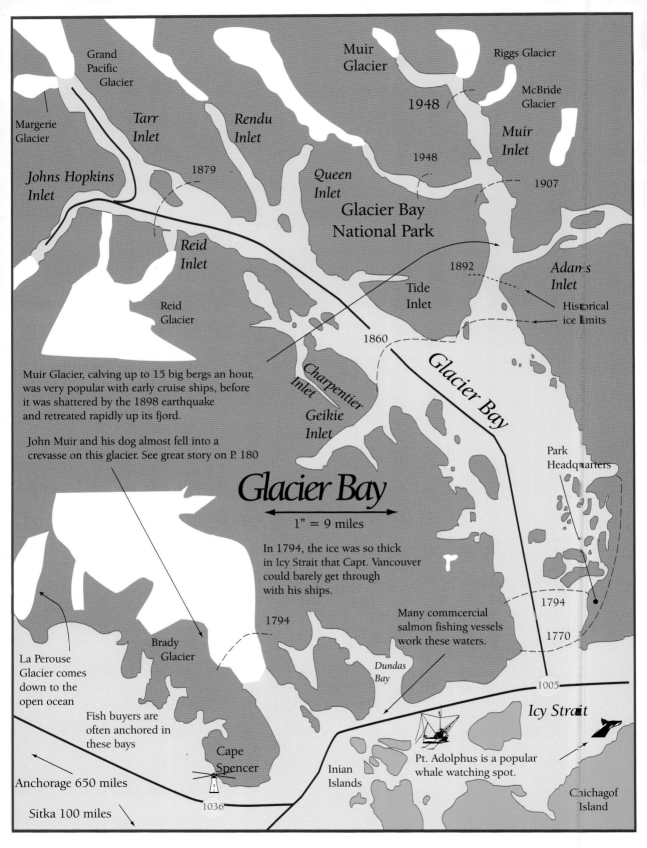

Grand
Pacific
Glacier

Muir
Glacier

Riggs Glacier

McBride
Glacier

Margerie
Glacier

*Tarr
Inlet*

*Rendu
Inlet*

1948

*Muir
Inlet*

*Johns Hopkins
Inlet*

1879

*Queen
Inlet*

1948

1907

Glacier Bay
National Park

*Reid
Inlet*

1892

*Adams
Inlet*

Reid
Glacier

*Tide
Inlet*

1860

Historical
ice limits

Muir Glacier, calving up to 15 big bergs an hour,
was very popular with early cruise ships, before
it was shattered by the 1898 earthquake
and retreated rapidly up its fjord.

*Charpentier
Inlet*

Glacier Bay

John Muir and his dog almost fell into a
crevasse on this glacier. See great story on P. 180

*Geikie
Inlet*

Park
Headquarters

Glacier Bay

1" = 9 miles

In 1794, the ice was so thick
in Icy Strait that Capt. Vancouver
could barely get through
with his ships.

1794

Many commcercial
salmon fishing vessels
work these waters.

1794

1770

1794

*Dundas
Bay*

1005

La Perouse
Glacier comes
down to the
open ocean

Brady
Glacier

Icy Strait

Fish buyers are
often anchored in
these bays

Cape
Spencer

Pt. Adolphus is a popular
whale watching spot.

Anchorage 650 miles

*Inian
Islands*

Sitka 100 miles

1036

*Chichagof
Island*

CHAPTER 5

Into The Ice

Glacier Bay to Cape Spencer, Mile 975 to Mile 1035

"This spacious inlet presented to our party an arduous task, as the space between the shores on the northern and southern sides, seemed to be entirely occupied by one compact sheet of ice as far as the eye could distinguish."

    -George Vancouver, *A Voyage of Discovery to the North Pacific Ocean and Around the World*

This was Vancouver's Lieutenant Joseph Whidbey looking east to Icy Strait from near the entrance to what is today Glacier Bay. The Strait was completely choked with ice and appeared to be impassable. And to the north, the bay was closed by "compact solid mountains of ice, rising perpendicularly from the water's edge." Glacier Bay didn't exist; it was solid ice.

A month or so after this discovery, Vancouver and his men finished their three summer exploration of the Northwest Coast (and determining that there was no ice free Northwest Passage back to the Atlantic) and headed off to England around Cape Horn. And Glacier Bay disappeared into the mists of time for some 80 years.

The Tlingits, of course, from the nearby village of Hoonah, and the Chilkats, hunted seals and had found that often the best

Into the ice; slowly! Passengers always want to go as far into the ice as possible, so as to observe wildlife and see and hear the dramatic calving of icebergs. But for the Captain, like the one below of a small cruise ship, the concern is not to damage the ship's propellors.

hunting was on the very edge of the ice, where seals would often go to calve and nurse their pups. So it is very likely that during this period, if the ice had been receeding, they would have been moving north with it, setting up hunting camps in Glacier Bay, but left no written records. Then in 1877, an explorer, Charles Wood, seeking to climb Mt. St. Elias, entered a now much bigger Glacier Bay and noted he had to travel 40 miles to reach the ice front. While there, he stopped at a Tlingit seal hunter's camp and recorded another bit of information that gives an insight to the ice's rapid recession. The chief, around 30 years old, said that within his lifetime the whole area around them had been solid ice.

This was startling: it meant that **within that relatively short period of 30 years, 10 or 20 cubic miles of ice had disappeared.** What caused such a great recession of the vast ice sheets during this period—some earlier version of global warming? No one really yet knows. But events in the late 1890s suggest substantial seismic activity in the Glacier Bay area. As these events were to prove, earthquakes seem to have the ability to shatter the ice in glaciers. Where such glaciers face the water, they will calve off immense amounts of ice after an earthquake, causing them to recede rapidly.

"Then setting sail, we were driven wildly up the fiord, as if the storm wind were saying, 'Go then, if you will, into my icy chamber; but you shall stay in until I am ready to let you out.' All this time sleety rain was falling on the bay and snow on the mountains; but soon after we landed the sky began to open. The camp was made on a rocky bench beneath the front of the Pacific Glacier, and the canoe was carried beyond the reach of the bergs and berg waves. The bergs were now crowded in a dense pack against the discharging front, as if the storm wind had determined to make the glacier take back her crystal offspring and keep them at home."

—John Muir, *Travels in Alaska*

The modern history of Glacier Bay really began in October of 1879, when John Muir, a noted naturalist and early preservationist, left Wrangell by canoe with a missionary friend, and three native paddlers. He had heard rumors of ice mountains in Alaska and had come to find out for himself.

He had neither gore-tex nor fleece, his canoe was overloaded, and the route was one today's kayakers probably wouldn't even attempt at that time of year. They paddled west through Sumner Strait, up through Rocky Pass (Keku Strait) and across Frederick Sound to follow the west shore of Admiralty Island north. Their canoe was small, the waters big. When they'd finally crossed the

When Muir and his group arrived at the inlet that now bears his name, it was a canyon full of solid ice, but actively calving very large icebergs. Below: John Muir in Glacier Bay, drawing by Christine Cox..

What's wrong with this picture? (Other than no life jacket...) Well the danger for small craft around icebergs is that as they melt, their center of gravity changes, and they can topple over without warning. See drawing below.

choppy 7 mile stretch of open water between Kuiu and Admiralty Islands, his chief paddler told him he hadn't slept for days worrying about it.

On they came, through Chatham and Icy Strait. As they traveled, the youngest native, Sitka Charley, told Muir he'd hunted seals as a boy in a bay full of ice and thought he could show Muir the way.

Muir was skeptical. Sitka Charley said the bay was without trees, that they'd need to bring their own firewood. The other paddlers, in all their lives throughout the region, had never seen a place without firewood.

They came to a bay cloaked in fog and storm. Sitka Charley became uneasy; the bay was much changed, he said, since he had seen it before. Even Vancouver's chart, a copy of which Muir so much relied upon, failed them, showing only a wide indentation in the shore.

Fortunately, they found a group of natives hunting seals and staying in a dark and crowded hut. One of the men agreed to guide them, and northward they paddled, off the chart and into that astonishing bay that had been birthed from the ice almost within their lifetimes.

The weather got worse, and Muir's paddlers wanted to turn around:

"They seemed to be losing heart with every howl of the wind, and, fearing that they might fail me now that I was in the midst of so grand a congregation of glaciers, I made haste to reassure them that for ten years I had wandered alone among mountains and storms, and good luck always followed me, that with me, therefore, they need fear nothing. The storm would soon cease and the sun would shine to show us the way we should go, for God cares for us and guides us as long as we are trustful and brave, therefore all childish fear must be put away."

—John Muir, *Travels in Alaska*

And so on they went, camping in rain, on snowy beaches, pushing farther and farther, only glimpsing the vastness and grandeur of the land.

Finally Muir climbed the flanks of one of the mountains just as the clouds passed, and he gazed, stunned, at the grandeur and the size of the many-armed bay that was revealed below him, full of slowly moving ice.

When the party headed back, the lateness of the season was evident. Each morning before they reached Icy Strait, the ice was frozen a little thicker, and the men had to cut a lane for their canoe with an axe and tent poles.

Muir's description of the moment of their departure is a shining icon of Alaskan literature:

"The green waters of the fiord were filled with sun spangles; the fleet of icebergs set forth on their voyages with the

Steamer Queen at Muir Glacier, about 1890. This graceful liner was one of the first to regularly bring visitors to Glacier Bay. Passengers could go ashore by small boat and climb ladders up to the top of the glacier. Imagine the Park Service allowing that today! Photo courtesy of Dave Bohn.

Reid Glacier in 1998. A lone prospector, Joe Ibach, made a modest gold claim at the two thousand foot level on the hill at the right. Ibach, and his wife, Muz, who lived in a homestead on Lemesieur Island, south of Glacier Bay, began spending their summers at Reid Inlet as the glacier receded. In 1940 they built a small cabin on the right of the spit above, bringing in soil from Lemerieur for their gardens. They never made much money from their gold claim, but kept coming back summer after summer. Friends said rather than the gold, it was the exquisite beauty of the place and of living close to the glacier that brought them back, year after year.

Your ship will stop in southern Glacier Bay to pick up a U.S. Park Service Ranger.

upspringing breeze; and on the innumerable mirrors and prisms of these bergs, and on those of the shattered crystal walls of the glaciers, common white light and rainbow light began to burn, while the mountains shone in their frosty jewelry, and loomed again in the thin azure in serene terrestrial majesty. We turned and sailed away, joining the outgoing bergs, while 'Gloria in excelsis' still seemed to be sounding over all the white landscape, and our burning hearts were ready for any fate, feeling that, whatever the future might have in store, the treasures we had gained this glorious morning would enrich our lives forever."

—John Muir, *Travels in Alaska*

After Muir's discovery and powerful writings about what he'd seen, the bay soon became one of the premier sights of the Western Hemisphere, and a regular stop for steamers such as the *Ancon*, the *Idaho*, and the *Queen*.

For many of the early steamer excursions, part of the trip was taking the ship's boats to shore and if conditions permitted, taking groups to the top of the glacier itself to climb around amongst the crevasses!

The destination was Muir Glacier, the face of which was an ice cliff towering above the decks of the approaching steamers, and calving up to 12 icebergs an hour.

"The Muir presented a perpendicular ice front at least 200 feet in height, from which huge bergs were detached at frequent intervals. The sight and sound of one of these huge masses of ice falling from the cliff, or suddenly appearing from the submarine ice-foot, was something which once witnessed was not to be forgotten. It was grand and impressive beyond description."

—Fremont Morse, *National Geographic*, January, 1908

THE 1899 EARTHQUAKE—At midday on September 10, 1899, as he was waiting for lunch at his salmon saltery in Bartlett Cove, now site of Glacier Bay National Park headquarters, August Buschmann was surprised to see his trunk come sliding across the floor at him. Moments later, the cook's helper came running into the building, frightened. He had been up on the hill at the native cemetery as the ground started to heave around him, and he thought the dead were coming to life.

The earthquake shattered the front of Muir Glacier and others, and within 48 hours Glacier Bay was a mass of floating ice so thick that ships could not reach the saltery at Bartlett Cove for two weeks. Icy Strait filled with ice, making Dundas Bay, 10 miles to the west, inaccessible.

Looking for mountain goats—from the deck you will see what look like moving white dots. Binoculars will reveal the goats, grazing on amazingly steep slopes. Below: How many mountain goats can you find?

LOOKING FOR WILDLIFE

Glacier Bay is actually one of the best opportunities to see bears and goats from your ship. However, you will need the strongest binoculars you can lay your hands on!

For bears, there are a couple of places to look. After about mid summer, there will be lots of berries on the slopes around the bay. So "glass" these hillsides carefully. What you will be looking for will be something that looks like a black spot that appears to be moving as it forages through the berry bushes. Another good place to look is along the shore, especially at low tide, as bears will forage for clams, crabs, etc. They'll scoop up a clam with one big paw, then smack it with the other to break the shell and then lift the whole dripping mess up to their mouth!

Mountain goats will be on the higher, steeper hillsides, and will be the white dots slowly moving!

Above: As glaciers recede, they leave a dramatically austere landscape behind them. This glacial moraine, as it is called, is created by the ground up rock left when the glacier melts.

It wasn't until the following July that the steamer *Queen* ventured close enough to Muir Inlet to see what had happened. The bay was still full of ice; only by picking their way along the shore west of Willoughby Island could they make any progress. The closest they could get to Muir Glacier was 10 miles; the rest was solid ice.

Hidden behind a fleet of icebergs, Muir Glacier commenced a rapid retreat up the inlet; today the face is 25 miles north of where Muir found it in 1879.

YOUR DAY IN GLACIER BAY: In order to allow each visitor to have the richest experience of the Park's unusual beauty, cruise ship visits are limited to two or less daily, and Park Rangers will board your ship to offer information and give presentations. A free informative map will be placed in your stateroom the night before. To get the most out of your Glacier Bay visit, I suggest stopping by the onboard ranger station with any questions, attending the presentation in the theatre, as well as viewing the video, *Beneath the Reflections* on stateroom TV. If young children are with you, consider the Junior Ranger program.

Usually large cruise ships travel up the west side of Glacier Bay, often slowing or stopping to allow passengers a good view of Reid Inlet. (See photo and caption on 172.) Next to the north is the entrance to Johns Hopkins Glacier,

very active in recent years, and the outgoing stream of ice is often so thick that ships often do not enter, for fear their propellors would contact ice pieces large enough to damage them. Additionally, seals use the ice flows in this inlet to birth their pups, and during the period when they are actively birthing pups, ship traffic is prohibited here.

However, while seal activity is the thickest in the inlet itself, you are apt to see seals, and perhaps even with their pups on ice flows anywhere in Glacier Bay, so be sure to have your binoculars ready whenever you leave your cabin in this area.

Then most big ships will travel up and stop as close to Margerie Glacier and Grand Pacific Glacier as they can. In recent years there has been less ice here than John Hopkins, and ships are often able to approach fairly closely.

Waiting for some calving action: when your ship is close to the ice, look for signs of imminent calving (see below.) Usually when they are at the face of a glacier, the Captain will often rotate the ship so that passengers watching from their balconies will also be able to see it.

WATCHING FOR CALVING ICEBERGS

Your naturalist and ship's staff would be thrilled if every glacier was as active as Muir Glacier was in the early 1900s: 12 big icebergs crashing down into the bay every hour! Seeing this up close would be the the the highlight of your cruise. However, much calving activity today is more modest. Things to look for that might signal calving is approaching include a section of much bluer ice than the rest of the glacier face and or small showers of ice and snow tumbling into the water, and cracking and rumbling sounds. Also remember that the ice face often extends several hundred feet beneath the surface, and icebergs the size of houses or larger can break off from the underwater part of a glacier and suddenly surface (another reason for small craft to give icebergs a good berth.)

WHALES IN GLACIER BAY

It's not clear why whales breach. Theories include trying to get rid of barnacles, establishing dominance over smaller males at mating time, and just wanting to have a bit of fun! Kay Gibson photo. Below: This pod of whales came so close to where we were watching from the promenade deck of the Dawn Princess that we could hear their trumpeting and smell their rotten fish breath when they surfaced close to us!

Glacier Bay has traditionally been a good spot to see humpbacks and other whales, so be sure to have your binoculars with you on deck and remember to keep a sharp eye peeled–your ship will have a naturalist, but there may be whales that he or she doesn't see.

Another good spot for whale watching is **Point Adolphus, Mile 1000**, directly south of the entrance to Glacier Bay. Your Captain may query the local whale watching boats and if he gets a report of sightings there may take a loop through before continuing on his course.

I was here in 1997 on the *Dawn Princess* when our Captain got a tip and, taking a loop through, spotted a group of humpbacks and let us ship drift, in hopes they might come closer. Regulations require big ships to keep a quarter of a mile away from whales, but in this case, after we stopped, the whales swam right over to us. I was on deck 7, the promenade deck, and had my camera handy as our fascinated group peered over the rail as the pod of five big humpbacks moved closer and closer until they were almost directly below where we were standing!

I had seen humpbacks blow at a distance before, but this time they were close enough to hear their distictive 'trumpeting' when they exhaled after a long dive. This was actually too close as their breath was bad, bad, bad!

WHEN HUMPBACKS "TRUMPET"

When humpback lift their tails and sound–dive deep–they are often gone for as long as five to twelve minutes. As you would after a long time underwater, they are anxious to exhale and inhale as soon as they surface. The force of exhaling creates a spume of water as well as a trumpeting sound, only audible from a short distance, so if you can hear the trumpeting, consider yourself lucky!

A Tale of Inian Cove

I spent much of my 19th summer in this cove, south of **Mile 1025**, buying fish from big native-owned fishing boats aboard the 75' tender *Sidney*. These were powered with immense, straight 8 Chrysler Royal gas engines, and one of my jobs was to keep them tuned and running smoothly. In these 58-footers, the fo'c's'le, or crew area, was right in front of the engine, and as I worked, replacing spark plugs and filing points, I could hear the natives talking. Sometimes they spoke their native language, but other times it was English. They spoke of the fishing, but also of the legend of Lituya Bay, over and beyond the ice mountains to the north. I didn't understand all that was said, but they seemed to be speaking of an angry spirit that sometimes lashed out, creating great waves that washed away villages.

And once or twice that summer, ice drifted into the anchorage at night, a powerful, almost magical experience for me:

"**August 17, 1965, Inian Cove**. Something woke me in the night, and I sat up in my bunk, wondering what it was. And then it came again, a faint but insistent scraping, as if another boat had drifted down on us in the night. I stumbled out on deck and, there, eerily lit by the three-quarter moon, was a big iceberg, moving gently down our port side, pushed by the tide. Its irregularly shaped top was even with my head; I reached out to touch it, to try and retrieve some of the gravel clearly visible within its pale, translucent flank. The gravel had been scraped off a canyon floor, dozens of miles away, hundreds of years before I was born. But the ice was hard, its contours softened by melting. My hand could find no purchase, and after a moment the berg moved away in the tide.

"Outside the point I saw a ghostly armada moving in the seven-knot current of North Inian Pass: eight or nine little bergs, maybe a thousand tons each, showing as big as medium-sized boats above the surface. In the moonlight they seemed to glow as if lit from within. I wanted to wake my shipmates, but then the tide pushed the bergs around the corner and they were gone."

ICY STRAIT POINT

Top: Hold on tight; the zipline here is the longest of its kind in the world, 5,330' long and with a 1330' vertical drop. Six riders can zip at once, and at one point you are almost 300' above the cannery with a spectacular view out to Icy Strait, Port Frederick, and your ship. Other excursions include a Hoonah bike tour, wildlife and bear watching expeditions, a forest/nature tram ride, salmon sports fishing, flightseeing over nearby Glacier Bay, Tlingit dancing and a wild Alaska seafood cooking lesson/meal. Photos courtesy Icy Strait Point.

Opening its doors for the first time in 2003, Icy Strait Point is unique among Alaska cruise ports–ship visits are limited to one a day, and the facility–a renovated cannery next to a Tlingit native village is surrounded by wilderness. If you've cruised Alaska before, you know how congested the other towns can get with four or five ships in port at once, so making a visit here is a welcome change.

Passengers come ashore by lighter to the cannery dock, where there is a museum, cafe/restaurant, and numerous shops. Cannery life was a major cultural and economic element in coastal Alaska and this is an excellent chance to get a close look. There are walking trails around the site and additionally there is a shuttle bus to nearby Hoonah, the largest Tlingit village in Alaska. The facility is owned by a native corporation and the richness of Tlingit culture is a strong element throughout.

Icy Strait Point is located in Port Federick, just across Icy Strait from the entrance to Glacier Bay.

Look north at mile 1,029 to Taylor Bay and Brady Glacier. Glaciologist extraordinaire Muir was here the summer after his 1879 Glacier Bay trip, hiking with a dog over the flats and up to Brady Glacier on a cold and rainy August day. In the late afternoon, he had to take a running jump across a very wide crevasse. Fortunately the other side was lower, but even so he barely made it: a few minutes later he realized he and the dog had jumped onto a sort of island, surrounded by wide and deep crevasses. The only ways out were back across the wide crevasse that he had barely managed to jump over, or across a frighteningly precarious ice bridge: curved, drooping, knife-edged, eight feet down in the abyss of a crevasse from the surface of the glacier.

Muir chose the ice bridge, notching steps into the side of the crevasse, and sliding across, straddling the ice, chipping away the sharp-edged top as he went so that the dog could also use it. As he worked, the dog whimpered and cried, refusing to follow. See drawing on right.

Above: Drawing of Muir and dog on Brady Glacier by Christine Cox
Below: The glacier at the head of Taylor Bay is part of a huge icefield, which also feeds into LaPerouse Glacier, which meets the open sea north of Icy Point, and which is a major landmark.

Only with difficulty did he get across. It began to get dark, and Muir could wait no longer. He moved away, calling to the dog that he could make it if he only tried.

"Finally, in despair, he hushed his cries, slid his little feet slowly down into my footsteps out on the big sliver, walked slowly and cautiously along the sliver as if holding his breath, while the snow was flying and the wind was moaning and threatening to blow him off. When he arrived at the foot of the slope below me, I was kneeling on the brink ready to assist him in case he should be unable to reach the top. He looked up along the row of notched steps I had made, as if fixing them in his mind, then with a nervous spring he whizzed up and passed me out on to the level ice and ran and cried and rolled about fairly hysterical in the sudden revulsion from the depths of despair to triumphant joy. I tried to catch him and pet him and tell him how good and brave he was, but he would not be caught. He ran round and round, swirling like autumn leaves in an eddy, lay down and rolled head over heels."

—John Muir, *Travels in Alaska*

Look for fishing boats coming out of the community of **Elfin Cove**, southeast of **mile 1,029**. This tiny settlement, with its boardwalk and its anchored fish buyers, is the center for the salmon trollers working this area. It's most recent addition is a seasonal floating espresso bar!

The End of The Inside Passage—the conspicuous lighthouse to the north at **mile 1,036**, is Cape Spencer Light, which marks the end of the Inside Passage. From here on to Prince William Sound, travel is along a rugged and spectacular coast, almost totally untouched by human settlement and unchanged except by the powerful forces of nature.

It is also a coast where small vessels travel with extreme care for the harbors are few and far apart...

Top: The 'excercise room' on the back deck of a small ship, somewhere in the vastness of Southeast Alaska. Bottom left: Not for the weak of heart: salmon troller working the rugged 'outside' coast. Bottom right: A welcome sight to many a beat up mariner: the lighthouse at Cape Spencer that marks the entrance to the sheltered waters of the Inside Passage.

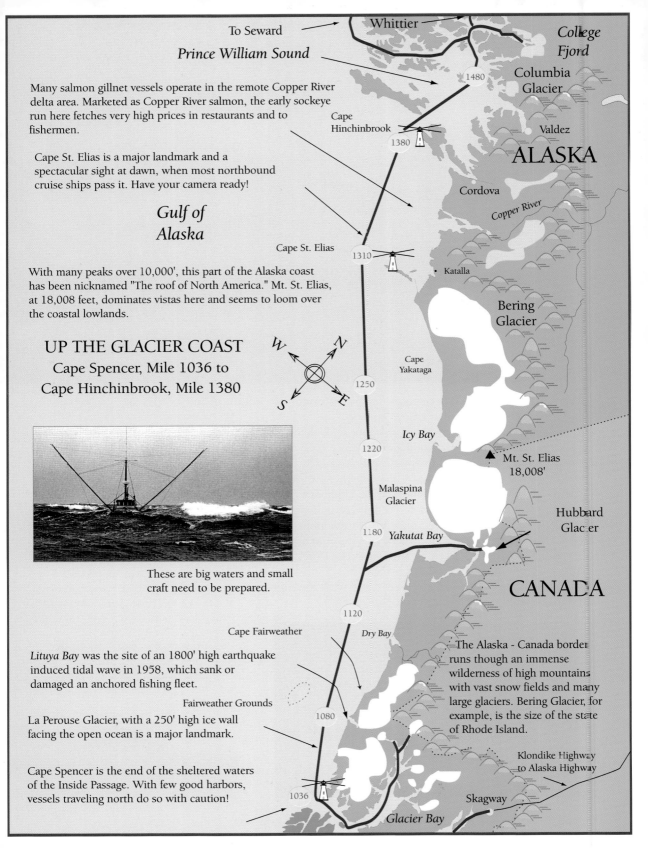

To Seward

Whittier

Prince William Sound

College Fjord

Columbia Glacier

1480

Cape Hinchinbrook

1380

Valdez

ALASKA

Many salmon gillnet vessels operate in the remote Copper River delta area. Marketed as Copper River salmon, the early sockeye run here fetches very high prices in restaurants and to fishermen.

Cordova

Copper River

Cape St. Elias is a major landmark and a spectacular sight at dawn, when most northbound cruise ships pass it. Have your camera ready!

Cape St. Elias

1310

• Katalla

Gulf of Alaska

Bering Glacier

With many peaks over 10,000', this part of the Alaska coast has been nicknamed "The roof of North America." Mt. St. Elias, at 18,008 feet, dominates vistas here and seems to loom over the coastal lowlands.

Cape Yakataga

UP THE GLACIER COAST
Cape Spencer, Mile 1036 to
Cape Hinchinbrook, Mile 1380

W · N · E · S

1250

Icy Bay

1220

▲ Mt. St. Elias 18,008'

These are big waters and small craft need to be prepared.

Malaspina Glacier

1180 *Yakutat Bay*

Hubbard Glacier

CANADA

1120

Cape Fairweather

Dry Bay

The Alaska - Canada border runs though an immense wilderness of high mountains with vast snow fields and many large glaciers. Bering Glacier, for example, is the size of the state of Rhode Island.

Lituya Bay was the site of an 1800' high earthquake induced tidal wave in 1958, which sank or damaged an anchored fishing fleet.

Fairweather Grounds

1080

La Perouse Glacier, with a 250' high ice wall facing the open ocean is a major landmark.

Klondike Highway to Alaska Highway

Cape Spencer is the end of the sheltered waters of the Inside Passage. With few good harbors, vessels traveling north do so with caution!

1036

Skagway

Glacier Bay

CHAPTER 6

Up the Glacier Coast

Cape Spencer to Cape Hinchinbrook, Mile 1036 to Mile 1380

"We thought it was an iceberg at first, way out past Spencer - you used to see 'em out there sometimes—but then when we got closer, we could see it was a big crab boat. But ... wasn't she iced over! Just like one big hill of ice, with some rigging and antennas sticking out of the top, and ragged pieces of plywood covering where the pilothouse windows were broken out. Pretty soon we could see the crew was all out on deck, knocking off the ice with baseball bats and shoveling it over the side as fast as they could. It gets bad out there..."

—Crab Fisherman Russell Fulton

Mariners tread cautiously here. Gone are the harbors with easy access when the wind blows. (Except for a few bays just north of the Cape.) This is the outside coast: bold, rugged, with few harbors, and backed by the stunning and rugged St. Elias Range. Take the time to go on deck with your binoculars. In North America, only Alaska has a coast like this.

If the coast of British Columbia had been like this, the development of coastal Alaska would have been very different. The myriad harbors and sheltered passages of the

This is a spectacular coast—there is a lot going on aboard your ship each evening especially, but you won't get many chances to see a coast like this, so dress warm, and find a place out of the wind, and just have a good look at the passing landscape. Roadless and very wild, with a mountain wall behind rising almost to 20,000' peaks, this part of Alaska has been nicknamed, "The Rooftop of North America." Also, especially on September cruises, go up just before you go to bed, let your eyes get used to the dark and look around—you might even see the Northern Lights!

Evening light off La Perouse Glacier, a major coastal landmark. Below: Salmon trollers headed out for the Fairweather Grounds, one of the best king salmon fishing spots on the Alaska coast.

Passenger Tip:

Spend some time on an outside deck along this coast especially in the evening or early morning, and bring your camera! On early and late season sailings, northern lights are also occasionally seen here!

Inside Passage allowed very small craft to travel to Alaska. Many would never have dared head north if their only route was outside, along a coast like this.

Look for La Perouse Glacier at mile 1060. With its almost perpendicular 200-300' face, it's an outstanding landmark along this section of coast. This is an active glacier: in some years, like 1997, advancing into the ocean, while just a year earlier receding enough to allow foot passage across the front at low tide.

To the west at mile 1090, is the Fairweather Ground, an area of legendary king salmon fishing. This is fishing only for the hardy—when the wind comes up you are a long ways from any harbor.

The land to the east, from the coast up over the Fairweather Range, and into the Yukon Territories of Canada, almost to the Alaska Highway, is for the most part a vast wilderness. It does present, however, an opportunity for kayakers or rafters willing to travel for long distances far from any help or source of supplies.

For the truly brave hearted, the **Dezadeash-Kaskawulsh-Alsek route** includes the infamous **Turnback Canyon.** It was named after the 1898 gold prospectors who tried the Alsek as a route to the interior, had one look at the ten-mile chute of churning icy water and turned around.

This unforgiving canyon has become to kayakers what K2 or Everest is to climbers. A word of caution—sometimes high water and fast currents make this canyon truly impassable and kayakers are urged to have a contingency plan for a helicopter to shuttle them around the canyon.

Three bare, light colored bluffs distinguish Ocean Cape, the entrance to Yakutat Bay, at mile 1162. This bay is the only really good anchorage for large vessels, in the 350 miles between Cape Spencer and Prince William

Sound. Nevertheless, in very heavy weather, breakers or very high swells have been observed all the way across this 15 mile-wide entrance.

Yakutat, some 5 miles inside the bay from Ocean Cape, is the northernmost village of the Tlingit Indians, many of whom fish for salmon nearby.

HUBBARD GLACIER BLOCKS RUSSELL FJORD

In April of 1986, Curt Gloyer, a pilot for Gulf Air Taxi, in Yakutat, returning from dropping off a climbing party, noticed that Hubbard Glacier had surged all the way across the channel and essentially dammed off the mouth of Russell Fjord. He circled lower to make sure, amazed at the unusual sight.

This was an event without precedent in recent geologic history, and as soon as word got out, people and groups from all over the world converged on Yakutat to try and rescue the marine mammals trapped by the ice dam—primarily seals, sea lions, and porpoises. As the weather got warmer and the streams filled with snow melt, the water behind the glacier/dam began rising rapidly, eventually reaching almost 90 feet higher than the level of Disenchantment Bay on the other side. Finally, in the middle of an October night, the water pressure became too great and burst through the glacier wall. By the time the first pilots got out the next morning, the big lake in Russell Fjord was pouring out a crack in the ice like a huge waterfall! The glacier eventually receded, only to surge again in 2002 to briefly block the Fjord again.

Near Dangerous River, Mile 1140. At times the river water is almost blue, from the fine as flour glacial silt it carries, and a plume may be seen in the ocean for many miles. The entrance is guarded by sandbars and heavy breakers, and vessels should not attempt to enter, except with local knowledge and in calm sea conditions.

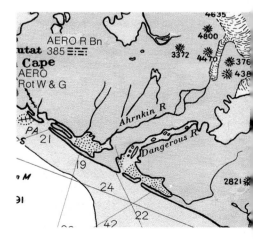

The evening of August 9, 1958 was gorgeous in Lituya Bay—several salmon trollers had come in to anchor for the night as was their custom, and turned in early. Around 10:20 p.m. Howard Ulrich, on his troller *Edrie*, was awakened by the sudden pitching and rolling of his boat. Still half asleep, he jumped up into the little pilothouse to see what was going on. What he saw became etched into his mind forever:

"These great snow-capped giants [the mountains at the head of the bay] shook and twisted and heaved. They seemed to be suffering unbearable internal tortures. Have you ever see a 15,000- foot mountain twist and shake and dance?

At last, as if to rid themselves of their torment, the mountains spewed heavy clouds of snow and rocks into the air and threw huge avalanches down their groaning sides.

During all this I was literally petrified, rooted to the deck. It was not fright but a kind of stunned amazement. I do not believe I thought of it as something that was going to affect me.

This frozen immobility must have lasted for two minutes or longer. Then it came to a dramatic end. It so happened that I was looking over the shoulder of Cenotaph Island toward the head of the bay, when a mighty seismic disturbance exploded and there was a deafening crash.

I saw a gigantic wall of water, 1,800' high, erupt against the west mountain. I saw it lash against the island, which rises to a height of 320 feet above sea level, and cut a 50-foot-wide swath through the trees of its center. Then I saw it backlash against the eastern shore, sweeping away the timber to a height of more than 500 feet.

Finally, I saw a 50-foot wave come out of this churning turmoil and move along the eastern shore directly toward me."

— Courtesy of *Alaska Magazine*

This was an earthquake so severe that it knocked the needle completely off the seismograph at the University of Washington.

Ulrich put a life jacket on his six-year-old son, started the engine, ran all his anchor chain out (there wasn't time to pull it in) and headed into that wave as his only chance. Fortunately the chain snapped and the giant wave carried the *Edrie* on a wild ride over what had been dry land and forest just minutes before. Ulrich got off a quick radio call: "Mayday!, Mayday! This is the *Edrie* in Lituya Bay. All hell has broken loose in here. I think

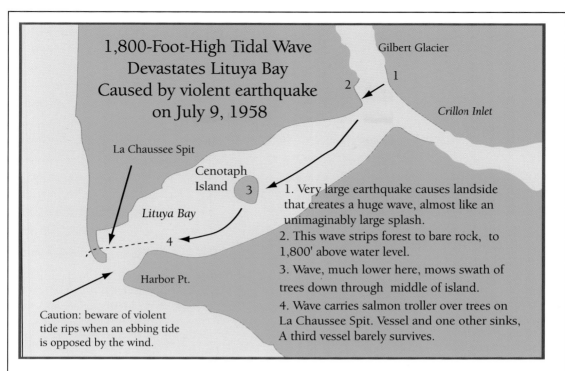

1,800-Foot-High Tidal Wave Devastates Lituya Bay Caused by violent earthquake on July 9, 1958

Gilbert Glacier

Crillon Inlet

La Chaussee Spit

Cenotaph Island

Lituya Bay

Harbor Pt.

1. Very large earthquake causes landside that creates a huge wave, almost like an unimaginably large splash.

2. This wave strips forest to bare rock, to 1,800' above water level.

3. Wave, much lower here, mows swath of trees down through middle of island.

4. Wave carries salmon troller over trees on La Chaussee Spit. Vessel and one other sinks, A third vessel barely survives.

Caution: beware of violent tide rips when an ebbing tide is opposed by the wind.

we've had it. Good-by."

Dancing and weaving for survival among heaving seas, icebergs and thousands of floating trees, the *Edrie* finally escaped the wave and managed to stay afloat.

The two other vessels in Lituya Bay that night weren't so lucky. The *Badger* was carried by the wave over the trees and the land on the north spit, finally to sink outside the bay, her crew safe in a tiny skiff. The third, the *Sunmore* was last seen running full speed toward the bay's entrance before the wave engulfed her, never to be seen again.

Bill Swanson, who with his wife Vivian survived the sinking of their troller *Badger*, saw a sight that gave geologists a clue to the almost unbelievably powerful forces at work that night in the mountains behind Lituya Bay:

"...The mountains were shaking something awful, with slides of rock and snow, but what I noticed mostly was the glacier, the north glacier, the one they call Lituya Glacier.

I know you can't ordinarily see that glacier from where I was anchored. People shake their heads when I tell them I saw it that night. I can't help it if they don't believe me. I know the glacier is hidden by the point when you're in Anchorage Cove, but I know what I saw that night, too.

"The glacier had risen in the air and moved forward so it was in sight. It must have risen several hundred feet. I don't mean it was just hanging in the air. It seems to be solid, but it was jumping and shaking like crazy. Big chunks of ice were falling off the face of it down into the water. That was six miles away and they still looked like big chunks. They came off the glacier like a big load of rocks spilling out of a dump truck. That went on for a little while—it's hard to tell just how long—and then suddenly the glacier dropped back out of sight and there was a big wall of water coming over the point. The wave started for us after that, and I was too busy to tell what else was happening up there."

— Bill Swanson, in "Where Hell Breaks Loose",
in *The Alaska Sportsman*®, October 1958

The 200 foot tall snout of Hubbard Glacier threatens to close off Russell Fjord. In 1986, it completely closed off the entrance. Below: Lituya Bay hermit Jim Huscroft was host to many climbing parties, headed to the rugged country to the east. Bradford Washburn photo

The Roof of North America—East and north of Hubbard Glacier is an area that has been nicknamed 'The Roof of North America'—an immense rock, ice, and snow world with many of the continent's highest peaks. Ten thousand-footers are common here, and there are at least four over 15,000'. Much of this area is the Wrangell St. Elias National Park and Wilderness. This mountain wall catches the eastward flowing moisture-laden air, which falls as heavy snow. The immense weight of the snow pack creates the largest glaciers on the entire Pacific coast. Hubbard Glacier is part of a vast ice mass that extends along a few miles behind the coast in an unbroken line (except for two places) almost to Anchorage, nearly 400 miles away. Today the glaciers have all receded substantially back from the shore, but a century ago, the ice reached the ocean in many places.

Icy Bay, to the north at Mile 1220, has the usual shallow entrance, though in recent years it has been the scene of considerable logging activity. One hundred years ago, the bay wasn't even there—it was filled with a glacier that extended several miles out into the ocean!

These are active glaciers—there is often much ice in the bay, and sometimes icebergs will drift out of the bay and form a regular line of stranded bergs along the outside shore, all the way northwest to Cape Yakataga.

"**Cape St. Elias, the south end of Kayak Island, is an important and unmistakable landmark**. It is a precipitous, sharp, rocky ridge, about one mile long and 1,665 feet high, with a low, wooded neck between it and the high parts of the island farther north. About 0.2 mile off the cape is the remarkable Pinnacle Rock, 494 feet high."

—*U.S. Coast Pilot 9*, 1964 ed.

Mt. St. Elias marks the spot where the Alaska border changes from an irregular zigzag along the top of the coastal range to veer sharply north to follow the 141 degree west longitude line, arrowing across rivers, lonely mountains and tundra to Demarcation Point on the Beaufort Sea, some 650 miles north.

The Copper River emerges from the mountains between Miles and Childs Glaciers, and spreads out into a delta with many islands as it enters the Gulf of Alaska. The river delta and the myriad sand bars are the scene of considerable activity in the late spring and summer with shallow draft salmon gillnetters seeking the well-known Copper River Red Salmon. Marketed as **Copper River Reds**, they are some of the first fresh Alaska sockeye on the market and traditionally command a high price. Much of the fishing is in and among the sand bars on the flats, in and out of the breakers, a challenging fishery. Tenders (fish buying vessels) typically anchor in sheltered coves nearby.

The nearest town and the home port for these vessels, is **Cordova**, northeast of **mile 1380**. There is a native settlement, Alaganik, 10 miles up Alaganik Slough, the main channel of the Copper River.

A shallow channel for vessels with local knowledge exists over the shifting sand bars east of Hinchinbrook Island.

Early morning risers get a great view of Cape St. Elias with dramatic 500' Pinnacle Rock, just offshore. Northbound cruise ships are usually off the cape just at dawn, so if you're an early riser, get your camera and get out on deck!

Something woke me around midnight—the motion of our new steel king crabber that had seemed so big tied to the dock in Seattle: slow and loggy, hesitating at the end of each roll, as if it weren't sure it was going to roll back the other way. I dressed and took the steps up to pilothouse and immediately saw the problem.

Ice! A bitter wind had come up, ripping the spray off the ocean and freezing to our hull and rigging. Enough had accumulated to make us so top heavy that capsizing was a very real possibility. This was how vessels died, I suddenly realized.

We dressed quickly in warm clothes and rain gear, and, secured by a safety lines, inched out onto the bow, knocking the ice off with hammers and baseball bats and kicking the pieces over the side.

Once a large sea loomed suddenly out the night and the bow dipped into it and we were suddenly hip deep in the dark swirling water. Our skipper stared out in alarm from the pilothouse through the tiny circle of ice-free glass, and then the bow rose, and sea poured back over the side.

On the back deck, our double stacked pots were a hill of smooth ice and we struggled, hammering and shoveling until we were wet with sweat. Finally our boat seemed to ride a little safer, and we jogged slowly to the shelter of a tiny island, hammering and shoveling all the way.

We pulled the big steel hatch covers off, loaded as many of the heavily iced pots into the holds as

would fit, laid the rest flat on the deck, lowered the boom and lashed it to the stern. The icy wind still clawed at us, but there was no sea. When we were finally done I looked around. We were probably the only humans within 50 miles and the vista—frozen islands, shore and mountains, now hidden, now revealed by moon and racing clouds, was unspeakably bleak.

"It's the Copper River wind, boy," the skipper's brother told me in the galley when we were done and warming up. "It just sucks down off the flats and ice after a little sou'west breeze. All that ocean air just gets frozen up there, and all of a sudden decides to roll back to the sea."

Ready for the ice: after icing badly our only choice to lower our center of gravity was to put as many pots as we could in our big steel holds below decks, and lower our heavy steel boom to a horizontal position.

"Ah, I shouldn't have let Dad steer at night... that's how it all started—he was almost seventy then and his eyes were starting to go. We were headed up to fish Prince William, and I just laid down for a bit. There was a moon, and not much wind, so I thought he'd be OK. But then the next thing I knew we were in the breakers— he'd just gotten in too close to the beach. The boat started to break up and that was way before survival suits, so we just ended up on the beach in our woolies (long woolen underwear).

"It all happened so quick there really wasn't any time for a radio call. The snow was right down to the water's edge in places—it was late April—so I figured our only chance was to try and make it back to Cape Yakataga. I knew there was at least a lodge or something there...

"It was really tough going—seemed like every mile there was a stream that we either had to wade across, sometimes up to our chests, and all snowmelt—just icy cold.

"We slept just huddled together, and then on the afternoon of the second day, Dad told me to leave him—that he couldn't go on any longer... The worst part of it was that we'd lost our

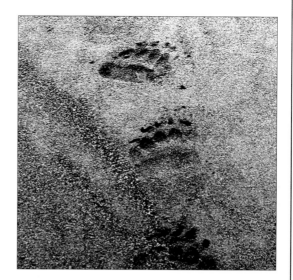

snoose (powdered or so called 'smokeless' tobacco) and our chew both with the boat.

"If we hadn't stumbled across an old trapper's cabin, and found some old moldy pipe tobacco that we could chew on, I don't think we would have made it. But we spent the night in there, and each of us got a good chew in our mouths so the next morning life seemed a little more bearable...

"Turns out BP had some sort of drilling operation at the Cape back then, and the first building we came to was the mess hall. It was noon, and we walked in the door, all scratched up, just in bloody ripped woolies and our rubber boots. Everyone turned as we came in the door, and for a long moment, you could have heard a pin drop in there..."

—Dick Kietel, fisherman

Left: Some sort of weird Halloween? Actually this is my crew, practicing putting on their survival suits. Developed in the late 1970s the buoyant and insulating foam suits were quickly embraced by much of the Alaska fleet. Boats with no room to store them sometimes tied the suits to the mast. Top: If hypothermia doesn't get you, the bears might: tracks along the beach north of Dangerous River. Brenda Carney photo

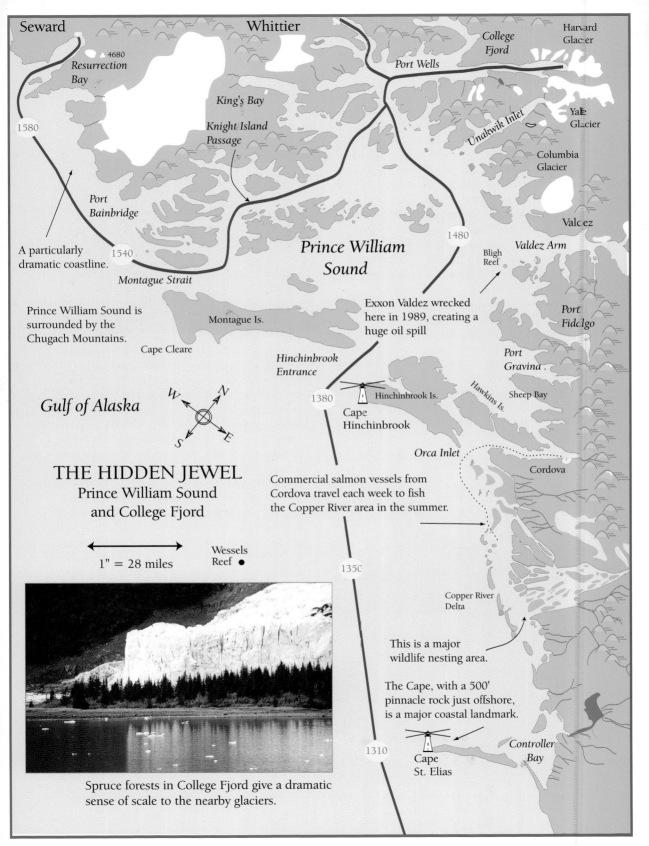

Seward

Whittier

4680

Resurrection
Bay

King's Bay

*Knight Island
Passage*

1580

*Port
Bainbridge*

A particularly
dramatic coastline.

1540

Montague Strait

Prince William Sound is
surrounded by the
Chugach Mountains.

Montague Is.

Cape Cleare

Gulf of Alaska

THE HIDDEN JEWEL
Prince William Sound
and College Fjord

1" = 28 miles

Wessels
Reef ●

*College
Fjord*

Port Wells

Harvard
Glacier

Unakwik Inlet

Yale
Glacier

Columbia
Glacier

Valdez

1480

Bligh
Reef

Valdez Arm

Exxon Valdez wrecked
here in 1989, creating a
huge oil spill

*Prince William
Sound*

*Port
Fidalgo*

*Port
Gravina*

*Hinchinbrook
Entrance*

1380

Hinchinbrook Is.

Hawkins Is.

Sheep Bay

Cape
Hinchinbrook

Orca Inlet

Cordova

Commercial salmon vessels from
Cordova travel each week to fish
the Copper River area in the summer.

1350

Copper River
Delta

This is a major
wildlife nesting area.

The Cape, with a 500'
pinnacle rock just offshore,
is a major coastal landmark.

1310

Cape
St. Elias

*Controller
Bay*

N
W   E
S

Spruce forests in College Fjord give a dramatic
sense of scale to the nearby glaciers.

CHAPTER 7

The Hidden Jewel

College Fjord and Prince William Sound

Cape Hinchinbrook, mile 1380, is the entrance to many-armed Prince William Sound, an area about the size of some small states. Except for three towns—Cordova, Valdez, and Whittier, and a few settlements, the area is mostly uninhabited, a dramatic island archipelago wilderness with many active glaciers.

If you are on a northbound ship, the early morning light here can be truly spectacular. First light comes real early in the summer, so as soon as you wake up, have a look out your window or if you have an inside cabin, dress warmly and step outside with your camera. The shining 12 and 13,000 footers of the Chugach mountains are sometimes clearly visible from 80 miles away.

It was here that the square-rigged ships full of Chinese workers and Italian and Norwegian fishermen came to build canneries and harvest salmon in the earliest days of the salmon fishery in Prince William Sound beginning in the 1890s.

In September, when the salmon runs were over, the cans and workers would be loaded aboard ship and sail hoisted for the run south to San Francisco or Puget Sound.

Procession Rocks, in the southwest corner of Prince Wil iam Sound, is a major sea lion rookery. But you don't want get too close as the big bull males have their own harems on the rocks and get aggressive if Zodiacs approach too near! Bottom: Once hunted almost to extinction, the friendly sea otter has repopulated its range. They especially like to swim on their backs, often placing food on their bellies as they eat.

Top: Headed out to find sea lion rookeries in the fog at Procession Rocks. Below: The remains of a fox farm, overtaken by brush, in the woods. In earlier years, such operations could be found on many Alaska islands.

Early Explorers: Captain James Cook briefly explored this area in 1778. Setting out from England in the spring of 1768, he made three voyages to become one of the most famous explorers in history. Much of his work was spent in filling in the vast blank space on the map that was the Pacific Ocean. Exploring this section of the coast was to be his last hurrah. Returning to Hawaii, he was tragically killed in a scuffle with natives in February of 1779.

But when Cook's men beached and caulked his ship in Prince William Sound, they traded a few fish hooks and trinkets for sea otter pelts, which were made into clothes to protect themselves against the cold. A year later, returning to England via China, the crew was amazed at what the worn-out clothes fetched—$10,000! They nearly mutinied, wanting to get back to Alaska and get more furs.

The Sound teems with **sea life** such as sea lions, seal, and frequently, humpback whales. Sea otters in particular have made a remarkable comeback. After being hunted almost to extinction, their population has risen to over

100,000 statewide. A particularly good place to watch for them is on small floating ice pieces in College Fjord.

But it is salmon that has been the bread and butter for most fishermen here. During the summer season, tenders or fish-buying vessels spread out to the farthest reaches of the many fjords of the region, to buy fish from both purse seiners and gill-netters. These tenders acted like mother ships, often supplying groceries, water, and fuel for their boats, fishing too far from town to return at night. Many fishermen live in remote communities like Cordova where fishing was about the only game in town.

In the hierarchy of salmon fishermen in Alaska, (there are many salmon fishing districts in Alaska, each with its different style of vessel and gear) the "Prince William Sound Boys" in the 1980s were doing well. Salmon prices were high, and catches were good, and it was a scenic and reasonably calm place to fish. Life was good.

This comfortable world was shattered on March 23, 1989, when a long nightmare began—the oil spill.

A sea lion harem at Procession Rocks. The enormous bu l on the left rules the roost and will oppose the arrival of any other males. He doesn't much like Zodiac inflatables, either...

195

ICE, OIL, AND THE EXXON VALDEZ

On a calm night the Exxon Valdez slid up on a well marked reef and sliced open her single skinned hull to release 11 million gallons of oil. Below: As was often the case, Columbia Glacier was calving huge amounts of ice directly across the tanker route. It was during evasive action to avoid the ice that the Exxon Valdez ran up on Bligh Reef. John Van Amerogan photo

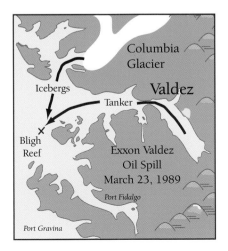

"The only guys that win are the lawyers."
— PWS fisherman

The evening of March 23, 1989 was calm, with a little fog, when the *Exxon Valdez* carrying 211,000 tons of North Slope crude oil departed Valdez. Two hours later the ship slowed near Rocky Point, about 15 miles out of town, to drop the pilot.

As was frequently the case, a substantial amount of ice—small icebergs and drift ice—was moving with the current across the shipping lane near Bligh Reef, just to the east of the channel, some seven miles farther south.

Captain Joseph Hazelwood elected to dodge the ice by crossing from the southbound traffic lane to the northbound lane (tanker traffic in this area is restricted to special traffic lanes), and then out of the channel entirely. Such a maneuver was neither dangerous nor uncommon, but required careful execution, as in this case, the course he elected to take would carry the *Exxon Valdez* perilously close to a dangerous, but well marked reef.

In a move he was to regret deeply later, Captain Hazelwood stepped into his stateroom to take care of some paperwork during this maneuver, leaving Third Mate Gregory Cousins in charge.

The problem with very large vessels like this one (987 feet long by 166 feet wide) is that they have such terrific mass and inertia. Even after the rudder is turned, the huge momentum of 211,000 tons of steel and oil tends to keep the ship traveling in the original direction.

In this case the ship wasn't turned quickly enough and shortly after midnight, the *Exxon Valdez* slid up on Bligh Reef, instantly rupturing several of her crude oil tanks.

About three hours later, the first small Coast Guard cutter arrived on scene and its officers were stunned by what they found, a huge tanker aground on a well marked reef, with crude oil literally blowing out of the hull, bubbling almost two feet out of the water. It was their worst nightmare and more.

Within 24 hours some 10 million gallons of crude oil had spread into a slick that covered about 18 square miles. Fortunately, the three days following the grounding were unusually calm—perfect weather for skimming and recovering oil from the surface of the water.

Unfortunately, much of the oil spill response equipment was temporarily unavailable. The reaction of fisher Riki Ott after arriving on the scene the day after the spill said it all:

"I was stunned. There was no (oil spill) boom, no containment. Just a tanker on the rocks with two fishing boats coming up to it. Where was everybody?"

By the time a modicum of oil spill recovery equipment arrived on scene, the opportunity had been lost—the oil had thickened into a hard-to-skim "mousse," and the wind and tide had started it on its journey to blacken many thousands of miles of shoreline, and wreck economic havoc on many of the state's salmon fishermen.

The state of Alaska was very concerned about oiled fish getting into the chain of product that stretched from the remote coves where it was caught to valuable markets in Asia and other places. So as the oil spill approached any of the state's numerous fishing areas in western Alaska, the areas were closed and fishermen were forced to stop fishing and wait. For these fishermen who had perhaps hundreds of thousands of dollars invested in their operations, and were substantially in debt, as is usually the case at the beginning of any fishing season, the oil spill and the closure of their fisheries, even if it was just for a few weeks, was a financial disaster.

Worse hit were Prince William Sound and particularly those fishermen who depended on the area's salmon and the herring stocks, which were closed to commercial fishing for almost all of the rest of the 1989 season.

To Exxon's credit, the company instituted a hugely expensive, if late, effort to recover some of the 11 million gallons of spilled oil. Part of the equipment included big barges with boilers to create steam and long hoses to reach the beaches where workers tried to remove the oil by

Oiled sea otter at washing station. These small, graceful critters suffered most from the oil spill. Many died from hypothermia, when their coats became oiled, losing their insulating property. John VanAmerogan photo.

While the oil is mostly gone from the beaches, salmon and herring catches have been substantially below pre-spill levels. And Alaska fishermen and processors are still waiting for their checks for damages, almost 20 years later.

After the 1989 oil spill a system of tug escorts were instituted to accompany outbound tankers safely past the rocks that impaled the Exxon Valdez. Top: An escort tug returning to Valdez after accompanying its tanker as far as Cape Hinchinbrook. The Chugach Mountains are in the background.

essentially steam cleaning the rocks. This 'hurry up and get it cleaned at any cost' attitude created a mini boom for thousands of scientists, technicians, reporters, and clean-up workers. Fishermen chartered their vessels at top dollar to work on the clean-up, and marine suppliers gladly wrote up orders for tons of buoys, line, boots, foul weather gear, etc.

The surprising recovery: in Prince William Sound, nature has shown itself to be remarkably resilient. Many affected sea life populations have returned to previous levels and the area appears to be as pristine as it always was. But neither herring nor salmon have returned to pre-oil spill levels.

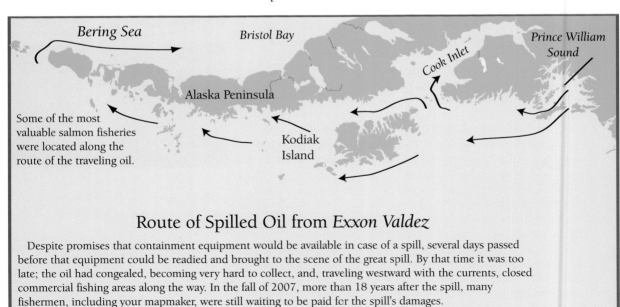

Route of Spilled Oil from *Exxon Valdez*

Despite promises that containment equipment would be available in case of a spill, several days passed before that equipment could be readied and brought to the scene of the great spill. By that time it was too late; the oil had congealed, becoming very hard to collect, and, traveling westward with the currents, closed commercial fishing areas along the way. In the fall of 2007, more than 18 years after the spill, many fishermen, including your mapmaker, were still waiting to be paid for the spill's damages.

The Columbia Glacier, 40 miles west of Valdez, is a big one, even by Alaska standards—some 450 square miles—and with its towering (over 200 feet high in places) six-mile-long face is as dramatic a sight as any in Alaska. It was ice from this glacier that the *Exxon Valdez* made its ill-fated turn to avoid.

Did you know? Probably the fastest-moving glacier in history was the **Black Rapids Glacier**, north of Valdez. In 1927 it was big news when it began surging, hitting <u>almost ten feet an hour</u> at one point, headed for the road link to the outside world, the Richardson Highway. Reporters were disappointed when it stopped just short of the road and began a slow retreat.

All of Prince William Sound was hit hard by the 1964 Good Friday earthquake. In many areas the whole sea floor was lifted, destroying what had been a prosperous clam fishery. Valdez was particularly hard hit as, being built on less stable silt, felt the violence of the quake more acutely than Whittier, just 75 miles west. Then after the shaking had essentially destroyed much of the town, four tidal waves or tsunamis demolished what was left. The damage was so bad that the town was rebuilt at a different and hopefully, more earthquake resistant site, four mile west.

Valdez—This town of some 4,000 residents, backed by high mountains, has been called Alaska's Little Switzerland. Valdez' main feature, of course is the terminal for the Alaska pipeline. It takes roughly one supertanker a day to keep up with the flow through the insulated four-foot diameter pipe that stretches 800 miles from Prudhoe Bay on the frozen Beaufort Sea.

Jack Dalton, a native Alaskan story-teller and dancer, entertains aboard the 100 passenger Spirit of Oceanus, operated by Cruise West.

Passenger Tip

Have a look to the north when you enter Prince William Sound; you may get a glimpse of Columbia Glacier, the largest and also fastest receding tidewater glacier in Alaska. It was ice from this glacier that forced the Exxon Valdez to alter course and eventually hit Bligh Reef.

With so many islands and sheltered waterways, Prince William Sound has become very popular with kayakers. Many outfitters offer complete trips where they supply the kayaks, gear, tents, food, etc. Then you would be dropped by boat at a remote, sheltered bay and picked up at a later date. For those seeking a bit more of an upscale experience, some outfitters travel with you, set up the tents, cook up the food and provide the entertainment.

The town has a truly spectacular setting, and is particularly popular with skiers and snowboarders seeking long runs and deep power snow. But with no ski lift to get the customers up to the snow, local entrepreneurs have invested in helicopters to take their clients up to the mountains, at around $100 a ride. The main base for heli skiing is at Thompson Pass, about 30 miles north of town. The location is far enough away from the salt water so that the coastal weather systems affect the flying much less than if it had been based in Valdez itself.

Cordova, in the far southeast corner of Prince William Sound, is only accessed by boat and plane. Originally settled to support the copper boom in the interior to the east, Cordova has become the main fishing port of Prince William Sound, and the population almost doubles in the summer when processing workers and commercial fishermen from the lower 48 come up to fish the Copper River and work in the canneries and freezer plants.

Faced with declining salmon runs in the 1970s for pink salmon, Prince William Sound fisherman invested in a substantial hatchery program to breed and release pink salmon. The program's success went a long ways to providing a stable base for the region's fishermen.

Before the tunnel into Whittier was modified in 2000 to allow cars to drive directly through (instead of being carried on rail cars,) Prince William Sound was fairly remote. But today, because of the easier access, more and more Anchorage and lower 48 residents are discovering the charms of this sheltered archipelago.

THE 1899 HARRIMAN ALASKA EXPEDITION

After suffering a nervous breakdown, railroad magnate (Union, Southern, and Northern Pacific) Edward H. Harriman was ordered by his doctors to have a "long vacation at sea." Prohibited from taking railroad men, he instead assembled one of the most remarkable literary, scientific, and artistic expeditions ever to come to Alaska. Chartering the steamer *George W. Elder*, Harriman arranged for a well-stocked library and some of the leading naturalists, artists, and scientists of the day including naturalist **John Muir**, photographer **Edward Curtis**, and many others.

Perhaps their biggest contribution was their extensive observations in Glacier Bay in June of 1899, just three months before a huge earthquake shattered many of the glaciers.

Entering Prince William Sound, they again found what some have called the two Alaskas—the spectacular beauty of the land in stark contrast to the grubbiness and even squalor of those who lived there, or like gold miners or cannery workers, exploited the resources.

Several days later, as their ship approached what is now

Top: Seal hunter's camp with hides stretched out for drying. UW NA2103
Below: Native visitors come alongside the expedition steamer in graceful carved cedar canoes. UW NA2098

201

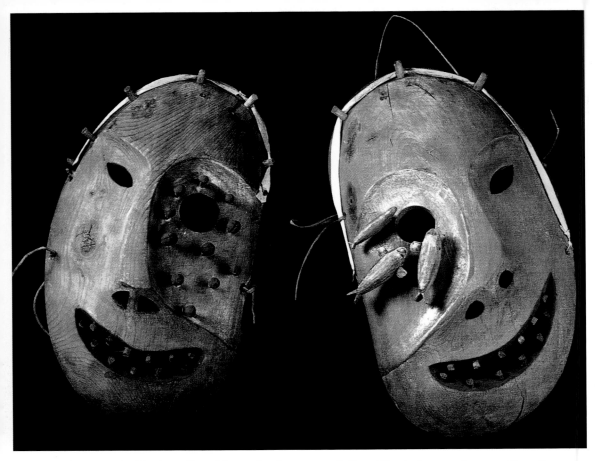

It's fortunate the Harriman Expedition came along when it did. For as Christian Missionaries came to Western Alaska, they viewed masks such like these as pagan and many were destroyed. ASM, IIA1451 & IIA1452 Below: Masks were mostly used by dancers in ceremonies that celebrated events in local culture. UW NA2006

known as College Fjord, they made a startling discovery—while the chart showed Barry Arm ending at Barry Glacier, in fact, the glacier had receded enough for the ship to squeeze through, into the uncharted and unknown waters beyond. It was a genuine thrill for the group to discover and map this new territory that came to be named Harriman Fjord. A group including John Muir (naturally) spent two days camped in the new fjord while the ship returned to Orca for propeller repairs, after striking a rock.

Next was another unique opportunity—to name a fjord and its glaciers. As many of his party were "Easterners," they surveyed many of the glaciers here, and named them for their New England colleges like Dartmouth, Harvard, Wellesley, and Vassar.

After leaving Prince William Sound, the *George W. Elder* proceeded "to the west'ard," touching at many places that are still extremely remote almost 100 years later, including King Island, Alaska, and Plover Bay, Siberia, on the Bering Strait. It was a remarkable expedition and they brought back a wealth of photographs, scientific data, and artifacts.

COLLEGE FJORD

The hidden jewel of Prince William Sound is remote College Fjord. Within an eight-mile stretch at the upper end of this fjord five major tidewater glaciers reach the salt water. While Glacier Bay has emerged from the ice so recently that substantial trees have not gained foothold close to the ice, College Fjord is a place where the forests and glaciers have coexisted for centuries.

The result is a perspective on the great rivers of ice not seen in Glacier Bay. To see a glacier towering above the 100-foot-tall trees of a spruce forest, like **Wellesley Glacier** is really impressive.

Study the hillsides here. The upper slopes of these big glacial fjords, stripped of trees and covered with many berry bushes, are excellent bear watching territory. What you are looking for are brown or black dots that appear to be moving—these will be bears foraging for berries. Look also for white dots, often found in small groups—these will be mountain goats. Sometimes you will see goats in places that an experienced rock climber would probably have trouble on.

With so many glaciers crowded around a single narrow body of water, College Fjord presents a much more dramatic vista than Glacier Bay. Bottom: Large cruise ship passing carefully next to a small iceberg, but still the size of a pickup truck and able to damage a propeller.

Bears are also found down on the beach, especially if the tide is low. They are pretty good clambers, despite a crude technique. It goes like this: they look for the telltale water spurts of clams, dig them up with a big paw, smash them open with their other paw, and press the whole mass, shells and all, up to their mouth.

So where are the really big icebergs? By the time most of this ice gets to the salt water, it has been fractured so much by those twisting mountain valleys, that most of the ice that breaks off is fairly small, say the size of a small apartment building at the most.

But remember that roughly 7/8 of an iceberg is below the surface of the water, so that something that looks small on top, like the size of a garage, still poses a significant danger to ships. (Small icebergs and so-called "bergy bits" are notoriously difficult to see on radar.)

Calving bergs: before Alaska cruising got so popular, few big ships penetrated right up close to the glaciers here and in other places. The captains of those ships that did discovered that if the glacier wasn't actively calving when they were there, they could often dislodge some ice with a blow of the ship's steam whistle. Today such practices are prohibited, so it's just a waiting game. Often major calving is proceeded by small bits breaking off. I was here aboard the *Dawn Princess* in 1997, and the captain spied an apartment building-sized ice spire that seemed to be tipping toward the fjord. We circled slowly for more than an hour, watching and waiting, and were finally rewarded with a

Spruce forests here grow right up next to some of the glaciers, giving you a sense of scale not seen in Glacier Bay. Below: compare the photo below of the same glacier taken from almost the same spot in 2007 with the photo above, taken in 1997. The amount that this glacier has receded is noticeable.

College Fjord will be your best opportunity to see sea otters. Look particularly for what look like long dark spots on top of ice flows. Look with your binoculars—chances are they'll be sea otters, perhaps with their pups.

splash that must have been 280 feet high and a huge boom that echoed up and down the fjord. See opposite photo. Directly astern as you swing to the east to leave College Fjord is **Passage Canal**, at the head of which is **Whittier**, a small fishing community. Before the new road was finished in 2000, the only access was via the Alaska Railroad and several tunnels through the mountains. Cars and buses drove onto flatcars for the scenic trip.

If your ship is headed for Seward, you'll continue west, swinging past Perry Island and into **Knight Island Passage.** The land is forested and wild. Around you passages lead back to bay after lonely bay: Copper Bay, Herring Bay, Mummy Bay.

Once many of these bays and islands were home to fox farms, herring plants, prospector's cabins and the like. But today, except for the settlements around **Sawmill Bay**, to the west at **Mile 1520** this part of the Sound is for the most part uninhabited. **Sawmill Bay** is also the site of the major salmon hatchery that supports the pink salmon fishery in the Sound.

West of Knight Island Passage, you'll enter Montague Strait, and then the open Gulf of Alaska for about 40 miles before entering the shelter of Resurrection Bay.

If your cruise ends at **Seward**, this is probably where you'll go to your stateroom and pack, figuring the drama and beauty of your cruise is pretty much over.

However, the area between Prince William Sound and

Seward is also some of the most dramatic of the whole trip. So try to find some time to go up to a lounge or viewing area where you have a view forward, and just take in some of this magnificent scenery. I have nicknamed the coast west of Prince William Sound, "The Ironbound Coast." and if you can take a few minutes in the late evening to study it, you will probably agree.

An ice spire the size of an apartment building topples into College Fjord, making a splash 250 feet high!

WHITTIER: REBIRTH - A ROAD AT LAST!

Top: Princess Cruises uses Whittier as the northern terminus of their Voyage of the Glaciers cruises. Below: There's a lot of snow here in the wintertime, so most of the population lives in a single building. Right: A creche, next to the Log Cabin Gift Shop waits for the next Christmas pageant.

Built originally as a World War II port alternative to Seward, 1940s and 50s era residents pretty much all lived in the ugly abandoned buildings east of the docks. In a place like this with heavy deep snow on the ground for most of the long winter, it was convenient to have all the homes and services, stores, movie theatre, etc. all under a single roof!

When the military pulled out in 1960, Whittier became almost a ghost town, the population plunging to around 70. The 1964 earthquake almost finished off the rest.

Finally rebuilt with a larger boat harbor that gave Anchorage residents a reason to come, (huge tides in the Anchorage area make it boater unfriendly) Whittier began to grow again. Access was still a problem—you could drive your car onto a flatbed railcar and get pulled through the tunnel with the rest of the train, but it was hardly convenient.

Finally, in 2000, a widened tunnel was opened that accommodated both cars (one way at a time) and trains. This better access was a boost for Whittier residents, and a number of businesses have sprung up to serve the increased numbers of visitors.

Most passengers transit Whittier quickly to and from their ship. If you do have the time, there are some modest places to shop and eat along the shore just east of the cruise ship docks. A popular whale and glacier excursion operates here as well.

Be sure to take the train in or out of Whittier instead of the bus; it's a delightful ride.

SEWARD: NORTHERN TERMINUS

Dawn Princess at Seward. Though the big ships bring a lot of seasonal jobs to this town, commercial fishing is still a strong part of the local economy.

The Good Friday Earthquake - If this town looks fairly new, it's because it is—much of the port and downtown was destroyed in the violent events of March 27, 1964. When the ground started shaking, it essentially created sort of an underwater landslide that dropped most of the waterfront 6 feet and into the bay. Next the big oil tanks east of town ruptured, the oil ignited in a flaming sheet across the bay in front of town and set the stage for the next tragedy: the tidal wave.

For as the shaken residents began to recover from the initial shocks, few noticed that the sea had receded substantially from the shore.

Then a 30 foot wall of water, carrying much of the flaming oil with it, blasted into what was left of downtown, basically destroying the entire waterfront, and it was more than a decade before the town had rebuilt and recovered.

Today, Seward's economy runs on commercial and sport fishing as well as tourism. Look just south of the boat harbor to the parking lot usually full of trailers and motor homes—mostly Anchorage residents combining a vacation away from the bright city lights with a salmon resource that allows them to take enough to can or freeze as a significant food resource for the winter, especially if several family members are all catching fish.

Have a walk around the parking lot. If it looks busy, chances are you'll see some home canning operations set up to process the fish being caught.

Why Don't Anchorage Residents Fish in Cook Inlet? Funnel-shaped Cook Inlet produces huge tides similar to the Bay of Fundy on Canada's east coast. These big tides make it very expensive to build marinas and create vast areas of mud flats at low tide. The result is that even though Anchorage is built on the water, most residents do their boating and salmon fishing in places like Homer, Seward, or Whittier.

Halibut are also usually plentiful here and available over the entire cruise season.

One of the region's few benefits from the Exxon Valdez spill is the **Alaska Sealife Center**, a major attraction in town. Funded with part of the oil spill mitigation money, it is part research, part educational combined with an facility that is probably one of the most unique small aquariums you will ever see. In addition to the tanks and exhibits, there is an unusual live video feed from the Stellar Sea Lion rookery at Chiswell Islands, about 35 miles south.

It's not just fish and marine mammals. Tufted Puffins, Red-Legged Kittiwakes, Murres and Pigeon Guillemots all live and breed in a rookery in the big tank as well.

Seward is also the headquarters for the **Kenai Fjords National Park**, a dramatic area of narrow bays, steep islands and glaciated fjords, west of town. Inland from the water and feeding all the glaciers is the **Harding Ice Field**, which once covered the entire Kenai Peninsula. As in most of Alaska, the ice is receding here, but the landscape is exceedingly fresh—most of the bays of

Chaos and destruction: the aftermath of the 1964 earthquake. The waterfront was essentially totally destroyed. Fortunately loss of life was light. UW 17947 Below: Fat and sassy—a harbor seal enjoys the easy living at the Alaska Sealife Center.

Exit Glacier is a good chance to get close to the ice. But not too close; falling pieces have occasionally killed or injured the unwary. Below: Sign on local road; winters are harsh here...

Kenai Fjords were solid ice just a hundred years ago.

If you haven't gotten a chance to get up close to the ice yet, consider a tour or a taxi to **Exit Glacier**, about 8 miles west of town. As you'll see from the extensive glacial moraine that you will cross to get to the glacier, it is also receding at a good clip, melting away all along its front. However, be careful to give the face a respectful distance; a visitor was killed by falling ice and others have been injured.

If you're planning to spend some time in the area before heading home and have a hankering for a wilderness, but not too rough, experience, the National Park Service does maintain four **remote cabins in Kenai Fjords**. You'll need to bring in a sleeping bag, groceries, and maybe your fishing rod. These are fly-in; there is no road access but air taxi outfits in Seward can get you in and out. Contact the NPS at 907-224-3175 for information and availability.

Leaving (or approaching) Seward, you'll pass just to the west of Fox Island, out toward the mouth of the bay. Today the island has a lodge and a day guest facility used by a tour boat operator.

It was here that noted artist and writer Rockwell Kent spent the hard winter of 1918-1919 with his nine-year old son.

Kent was a bit of a renaissance man as well as adventurer, liking a life that was close to the edge. He put his adventures here

(some of which he and his son were lucky to survive) into an excellent book, *Wilderness, A Quiet Adventure in Alaska*, illustrated with his dramatic woodcuts.

The Kents had come to Seward seeking an isolated place to winter and bond as father and son, and by chance, encountered a rough hewn homesteader who offered to share his island with them. Their only boat to get back and forth to town was a small dory and in it they had a few close calls:

"The aspect of the day had become ominous. The mountainous land appeared blue black, the sea a light but brilliant yellow green. Over the water the wind blew in furious squalls raising a surge of white caps and a dangerous chop. I was now rowing with all my strength, foreseeing clearly the possibility of disaster for us, scanning with concern the terrible leeward shore with its line of breakers and stern cliffs."

They survived. And later:

"The wind that night continued rising 'til it blew a gale. And that night in their bed Rockwell (Kent's son) and his father put their arms tight around each other without telling why they did it."

Top: Seal having fun in the Alaska Sealife Center. Below: In summer, when the fish are running, the beach at Seward is busy!

In 2005, the 100 passenger *Spirit of Oceanus* lay off these islands to send passengers exploring in Zodiac inflatable boats. I was helping, a bit of a swell was running, and it was awkward to get the passengers safely aboard. In particular, I was concerned about one particular 88 year old passenger who was eager to go but unsteady on her feet. After carefully guiding her down the narrow and steep stairway to the boarding platform, the Phillipino boat crew picked their moment, grabbed her together, and plunked her aboard.

The steep islands were spectacular bird rookeries and as we approached, clouds of kittiwakes, guillemots, and auklets lifted off and swirled around us. There were some very large sea caves and as we approached the big swells would boom in and out of them.

"Lets go in there, Joe," cried Millie, our elderly passenger.

"Millie," I exclaimed, " we can't go in there, you can see what the waves are doing. If we even tried to go in there, we'd be smooshed?"

"Ah," she answered cheerily, "but it'd be better than fading away in a nursing home..."

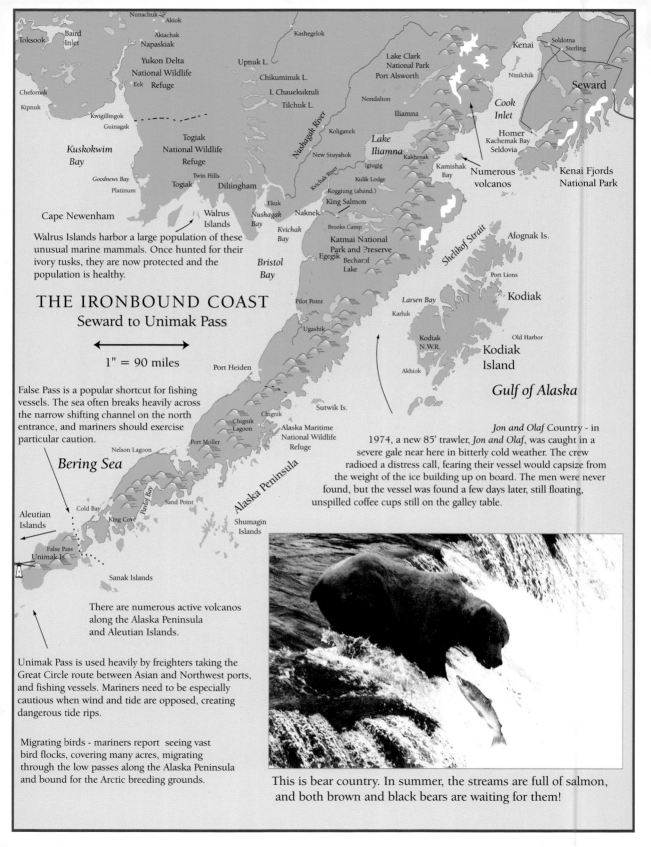

Nunachuk · Akiok
Toksook · Baird Inlet
Akiachak · Napaskiak
Kashegelok
Lake Clark National Park
Port Alsworth
Kenai · Soldotna · Sterling
Seward
Upnuk L.
Chefornak
Yukon Delta National Wildlife Refuge
Eek
Ninilchik
Chikuminuk L.
L Chauekuktuli
Tilchuk L.
Nondalton
Cook Inlet
Kipnuk
Kwigillingok · Guinagak
Iliamna
Homer · Kachemak Bay · Seldovia

Kuskokwim Bay

Togiak National Wildlife Refuge

Koliganek

Lake Iliamna

Kakhenak

Kamishak Bay

Numerous volcanos

Kenai Fjords National Park

Goodnews Bay
Platinum
Twin Hills
Togiak · Dillingham

New Stuyahok

Igiugig
Kulik Lodge
Koggiung (aband.)
King Salmon

Ekuk · Naknek

Nushagak Bay
Kvichak Bay

Brooks Camp

Katmai National Park and Preserve
Egegik · Becharof Lake

Shelikof Strait
Afognak Is.
Port Lions
Kodiak

Cape Newenham

Bristol Bay

Pilot Point

Larsen Bay
Karluk

Kodiak N.W.R.
Kodiak Island

Walrus Islands harbor a large population of these unusual marine mammals. Once hunted for their ivory tusks, they are now protected and the population is healthy.

Walrus Islands

Ugashik

Akhiok
Old Harbor

THE IRONBOUND COAST
Seward to Unimak Pass

Port Heiden

Gulf of Alaska

⟷

1" = 90 miles

Jon and Olaf Country - in 1974, a new 85' trawler, *Jon and Olaf*, was caught in a severe gale near here in bitterly cold weather. The crew radioed a distress call, fearing their vessel would capsize from the weight of the ice building up on board. The men were never found, but the vessel was found a few days later, still floating, unspilled coffee cups still on the galley table.

False Pass is a popular shortcut for fishing vessels. The sea often breaks heavily across the narrow shifting channel on the north entrance, and mariners should exercise particular caution.

Sutwik Is.

Chignik
Chignik Lagoon

Alaska Maritime National Wildlife Refuge

Bering Sea

Nelson Lagoon
Port Moller

Aleutian Islands

Cold Bay
King Cove
Sand Point

Pavlof Bay

Alaska Peninsula

Shumagin Islands

False Pass
Unimak Is.

Ⓐ

Sanak Islands

There are numerous active volcanos along the Alaska Peninsula and Aleutian Islands.

Unimak Pass is used heavily by freighters taking the Great Circle route between Asian and Northwest ports, and fishing vessels. Mariners need to be especially cautious when wind and tide are opposed, creating dangerous tide rips.

Migrating birds - mariners report seeing vast bird flocks, covering many acres, migrating through the low passes along the Alaska Peninsula and bound for the Arctic breeding grounds.

This is bear country. In summer, the streams are full of salmon, and both brown and black bears are waiting for them!

CHAPTER 8

The Ironbound Coast

Seward to Unimak Pass

This isn't your regular Alaska. The kind folks send postcards of. The tall trees, the calving glaciers. In fact, once you get west of Kodiak Island, there aren't many trees on the shore at all; the climate barely allows them to grow.

Out on the Alaska Peninsula and the Aleutian Islands, they pretty much disappear entirely, the landscape dominated by tall bushes and windblown grasses.

And more than in Southeast Alaska and Prince William Sound, the wind is stronger when it blows, and blows more often.

The large cruise ships make their turnaround in Seward or Whittier. Some, headed to Asia via the great circle route make a stop at Dutch Harbor, in the Aleutian Islands. But for the most part, the rugged coast west of Seward is lonely, visited only by fishing and workboats, Alaska ferries, and the rare small cruise ship on an 'adventure' itinerary.

Even the water is unfriendly here: in funnel shaped Turnagain Arm, near Anchorage, the bigger tides enter as a bore or wall of water, and quicksand waits for the unwary. And Shelikof Strait, northeast of Kodiak is dreaded by mariners in winter for its bitter winds and flying spray that freezes so rapidly vessels can capsize with little warning.

Top: Airport, Coffee Point, Egegik. Note the so called "tundra tires" on the airplane, able to land on short grass strips. Bottom: The typical waving grass scenery of western Alaska, with a setnetter's riverfront shack.

217

HOMER

Four-mile-long Homer Spit sticks south into Kachemak Bay. The harbor and many visitor-related businesses are located along the spit.. Below: This is a great spot for halibut fishing; and the annual Halibut Derby is a big event. In 2006, the winning fish was 342 pounds.

Once a remote coal mining settlement, today Homer is a town of 5,000 set in a truly exquisite location. Looking south across Kachemak Bay to the snow covered mountains on the Kenai Peninsula, it is becoming a well-known arts community as well and Artrageous August celebrate it for an entire month. Commercial fishing is the lifeblood here and in the surrounding small communities, with several seafood processors and fleets that fish the waters as far west as the border with Russia in the Bering Sea. Like Seward, Homer is at the very end of a road from Anchorage and is a gateway to many National and State Parks including Katmai, Lake Clark, McNeil River, and Kachemak Bay.

Visitors will see a lot of timber being harvested and shipped here. Logging restrictions in other areas of Alaska and a recent spruce bark beetle outbreak, requiring thousands of acres to be cut, contribute to the big harvests.

The Spit—Homer's most unique feature is a four-mile sand spit sticking out into Kachemak Bay. At the end of the spit is the harbor, marine support facilities, log dump, and shipping facility and a growing number of eateries, gift shops, whale watching and kayak excursions, and other businesses catering to visitors.

The headquarters of the Alaska Maritime National Wildlife Refuge is in town. Its 3.5 million acres are spread

across much of the coast of Alaska to the west. The visitors center has exhibits and displays of the wildlife found in the refuge.

Sportfishing, as you may have guessed, is excellent here. One of the local hot spots is the lagoon just north of the boat harbor—hatchery-raised fish are moved to cages in the lagoon, causing them to imprint the lagoon's location and return there as adults to try to spawn. Naturally they are a little disappointed when they get there and don't find a stream or river, just a big crowd of fishermen! Sometimes, toward the end of a run, "snagging," or dragging a bare hook through the water, is allowed to harvest all the rest of the fish. Kids especially like it; this way the fish are really easy to catch!

Halibut Cove, on the opposite shore of Kachemak Bay from Homer, is a roadless fishing settlement with a strong arts flavor, and a 12 block long boardwalk . Not having a road creates a community that is very different from any of the places visited by most cruise ships. One's schedule tends to revolve around the weather and the tides. A foot ferry connects the Cove to Homer; the noon sailing stops at a seabird nesting island and leaves time for several hours at the Cove before returning to Homer at 4 p.m.

Seldovia, 20 miles west of Halibut Cove, is another commercial fishing oriented community, accessible only by charter plane or boat.

Top: Partially framed by driftwood, a cabin goes up on Homer Spit. The view is to the south across Kachemak Bay. Cook Inlet is almost 50 miles wide here, but the sometimes smoking (or worse) volcanoes stick up over the horizon. Most of Alaska's coastal communities have a monument to their fishermen lost at sea. At Homer, the monument overlooks Cook Inlet, a particularly nasty patch of water.

Katmai
National Park

When 6,715' Mt. Katmai erupted in 1912, several feet of ash buried Kodiak and the blast was heard hundreds of miles away.

Cape Douglas

Shelikof Strait

Shuyak Is.

Afognak Is.

Marmot Is.

Raspberry Is.

Marmot Bay

Ferry

Mt Katmai

While we anchored here in March, 1971, the wind picked up pebbles and small rocks from the beach and drove them against our hull.

Port Lions

Kodiak

Puale Bay— known to mariners as the windiest bay in Alaska

Uyak

Karluk

Larsen Bay

Old Harbor

Chiniak Bay

Cape Chiniak

Kodiak Island

Ugak Bay

Cape Ikolik

Kodiak National Wildlife Refuge

Olga Bay

Dangerous Cape

Sitkalidak Is.

Kodiak Area:

⟷

1 inch = 45 miles

King Crabber

Akhiok

Alitak Bay

Trinity Islands

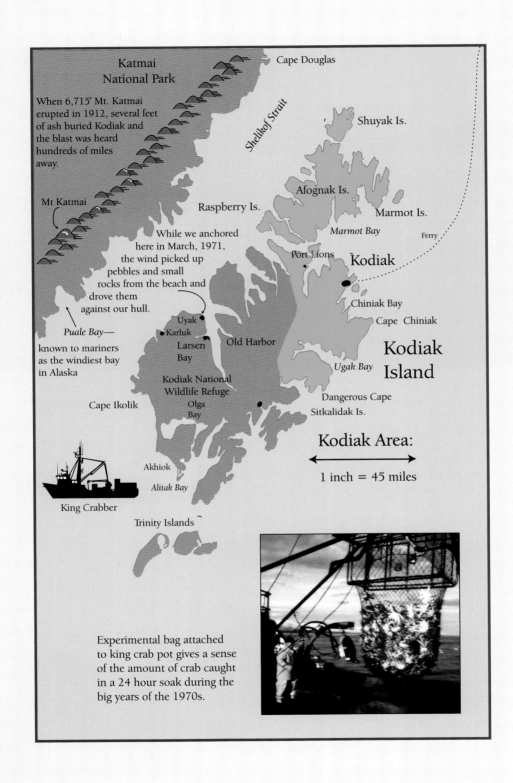

Experimental bag attached to king crab pot gives a sense of the amount of crab caught in a 24 hour soak during the big years of the 1970s.

220

KODIAK ISLAND

One of the largest islands in the United States, its early residents were the Koniag Indians, whom the Russians found to be particularly strong, cunning, and aggressive.

Kodiak today is the home of a particularly hardy group of Alaskans, most of whom depend on commercial fishing and live in or near the main town, also named Kodiak.

This town has had its share of natural disasters. On June 6, 1912, residents observed a curious-looking fan-shaped cloud, getting closer, higher and darker, with flashes of lightning inside the cloud. This was the tipoff that something very unusual was occurring as lightning was a rare event. The sky got even darker and then small earthquakes could be felt, and finally ash began falling from Mt. Katmai, some 100 miles away.

Visibility dropped to almost nothing—people groped their way toward the foghorn of the Coast Guard Cutter *Manning*, and some 500 sought refuge aboard as the cutter steamed away from the shore and anchored in total blackness.

Two days later, it seemed safe enough to return. The town was buried in almost two feet of ash and many roofs had collapsed. Ash piles may still be seen today in many parts of the Alaska peninsula.

Then in March of 1964, as the town was getting ready for the salmon season, it was shattered, like Seward and Anchorage, by the Good Friday Earthquake. After five minutes of terrifying shocks, the radio station broadcast

Both men and bears compete for the fish around Kodiak. Below: Tossing the buoy line, carefully, after another king crab pot goes over the side. If your arm or leg gets tangled in the line as it whips over the side, you will be quickly pulled overboard.

221

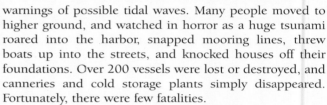

Most of the Kodiak fishing fleet ended up in the streets of town after the 1964 earthquake and tidal wave. Jo Keers, Kodiak Hist. Society P633.45 Below: Retorts, or steam cookers at a salmon cannery operate day and night during the frenzied peak of the fishing season.

warnings of possible tidal waves. Many people moved to higher ground, and watched in horror as a huge tsunami roared into the harbor, snapped mooring lines, threw boats up into the streets, and knocked houses off their foundations. Over 200 vessels were lost or destroyed, and canneries and cold storage plants simply disappeared. Fortunately, there were few fatalities.

After the earthquake devastated the town and essentially swept all the crab and fish plants into the bay, processors had to do something quickly. The easiest solution was to bring up ships and beach them with processing facilities built inside. The *Star of Kodiak*, an old World War II liberty ship, right by the docks, had a new life in Kodiak as a cannery.

Most of Kodiak Island is unsettled, roadless, and wild, with seasonal fishing settlements located in several of the larger bays. With less than a hundred miles of roads, many residents get around by boat or floatplane.

Of course, like other native groups up and down the coast, the Alutiiq people of Kodiak Island had no immunities to the diseases brought by the Russians and other traders. This combination of disease and murderous tactics to induce sea otter hunting took a heavy toll on the native population.

Kodiak became the first capital of Russian America (the capital was later shifted to Sitka). Today the biggest reminder of the Russian period is the Russian Orthodox religion, a major influence throughout much of western Alaska. Look for the blue onion domes of the Holy Resurrection Orthodox Church, just a block from the

docks. It is one of many active Russian Orthodox parishes in the state.

A Native Cultural Renaissance—in 1995, the eight Kodiak Island area native groups formed the Alutiiq Heritage Foundation as part of an effort to celebrate and preserve their native traditions.

The Foundation created the Alutiiq Museum and Archaeological Repository, located on Mission Road, just two blocks from the docks. Featuring an excellent display gallery as well as a gift shop, it is well worth visiting. If your schedule allows, you may also wish to see the Kodiak Alutiiq Dancers perform. Dancing, once discouraged by missionaries, is now part of this cultural renaissance, as these tribes celebrate their past.

Downtown Kodiak has most attractions within easy walking distance. In addition to those listed above, the Baranof Museum—just across the street from the visitor information center—has a good display on Kodiak's Russian and early American history.

How far did the the tidal wave carry boats? Three blocks from the harbor on Mill Bay Road, is a plaque marking where the 86' power scow *Selief* ended up after the water receded. Patched up and refloated, she is still working and fishing up and down the coast.

Want to see sea lions up close? You'll probably find a few hanging out near around the shore, just outside the harbor. Don't expect cute - these brutes are big, smelly and sometimes aggressive. Keep your distance!

A deck loaded fish buyer or tender waits for another tender to offload to so all the fish can be chilling in refrigerated sea water on their way in to the cannery. Below: A distinctive Russian Orthodox cross marks graves.

In the 1950s, the only outside contact for 19 isolated native villages on the Alaska Peninsula and Aleutian Islands was the 114-foot mailboat *Expansion*, which made regular round trips from Seward, skippered by owner Niels "Cap" Thomsen, one of those entrepreneurs that Alaska seems to attract. In his earlier years, "Cap,' operated a freight boat between Seattle and Ketchikan. Radar was expensive and rare on smaller boats then, but "Cap" impressed his Ketchikan investors when he cruised past their watefront houses with his radar antenna turning. Little did they know that all he could afford was the antenna and his son was turning it by hand from inside the pilothouse!

About the first thing "Cap" noticed on his stops was how some native villages seemed to have a lot of single young men, and another village, maybe a hundred miles away, single women, but neither group of singles was aware of the others:

"So I bought a Polaroid camera and took pictures of the unmarried natives. I'd write their names and towns on them: 'Nona Popalook from Gambrel Bay,' etc. I put the pictures up on two bulletin boards, one for single women and another for single men. Pretty soon after that the word was out, and any time we'd round a point to come into a harbor where a native village was, the singles would be jumping into their boats and rowing out as fast as they could to meet us even before we got the anchor down! They'd come aboard and head right for the singles bulletin boards. Also back in those days, to be legally married, the natives had to go to Cold Bay, a long way away. So I got a Justice of the Peace license, so I could marry them right aboard the boat!"

— "Cap" Niels Peter Thomsen

"Cap" Thomsen's boat also served as a general store, many times taking furs in trade for rifles, flour, etc. He also was a traveling branch of the Bank of Kodiak for the native villagers, some of whom had taken to burying the money they made fishing in jars in their back yards.

An early cruise ship? "FOR ROMANTIC ADVENTURE, Sail to The Aleutian Islands, 'Land of the Smoky Sea,' See majestic steaming volcanoes, Witness the drama of life at sea, See roaring sea lions, precious sea otter." So went the pitch on Thomsen's brochure, seeking travelers wanting an off the beaten path experience. He might have added, 'Help the Captain work on his crab processor,' for on each trip, Thomsen managed to lay over in remote Dutch Harbor, for three or four days—long enough for the passengers to see the local sights, as well as a little scraping and painting on Thomsen's floating crab processor, the *Bethel I*. These were the days when the king crab fishery was just starting. Most of the activity was in the Kodiak area, but wherever "Cap" anchored the *Expansion*, he set a crab pot over and noted how many of the big spiny fellows he caught. A few years later, when his crab processor was ready to go, he recruited some boats from Kodiak by telling them that he knew most of the good crab fishing spots in the Aleutian Islands. Thomsen was able to ride the king crab boom to the peak, eventually selling his little company for some five million dollars, and heading to the Caribbean to build a resort!

Thomsen also wrote a remarkable book, *The Voyage of The Forest Dream*, about some of his early sailing days as a lad of 18, aboard a big square rigger loaded with lumber on a trip across the Pacific.

"Cap" Thomsen aboard the iced-up Expansion after a difficult trip up Shelikof Strait to Seward in wintertime. Opposite page: Is this a boat? The Expansion iced up at Seward. Icing up was a constant problem for vessels traveling the western Alaska coast in winter.
Photos courtesy Niels Thomsen

New England based whalers worked this coast as early as the 1870s. Getting trapped by the ice was always a major worry. 1899 was particularly bad and numerous whalers were crushed by the ice and their crews only survived through great hardshiip.

Whaling has been a native tradition here from pre-history and continuing until the present day.

Cape Lisburne

Bering Land Bridge - during the last glacial period, 10,000 years ago, lower ocean levels created a land bridge to Asia in this area.

Global Warming: Northern Alaska has been seriously impacted by many of its effects. Melting permafrost, loss of ice protection, and loss of wildlife habitat are just a few of these. Polar bears are especially threatened by a warming Arctic.

Pt. Barrow

Pearl Bay

Icy Cape

Prudhoe Bay

Arctic National Wildlife Refuge

Chandlalar River

Porcupine River

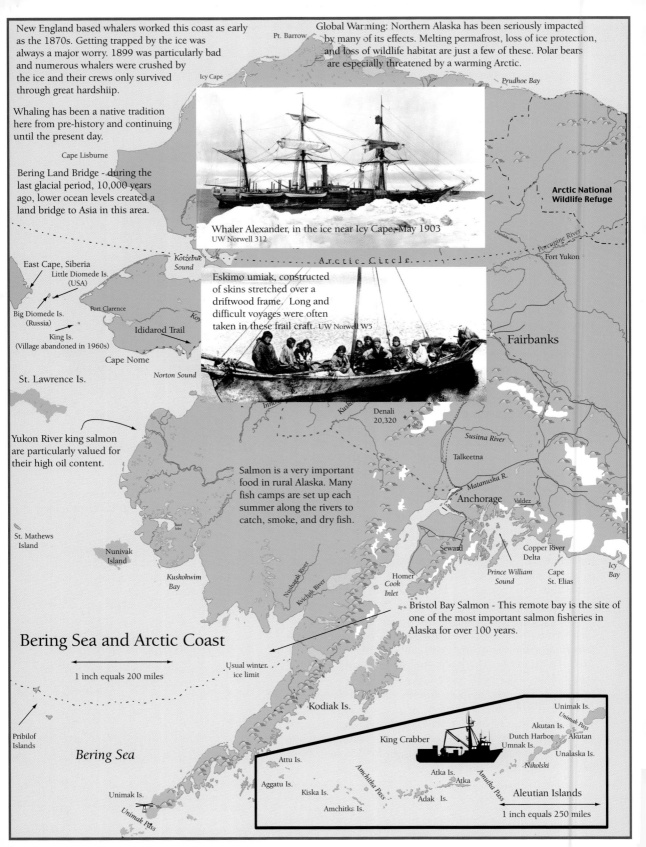

Whaler Alexander, in the ice near Icy Cape, May 1903
UW Norwell 312

Arctic Circle

Fort Yukon

Kotzebue Sound

Eskimo umiak, constructed of skins stretched over a driftwood frame. Long and difficult voyages were often taken in these frail craft. UW Norwell W5

East Cape, Siberia
Little Diomede Is. (USA)

Big Diomede Is. (Russia)

Port Clarence

Koy

Fairbanks

King Is. (Village abandoned in 1960s)

Ididarod Trail

Cape Nome

Norton Sound

St. Lawrence Is.

Innok

Kusk

Denali 20,320

Susitna River

Talkeetna

Yukon River king salmon are particularly valued for their high oil content.

Salmon is a very important food in rural Alaska. Many fish camps are set up each summer along the rivers to catch, smoke, and dry fish.

Matanuska R.

Anchorage

Valdez

St. Mathews Island

Nunivak Island

Seward

Copper River Delta

Kuskokwim Bay

Nushagak River

Kvichak River

Homer
Cook Inlet

Prince William Sound

Cape St. Elias

Icy Bay

Bering Sea and Arctic Coast

Bristol Bay Salmon - This remote bay is the site of one of the most important salmon fisheries in Alaska for over 100 years.

1 inch equals 200 miles

Usual winter ice limit

Kodiak Is.

Unimak Is.
Unimak Pass

Akutan Is.
Dutch Harbor   Akutan
Umnak Is.
Unalaska Is.

King Crabber

Nikolski

Pribilof Islands

Bering Sea

Attu Is.

Aggatu Is.

Kiska Is.

Amchitka Pass

Atka Is.
Atka

Adak Is.

Amukta Pass

Aleutian Islands

1 inch equals 250 miles

Unimak Is.

Unimak Pass

Amchitka Is.

CHAPTER 9

The Other Alaska
Bering and Arctic Sea Coasts

My wife's uncle told me this more than once. He told me that everything has a yuk, a spirit. He told me that he had seen them. He said that even a piece of wood that was split in half was half of a person. It was their life. Everything has a person."

—Paul John, Tooksook Bay, Alaska, quoted in *Agayuliyararput: The Living Tradition of Yup'ik Masks* by Ann Fienup-Riordan

Top: Abandoned boats on the Ugashik River. Below: Yup'ik style ceremonial mask, used in traditional dances. Author's collection.

The vastness of this coast is hard to grasp. From the border with Russia in the far west of the Aleutian Islands to Bering Strait in the north, the Bering Sea washes a length of coast longer than the distance from Maine to Florida.

The land is treeless and austere, the settlements few and many miles apart, few connected to each other and none to the 'outside' by roads.

The climate is dramatically harsher than that of Southeast Alaska. There is no gentle and sheltering forest, no warm offshore current to temper the extremes of weather. In the native communities of southern Alaska winter was often a time for crafts, for family, an often welcome change from the busy pace of salmon fishing and berry gathering that characterized the summers. But along much of the mainland Bering Sea coast, before the white man's processed food was available, winter could be another word for starvation. The sea along the shore froze, game was scarce. Family survival depended on the success of the man, the hunter.

Top: Little visited, seldom climbed, lonely Aniakchak Volcano rises from the tundra, west of Ugashik Village on the Alaska Peninsula. Note steam vent on left slope. Also if you look closely, there is a bald eagle over the building on the left. Stream vents, ash releases, and occasional dramatic lava burps are common among the volcanoes of the Alaska Peninsula and Aleutian Islands.

And far more than in any other part of coastal Alaska, the settlements of this coast are predominantly native Alaskans: Aleuts along the Aleutian Islands, Yup'ik Eskimos from Bristol Bay to Norton Sound and Inupiat Eskimos from there north.

All had evolved from tribes who migrated from Siberia over a land bridge across Bering Strait during an ice age some 30,000 years ago. Once across, they evolved into several native groups, each with its own language.

The coastal tribes depended on the sea. Salmon, crab, herring, and other fish were plentiful along the Bering Sea. But in the Arctic, there were few salmon, and seals, whales, and the occasional caribou were the diet staples.

Life was never easy for these peoples, and the arrival of the Russians and eventually the Americans was, like for all the Northwest native tribes, devastating.

The Russians were brutal in their single minded pursuit of sea otters, not hesitating to massacre entire Aleut villages when the hunters refused to hunt to their command.

But it was disease, alcoholism, and drugs, together with the loss of many traditions that, more than anything else has caused the shredding of the original native culture in many of the villages of western Alaska.

"It was so sad. I'd see these cute young little children playing with their mothers around the cannery houses when the men were out fishing. Each summer they'd come back and I'd get to know them all. Then they'd be teens and I'd see those same little children wasted on booze and drugs. It was so sad."

- A Bristol Bay cannery superintendent.

Salmon still drives the economy in much of the Bering Sea region. Beginning in June millions of red, king, and chum salmon make their way from the North Pacific to the region's rivers.

Yukon River kings are especially prized by processors seeking fish to smoke because of their high oil content. And for generations the chum or dog salmon run up the Yukon and its tributaries was caught and dried to provide winter food for the thousands of dog teams that were winter transportation.

But the biggest and most valuable salmon fishery in the whole state is in **Bristol Bay**, on the eastern shore of the Bering Sea, where 10 to 30 million red salmon return to their native rivers during a brief but very intense one month fishery.

The first cannery was built in 1885 and until 1958 no engines were allowed in the 32' fishing boats, as a way to protect the fish stocks, and employ many fishermen.

Today places like the Egegik River, which sleeps for most of the year, are transformed in June when as many as 900 fishing boats and perhaps 50 support vessels including big floating processing ships arrive to get their share of the fish.

The fish are caught by gillnetters—32' vessels—but also by setnetters, who work from the muddy beaches, live in modest camps and tend their nets with small skiffs.

In the glory days of the 1980s, limited entry permits went for over $200,000 and a crewman on a really good boat might earn $50,000 for six weeks work. Today fish prices have retreated substantially, but the fishing frenzy is just as intense.

On a lonely Bristol Bay river, busy only for two summer months, salmon gillnet boats hustle to unload. Below: Salmon crew and net. That's your mapmaker and his son on the right.

Ice is one of the biggest challenges in this fishery. The bitter wind freezes sea spray onto all the exposed surfaces, even the nylon meshes on these 600 pound crab pots. The danger is that as the heavy ice accumulates, it raises the center of gravity. If the icing continues, the vessel may capsize.

In the early 1960s Alaskan fishermen began to expand fishing for a remarkable spider-like creature—the king crab. Unlike most crab, king crab traveled in herds across the bottom of the Bering Sea. When fishing was good, the big pots would come up with up to 2,000 pounds of crab after less than 24 hours in the water. Boats would get a 200,000-pound load in 48 hours! It was legendary money, but legendary work as well—when you were on the crab, 18 - 20 hours on deck a day were routine.

The heaviest concentration of crab was found in the Alaska Peninsula - Bering Sea - Aleutian Islands area. In the winter, this area has some of the stormiest weather in the world, and many able vessels and crews were lost to violent winds, big seas, and low temperatures. Perhaps the biggest threat was the buildup of heavy ice on a vessel's superstructure and any crab pots on deck when below freezing temperatures combined with strong winds, a fairly regular event.

Of the many losses in the king crab fishery, none was more tragic and puzzling than the loss of the 123 foot sisterships *Americus* and *Altair*, in good weather on Valentine's Day, 1983. Both vessels, loaded with some 230 king crab pots, left Dutch Harbor, in the Aleutian Islands, and were never heard from again. Only the capsized hull of the *Americus*, which sank shortly thereafter, gave a clue to their fate.

It took months of detective-like work to find the cause. It turned out that after each vessel offloaded some 28,000 gallons of surplus fuel from their double bottom tanks, and loaded the heavy crab pots, the vessels, unknown to anyone aboard, had such a high center of gravity that they were rolled upside down by mild seas.

Today all crab vessels operating in these waters carry a certificate specifying exactly how many pots they may carry and in what conditions. (In summer, with no danger of icing, they may carry substantially more pots than in winter.)

The sea claims another. While riding out a severe Bering Sea Storm in 1978, several crab pots broke loose on deck aboard the brand new 150' Key West. It was too rough to try to secure the heavy pots, and one broke off a 12" air vent pipe, allowing water to flood into the vessel. Fortunately, another crab boat was able to rescue all aboard. Bart Eaton photo Right: Crab fisherman Walter Kuhr and friends are pictured at right. For many, this was nothing less than another "gold rush." Walter, who was a very experienced and talented fisherman, worked his way up from deckhand in 1971 to owning several large vessels a decade later.

After almost two decades of spectacular growth both in catch and fleet size, the crab population crashed in the early 1980's. For a while the joke in Alaska banks was that when you started a new account, you got a crab boat free as a premium.

Fortunately, it was in this period that foreign fishing effort in the rich waters of the Bering Sea was being reduced, creating much needed opportunities for the crab fleet to convert to trawling—towing funnel-shaped nets for cod, pollock, and other species.

Today the crab fishery continues, but at a much lower harvest level than in the boom days of the '70s and early '80s. In recent years the TV show, "The Deadliest Catch" celebrates the fishery and its risks. But actually the most dangerous years of the fishery are now in the past, as new management regulations reduced the fleet substantially and allowed more time in what was once a very dangerous, wild, and chaotic fishery.

THE ALEUTIANS

Austere Dutch Harbor, on the shore of the Bering Sea with its classic Russian Orthodox church. Alaskastock Photo. Below: The old graveyard at Dutch Harbor shows that the area was a crossroads for trade a hundred years ago.

Stretching almost a thousand miles from Unimak Pass to the border with Russia, and encompassing two time zones and crossing the international date line, the Aleutians are America's least visited islands. Even to Alaskans, the islands are a bit of a mystery, definitely separate from the rest of the state.

It's not hard to see why. The weather is bad—totally sunny days are rare, though 'sun breaks' are not. The wind is ferocious; Dutch Harbor officials recently elected not to pursue wind powered electrical generators there for fear the machines couldn't stand the not uncommon 120 mph winds!

Then there is the isolation. The 200 some islands are mostly uninhabited, with only five or six villages in the whole archipelago. A few hardy ranchers still try to make a go of it, and there are a few remote military installations. Getting in and out is a challenge; so many flights are cancelled that the main carrier, Reeves Aleutian Airways, built a bunkhouse/mess hall at Cold Bay, on the Alaska Peninsula, to house passengers from canceled flights.

At the time the Russians first arrived there were perhaps 25,000 Aleuts, scattered in many villages among the islands. Most men had at least one hand built baidarka, similar to today's kayaks, and basically hunted seals, sea otters, sea lions, and fished for salmon and other species.

Arriving in the 1740s, the Russians were primarily interested

in sea otter skins, which were prized in China. Initially relations with the Aleuts were mixed, but by the 1760s Aleut resentment was enough for Natives to attack and kill almost 200 Russians on wintering ships. The Russians responded by systematically attacking many Aleut villages.

By the time America purchased Alaska in 1867, the sea otter population was greatly reduced, and most attention was focused on the rich fishery resources of the chain, first codfish, then salmon.

Dutch Harbor, on Unalaska island, with its protected harbor and convenient location, became the main Aleutian town. In addition to sealers, whalers, cod and salmon fishermen, it also was a major crossroads as steamers carrying gold rush passengers to the Yukon and Nome gold rushes usually stopped coming and going.

In World War II, Japanese forces briefly occupied Kiska, triggering a major US military buildup and campaign.

In the 20th century things really started popping with the king crab fishery starting in the 1960s, then after the 200 mile limit, the trawl fishery, primarily for cod and pollock. By the 1990s, Dutch Harbor became the number one port in the entire U.S. in terms of value of product landed.

Today's Aleutian visitors might be kayakers seeking a wilderness experience, or bird watchers, but commercial fishing is a huge and active presence particularly during the king crab or pollock seasons.

Dutch Harbor in 1971, with big Japanese trawler next to U.S. king crab boat. The 200 mile limit, enacted in 1974, was a huge boom to American fishermen and processors. Below: Crabber with a big, big load of pots. You wouldn't want to run into icing conditions with a load like this one!

THE ARCTIC

"Shopping" - Inupiat Eskimos aboard a trading schooner, circa 1930. Notice the intricate details in their sealskin parkas. UW 17962

The Arctic Circle crosses the Alaska coast near Nome, on the Seward Peninsula, the approximate boundary between Yup'ik and Inupiat Eskimo native cultures.

The Yup'iks, living closer to the major salmon and herring fisheries at Norton Sound and Bristol Bay, had more opportunities to fish, or work in the canneries and participate in the cash economy early in the 20th century.

But Inupiats generally lived too far from sources of seasonal employment to travel easily back and forth. And so subsistence fishing, with the fish smoked and dried for the winter ahead, both for the dogs and for the people, was more of an integral part of their culture.

Crafts were also an important part of Inupiat culture and economy. As early as the 1910s and 1920s Eskimos would regularly travel to Nome to set up their tents on the beach and carve and sell ivory to the tourists of the day.

But winter, for a people dependent on hunting, remained a difficult time. When game was scarce, starvation could be very close. Before kerosene, gasoline, and the cash economy, cooking and heat was by seal oil; a poor hunt meant cold homes.

The Missionaries began coming to Western Alaska shortly

after the Russians sold Alaska to the US. Generally speaking, the missionaries (from many religions) misunderstood or failed to respect native beliefs. Native languages were an early target: after 1910 speaking native languages was banned in pubic and missionary schools and native families urged to speak English at home. On occasion, children were separated from their parents and sent to boarding schools distant from their homes.

One successful program initially operated by the missionaries was the importation of reindeer from Siberia, to see if they would flourish in Alaska as domesticated herds for food. The reindeer definitely liked Alaska, growing from the several thousand imported from Russia in 1892 to 640,000 estimated in 1930 (an additional 125,000 were used for food and skins!)

Until fairly recently many of the natives in the 'bush' weren't really in the cash economy. As late as the 1950s, traders would load up their boats in Seattle with trading goods: cans of gas and kerosene, rifles, ammunition, flour, bolts of cloth, canned goods, etc. They would travel to the remote native villages of the Arctic coast, anchor, and natives would come aboard with ivory, seal skins and other articles to trade for the materials that they needed.

The biggest event for Alaska natives in recent history was the Native Claims Settlement Act of 1971. This act, intended to clear land title issues to allow development of the Prudhoe Bay oil fields discovered in 1967, gave natives title to 40 million acres and approximately 900 million dollars, to be divided among 13

Top: Summer camp on the Arctic with father bringing in a seal. Ken Lisbourne painting. Many native families move to fish camps along the rivers where there was a good fish run for part or all of the summer. Below: Note roof on model, made of skin, weighted by stones against the strong winds off the Bering Sea. Both from Author's collection.

Top: Eskimo ivory carvers on the beach at Nome, around 1910. Note the cribbage board, being carved from a walrus tusk. UW 17963 Bottom: Hand made doll from author's collection.

regional corporations. The corporations, often with the help of high priced non-native managers, invested the funds, with the proceeds to benefit the tribe.

The results of these investments were mixed—some tribes, who invested well, returned dividends to their members. Others invested less well, with meagre returns.

For many in the Arctic, life is still hard. Older people feel the loss of their traditional ways. With satellite television, the young feel the seductive draw of western ways. The biggest challenge for most is economic: good jobs in the bush are scarce.

THE CUTTER BEAR

Originally built in 1874 in Scotland as a sealer, with six inch thick oak planking to withstand the pressure of the ice, the *Bear* was the most well known vessel in Western Alaska for over 40 years.

Owned by the U.S. Government, she worked the Bering Sea Patrol, a job that combined duties as mailboat, supply ship, hospital, police station, and district court. With her combination of sails and steam power, she rescued many a vessel from the grip of the ice.

When she was replaced by a newer vessel, she was purchased by Admiral Byrd, and then went to the Antarctic for several expeditions as well.

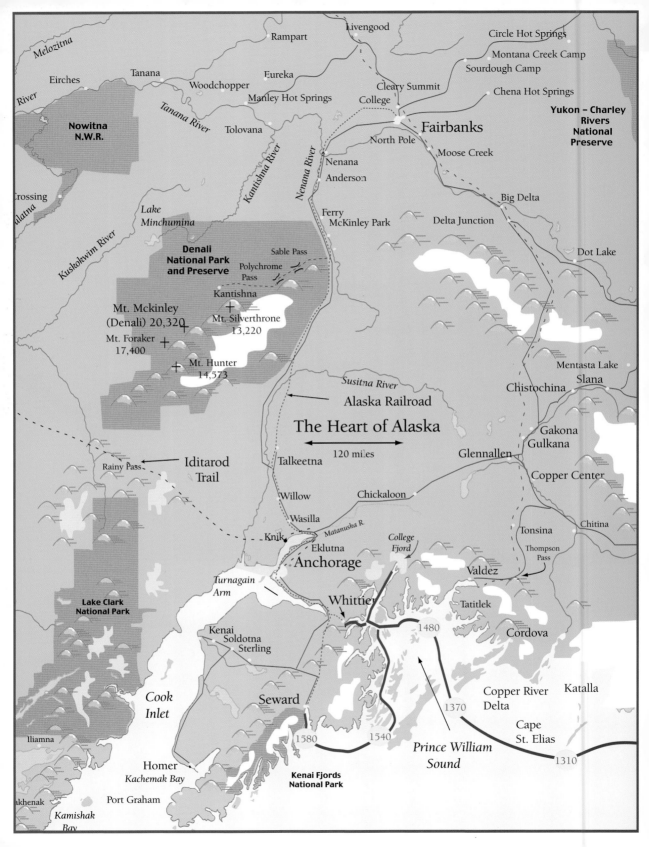

CHAPTER 10

The Heart of Alaska

Seward and Whittier to Fairbanks

"So off we went, the four dogs and I, to explore high mountains new to us.

"As the days went by, I wondered what the dogs got out of it. I had a supply of dried salmon on the sled, and they eagerly looked forward to their meal each evening. They loved to be in harness; as a matter of fact, as they were being hooked up in the morning, they were so happy that it was hard to handle them. The minute we were ready, off they would go in a great burst of speed."

— Olas J. Murie, *Journeys to the Far North*

When you plan your Alaska cruise, make time to explore a bit of the interior—at the minimum the Fairbanks-Anchorage corridor—it is so dramatically different from the coast. Cruise lines encourage people to take the Alaska Railroad. Several cruise lines have their own vistadome style rail cars and make at least an overnight stop at Denali, and then take the paddlewheeler excursion out of Fairbanks. But if you have time, consider additional side trips. Maybe renting a car to

For generations, the rivers of interior Alaska were the only highways. Paddlewheelers took freight and passengers to the most remote locations. But once the rivers froze up for the winter, travel was either by dog, horse-drawn sled, or by foot. The arrival of the first paddlewheeler in the spring with the first new food supplies and mail, was always a big event. This is the Discovery III, an excursion vessel out of Fairbanks, operated by a family that first started piloting paddle wheelers during the Yukon Gold Rush. It is a truly excellent excursion.

Passenger Tip

If at all possible take the train
either to or from Whitter and
Seward. If your cruise line—which
often offer the train as an add-
on—tells you there is no space,
contact the railroad directly at
www.alaskarailroad.com. There are
daily trains leaving Seward or
Whittier around 6 in the evening
for the 3- 4 hour trip.

Top: View from the train along the
shores of Turnagain Arm at low tide.
Keep your eyes peeled for beluga
whales here—they are white! Below:
A twin-engine floatplane on a lake
near Homer.

explore the Kenai Peninsula. The Homer area is a great
destination—see P. 218-219—as is the whole Arctic
coast via a bus or a plane excursion up to Prudhoe Bay
or Nome. If you want to see bears up close—best in
June and July—and the photos on pages 244-245 whet
your appetite, fly out to Katmai. There is a lot of great
country out there!

Until 2000, to drive to Whitter, you had to put your
car onto a flatbed railcar: fun, but only if you had the
time. Then the rail tunnel was widened to accommo-
date a one-way road as well. It's not as convenient as a
regular highway tunnel as one way traffic alternates
with the train, but it's a lot better than it used to be
and many Anchorage residents are enjoying Prince
William Sound, perhaps for the first time.

Early travelers headed over these mountains from
Whitter and Seward, had to fight the winter storms.
The low passes form a highway for the powerful weath-
er systems that march back and forth between the
Arctic highs to the north, and the North Pacific lows
out in the Gulf of Alaska. The power of these storms
became part of the lore of The North as soon as early
Alaska novels became popular reading:

"It was early in the afternoon when the Indian
stopped and began testing the air; Balt also seemed suddenly to scent a change in the atmospheric conditions.
"What's wrong now?" Emerson asked, gruffly.
"Feels like wind," answered the big man with a shake

"One of my jobs each summer is to run all the stream watchers out to the bays where they'll be working. Stream watchers are kids— usually college biology students—hired for a couple of months to camp in some remote bay and count the fish going up a creek—they put a white board across the bottom to make it easier to see. Then they radio in each night to the Alaska Department of Fish and Game, and ADF&G uses the data to manage salmon fishing.

"They were also sort of junior fish cops: ADF&G figured there would be less poaching if there was a stream watcher.

"So anyway, I pick up these kids—a couple, maybe in their early 20s, totally green, even a bit geeky, never been to Alaska before. Hell, I don't think they had ever spend a night out in a tent!

"They got a lot of stuff. All their own stuff, man they each brought about three duffels of clothes—plus all the ADF&G camping stuff, and boxes of food, the radios, etc. It was a full planeload, and I'd brought the Beaver.

"So we get in there—some bay on the back side of Prince of Wales—very lonely country - and I'm unloading all their crap, and I didn't see any guns. So I asked them,

"So, didn't you bring any guns?"

"'Ggggg-guns,' the kid stammered, 'No one told us about bringing ggg-guns?'

"'Well,' I said, 'what the hell are you going to do when bears come sniffing around your tent...?'

"'Bbb-bears,' the kid was pretty shook, 'no one told us about bbb-bears...'

"'Hell,' I told them, 'where's there's salmon there's bears. What d'ya think that is?' I walked over to the bear shit at the side of the stream.

"Man, when they saw that, they turned about three different shades of white. So I decided to fun 'em a bit, they were so green...'

"So 'Here,' I said, taking my little pistol out of my pocket, 'take this. It's only a .38. It'll never hurt a bear unless you get him in the eye with it. But if you get in a jam and the bear's about to maul you, you can shoot yourselves with it...'"

Top: Orca Cafe at Whittier looks out at Passage Canal. Below: Guide and happy out of state fishermen with a big Kenai Peninsula trout. Brenda Carney photo.

of his head. The native began chattering excitedly, and as they stood there, a chill draught fanned their cheeks. Glancing upward at the hillsides, they saw that the air was now thickened as if by smoke, and, dropping their eyes, they saw the fluff between their feet stir lazily. Little wisps of snow vapor began to dance upon the ridges, whisking out of sight as suddenly as they had appeared. They became conscious of a sudden fall in the temperature, and they knew that the cold of interstellar space dwelt in that ghostly breath which smote them. Before they were well aware of the ominous significance of these signs the storm was upon them, sweeping through the chute wherein they stood with rapidly increasing violence. The terrible, unseen hand of the Frozen North had unleashed its brood of furies, and the air rang with their hideous cries. It was Dante's third circle of hell let loose—Cerberus baying through his wide, threefold throat, and the voices of tormented souls shrilling through the infernal shades... There was no question of facing the wind, for it was more cruel than the fierce breath of an open furnace, searing the naked flesh like a flame."

— Rex Beach, *The Silver Horde*

242

The Iditarod—Today the famous dog sled race begins each year in Anchorage. But it's important to remember that the diphtheria vaccine to combat the outbreak in Nome actually arrived in Seward by ship in January of 1925. From here it traveled by train to Nenana to begin the 674-mile dog sled relay through blizzard conditions to Nome.

Another big event in those days was the arrival of the dog teams that brought the heavy loads of gold from the interior to meet the southbound steamers:

> "The town was stirred by the arrival of the Iditarod gold shipment...The populace stood packed about, but fully one half their interest was centered on the perfectly matched dog teams that had pulled the treasure from the banks of the Kuskokwim, four hundred miles to the northwest... Their harness was perfect from the silver bells that jangled so sweetly, to the red pom-poms that bobbed gaily on each furry back."
>
> — Terris Moore, *Mt. McKinley, The Pioneer Climbs*

Convenience store, Alaska style, along the Kenai Highway. Below: The old and the new: wringer washing machine and old log cabin, Ninilchik.

THE BEARS AT KATMAI

Waiting for that perfect fish. The bears don't catch the jumping fish with their paws, but actually grab it out of the air with their mouths! At the peak of the run, some 200-300 fish a minute are leaping these falls, so the bears have a pretty good chance.

The Valley of 10,000 Smokes at Katmai National Park is pretty quiet these days (most of the old fumaroles have stopped smoking), but this national park is known for another feature: the bears.

For the bears, the attraction is the salmon. The park encompasses several major salmon-producing lakes, and in spawning season, the streams that feed them are full of salmon jumping the falls on their way upstream.

The visitor center is at Brooks Lodge, built in the 1930s as a sportfishing camp. Today it is a classic Alaska lodge, with individual log cabins overlooking the lake and the mountains.

I flew in there in July of 1997, with my son, and some friends, after just finishing our commercial salmon fishing season in Bristol Bay, 80 miles to the west.

The only way in is by floatplane; it pulls up to the beach, and you walk up to a small log cabin that is both the park headquarters and gift shop. While our group was watching a "bear etiquette" video, there was a clatter outside, and we looked out to see a brown bear about the size of a Volkswagon, rattling the bolted-down, bear-proof trash cans.

As we walked the paths to the viewing platforms, we were accompanied by a walkie-talkie equipped park ranger, who was monitoring bear movements. Several times on the way to the viewing stand at the falls on the Brooks River, we had to move off the trail to let bears pass

as they have right of way!

Then we got to where we could see the falls through the trees, and my feet stopped walking. There, in plain sight were at least six very large brown bears, intent on the business of catching the fish that were leaping up the four- foot falls, oblivious to us humans.

We climbed the ramp to the viewing platform, our guide latching the gate behind us. In front, arrayed across the falls, and in the stream below were the bears, wading, chasing fish in the pools, snatching them out of the air as they leaped the falls.

In a tree, just twenty yards from the platform, were two 100-lb. bear cubs. When they got bored and began climbing down, their mother would amble quickly over from the stream and indicate to them in no uncertain terms that they were to remain where they were.

When a bear got a fish, it would walk into the shallows, hold the fish down with one paw, and neatly strip off a fillet with the other, flip the fish and do it again—an impressive performance.

The park ranger said there hadn't been a bear incident in 12 years, but we forgot to ask what the park's definition of an incident was—did you have to get stitches, or would just a few cuts and bruises do it?

Several viewing stands afford an excellent opportunity to watch and photograph the bears. This is not for the squeamish as sometimes the bears are literally rubbing on the posts that support the elevated platform. After a few minutes of watching, it's obvious that the big alpha males get the spot on the falls with the most fish coming by. When the fish are close enough, the bear just snaps them out of the air with his teeth, then retires to the shore. With one paw on the head, he fillets the fish with the other paw, eats the fillets, and lets the waiting gulls have the carcass.

ANCHORAGE - DOWNTOWN ALASKA

With the Chugach Mountains looming behind downtown and Cook Inlet in front, Anchorage has a dramatic setting. The eight-mile-long, paved Tony Knowles Coastal Trail, starting at the end of 2nd Avenue, is a great walk, and an opportunity to watch shore birds.

The old saying, "You can see Alaska from here," basically describes the relationship of Anchorage and the rest of the state. While some 40% of the entire state's population resides in the greater Anchorage area, it's a good bet a lot of them blast out of town each weekend, judging from the number of planes, campers, snowmobiles, 4-wheelers, kayaks, etc., in the back yards all around town. Don't be surprised to see a moose meandering around town, though wandering bears are also regularly seen.

Though Anchorage overlooks **Cook Inlet** and **Knik Arm**, it's hardly a waterfront town in the mold of Ketchikan or Juneau. There's no place for boats to tie up downtown—the rivers draining into the inlet bring a big silt load and there are extensive tide flats making it difficult to even get to the water in most places. Most marine activity is centered in Ship Creek, north of town.

The newest and shiniest high-rise office buildings usually belong to Big Oil in this town. The revenue from this industry basically redefined Alaska economics, and gave its citizens the unique distinction of getting the only state dividend checks in the country. Farsighted leadership in the early days of the oil boom

established a large and so far untouched "Permanent Fund" which yields enough income for checks typically in the $1,000 range annually for each of Alaska's citizens.

Cheating on the Permanent Fund. There's a lot of P.O. Box addresses in a state as rural as Alaska. There are also a lot of people who like to get that check, regardless if they qualify as a resident or not (Alaska's residency definition is pretty strict). Fish and Wildlife Protection officers (game wardens) who enforce the state's many fishing and hunting regulations, and other law officers, are usually alert to ID's with post office box addresses:

> "We were way back up the Koyukuk, fishing, and this fish cop appears out of nowhere in his boat and asks to see our licenses and our photo ID, I mean, that's lonely country up there—we hadn't seen anyone for days...
>
> "He checks my Alaska driver's license and says, 'Hey, pal, this here says you live in King Salmon. How come I've never seen you there?' I finally had to admit I spend most of the year in Idaho.
>
> "Damn. I had to go to court, and got fined a thousand bucks for falsifying a residency and another hundred bucks for not having a fishing license...and way up the Koyukuk."
>
> — A sportfisherman

Take a few minutes and walk to the **Captain Cook Memorial**, overlooking the water at the end of 3rd Ave. You

Orca mural at the old JC Penny building, downtown. Below: The statue of Captain Cook looks out at the inlet named after him.

247

When the earth shook: Some sections of town were so shattered that survivors could only be reached by helicopter. UW 14501 Decorated salmon sculptures in downtown, to be auctioned off as part of a fund-raiser.

can get a clear sense of the very different shoreline below, but also it's an opportunity to reflect on the many unusual deeds of this English sailor, who charted much of the vast reaches of the Pacific Ocean.

Good Friday, 1964—Most folks were just settling down to supper when the most powerful earthquake to hit North America this century struck. Anchorage was mostly built on unstable clay, which is particularly susceptible to movement in an earthquake. So move it did—splitting apart, dropping whole blocks and tumbling expensive waterfront homes down steep bluffs. Within minutes, much of the downtown core was a ruin of fallen storefronts, crumpled streets, and shattered businesses.

Property damage was extremely heavy, but fortunately only nine people died.

Shopping—if your cruise is over and you haven't done all of your shopping, it's all here in downtown. Take an evening to explore these shops and especially the galleries of native arts and crafts. There are pieces here that would be hard to find anywhere outside Alaska.

Galleries and other notable places—**Alaska Center for the Performing Arts**, 6th & F; **Wolf Song of Alaska**, inside J.C. Penny Mall, 6th & E; **Reeve Aviation Picture Museum**, 343 W. 6th; and **Museum of History & Art**, 121 W. 7th

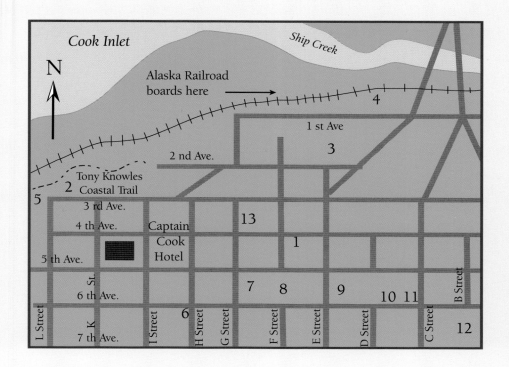

Downtown Anchorage

1. Log Cabin and Visitor Information Center
2. Tony Knowles Coastal Trail - ten mile trail that follows the shore with great views.
3. Alaska Statehood Monument
4. Alaska Railroad Depot
5. Resolution Park with Captain Cook Monument
6. Oomingmak Musk-ox Producers Co-Op— unique garments from strange creatures.
7. Alaska Center for the Performing Arts
8. Town Square Municipal Park
9. Reeve Aviation Picture Museum
10. Alaska State Trooper Museum
11. Wolf Song of Alaska - large wolf exhibit.
12. Anchorage Museum of History and Art— excellent collection; gift shop and cafe.
13. Alaska Public Lands Information Center

THE ALASKA RAILROAD

In the stillness of a September morning, dome cars wait for their northbound travelers. Below: Winding along the Susitna River Canyon. It was near here that pilot extraordinaire Don Sheldon landed his floatplane in a rescue mission that became legend. See story on following pages.

"**Anchorage, September 14, 1997, 7:45 A.M.:** Our train sits waiting on a siding, near the water. The other passengers board quickly, their breath white in the chill morning air, but I stand aside, let the bus leave, to take in the surroundings. The days get shorter quickly in the fall this far north and the sun is still behind the Chugach Mountains to the east, yet just illuminating the volcanoes along the snowy wall of the Alaska Range, across Cook Inlet. The shiny sides of the coaches are yellow and pink, reflecting the sky, while all around is almost dark. Here and there along the waiting train, steamy air vents from beneath the coaches, cloaking all in a mysterious otherworld feeling. The last whistle finally blows, and I have to board. Yet I linger until the very last, unwilling to leave the drama of this moment."

Until just 20 years ago, when the George Parks Highway north to Fairbanks was completed, the train was the only transportation there was for the folks along much of the Anchorage - Fairbanks corridor.

Whistle stops were an everyday part of train life as the "local" trains dropped homesteaders off with their bags and boxes of groceries and supplies, often at trail heads where horses or four-wheel-drive vehicles waited to take them down some lonely dirt track to a remote home.

Since the Highway was completed, the railway is strictly freight for seven months out of the year.

But every spring the passenger specials begin, with the domed cars that make it one of the most scenic rail rides in North America. Each day there is a northbound and a southbound passenger run. These trains generally have three different kinds of domed cars. The Alaska Railroad domed cars are essentially the Vistadome cars still seen on some routes through the United States west today—only part of the car has a dome, and passengers either pay extra or rotate through the domed section. Several cruise lines have had special railcars constructed for their passengers. These dome cars are usually a modification of dome cars used by railroads in the US western states. The domed section is usually made longer along with other improvements including gift shops and other passenger amenities.

However you travel, these dome cars provide a wonderful chance to experience this dramatic country.

Just north of Anchorage, the train passes just east of the runways of **Elmendorf Air Force Base**, essentially a self-contained town with its own schools, shops, etc.

Shortly after passing Elmendorf, you will be transiting an area of marsh and lakes around the **Knik River Delta**. This whole area is part of the Northern Flyway, the route that hundreds of thousands, perhaps even millions, of birds and waterfowl travel each spring and fall in their annual migrations.

Some of these birds, like the Arctic Tern (see drawing on

Crossing the Nenana River: it's mid-September and the leaves are flying! These rebuilt vistadome style cars, operated by several cruise lines, offer excellent viewing upstairs and elegant dining downstairs. Below: Some cars offer special areas for photographers, like this covered real platform.

Truly remarkable travelers, the Arctic Tern (black cap, red bill and feet, with a long, forked tail) summers in Alaska then takes off each fall for a 10,000 mile journey to winter in the Antarctic (it's summer there). Look for them in the Knik marshes.

Good soil and long hours of daylight in summer makes for some very large vegetables, like this cabbage near Fairbanks.

left) make truly remarkable migrations. Sometimes called the migration champion of the world, each year they summer along the shores of the North Pacific and Bering Sea, where they breed and hatch their young. Then in late August, they and their young start flying south—and keep going. down the British Columbia coast to Washington and California, along the Central and South American coasts, to wait in the Cape Horn area for good weather conditions for the last leg—across hundreds of miles of the stormy Drake Passage to the Antarctic Peninsula. When the southern hemisphere fall begins, they head north, 8,000 miles or so, back to Alaska, Greenland, and northern Canada.

The number of birds involved in these annual migrations is stunning. When I was a crewman on a king crab boat in the spring of 1971, we would often anchor in the bays on the north side of the Alaska Peninsula. At the head of the bays, valleys ran back to low mountain passes that connected to the North Pacific side of the peninsula. On some mornings we would look out in awe as dark clouds of birds flowed down from the passes, out low onto the water, dividing at our bow, rejoining behind our stern, hundreds of thousands of birds, driven by the mysterious power of their annual migration to the vast complex of lakes and marshes around the mouth of the Yukon River.

During the Great Depression, 202 families were chosen from the distressed northern Midwest, and brought by the federal government to found an agricultural colony and begin a new life in the rich bottomland of the Matanuska River valley, northeast of **mile 150**.

It didn't work out as the planners had hoped. The first summer was unusually wet; many children grew sick; the soil quality was uneven. The sizes of the plots weren't really big enough from which to make a living. Some families gave it up, but the remainder stayed, fighting the challenges of high latitude farming. Today the valley farmland is a natural target for developers creating more suburbs for Anchorage commuters; but the long hours of summer daylight still produce some spectacularly large vegetables, most notably the legendary 90-pound cabbages.

"Fer Cris'sake, all it would take is for one of those Alaska Airlines jets to cream into Mt. Juneau and it'd take the the whole legislature with it..."
— Heard around Alaska

Now that you've taken the cruise, seen Southeast Alaska and steamed up the wild and lonely coast to Seward, doesn't it seem a bit like there are two Alaskas?

The drizzly, grey one down there with Ketchikan and Juneau, and the wide open one up here with Anchorage, Fairbanks and the whole really, really, big rest of the state? And doesn't it seem odd that the capital, Juneau, is way down there, and well, so really isolated from the whole rest of the state?

Don't think that this same thought hasn't occurred to many Alaskans. In the 1970s when the state was flush with oil revenues—just the oil lease sale, in 1969, eight years before a drop of oil flowed down the pipeline, brought in 900 million dollars— "Move The Capital" was a bumper sticker seen all over the state.

The only problem was where to move it. In true Alaska fashion, Anchorage and Fairbanks were such rivals that neither would accept the other as capital. So why not pick some centrally located spot in between, and make that the capital? Brilliant! So, in 1976, Alaskans voted to build a new capital near Willow, mile 185.7. So where is it, you say? Cooler heads prevailed when the first cost estimates came out, and the capital remained in Juneau.

Now and again, through the trees, you'll glimpse a road, the George Parks Highway, just to the west, or left of the train. Between this highway and the Bering Sea coast, 500 miles to the west, there are no roads. (Well, O.K., there are a few exceptions—the 20 miles of bumpy pavement between Naknek and King Salmon, on Bristol Bay, a few miles around Dillingham and a few more around Nome. But, basically it's pretty lonely out there.)

The forest here is known as taiga, very different from that of Prince William Sound and Southeast Alaska. Gone are the tall hemlocks and cedars, replaced by low white and black spruce, poplar, birch, aspen and larch. Where the trees seem particularly stunted is a sign of either wet muskeg or frozen permafrost close to the surface.

Sometimes the train slows near mile 224, to let travelers get a good view of the Alaska range across the Susitna River: Denali at 20,320', and her lower sisters, Mt. Hunter, 14,573', and Mt. Foraker, 17,400'.

The Susitna is normally placid, but about 65 miles northeast of here the river turns violent in a five-mile rapids named Devil's Canyon. It was here in August of 1955, that one of the more remarkable feats of Alaska flying took place.

Talkeetna pilot Don Sheldon saw the wreckage of a U.S. Army survey boat in the canyon on a charter flight to a nearby lake, and upon returning, spotted survivors huddling on the rocky shore with almost no way out, unless he could somehow land in the river canyon. The rapids in the river created 6-foot waves—certain death to land on, but after a couple of passes through, Sheldon found a little

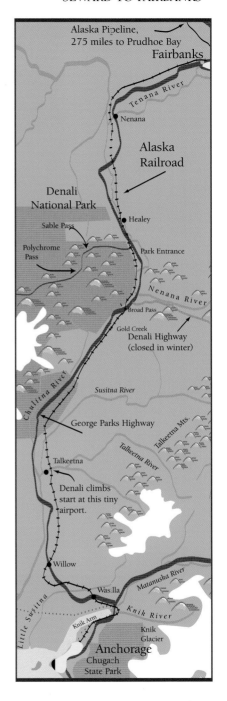

"THREE FRIENDS" DREDGE ON SOLOMON RIVER, ALASKA.

As these rivers grind their way down from the mountains, they accumulate minute amounts of gold in the silt and sand on the bottom. Huge dredges were built to slowly work their way along a river's sandbars, sifting through many tons of sand for those few elusive ounces of gold. Gold prices today are about 30 times what it was when these dredges were operating, but the environmental damage such mining would cause makes it almost impossible to get a permit for such an operation today. UW17960

strip of calmer water, just above the survivors, where he thought it might just be possible to land. Sheldon made his approach, swallowed hard, and set his little Aeronica down. Once he was in the water, he had to let the river carry him backwards, into the rapids, for him to get to where the survivors were:

"As the plane backed into the first of the combers, I felt it lurch heavily fore and aft. It was like a damned roller coaster. The water was rolling up higher than my wingtips, beating at the struts, and I could barely see because of the spray and water on the windows. All of a sudden the engine began to sputter and choke, and I knew it was getting wet down pretty good..."
—Don Sheldon, in *Wager With the Wind,*

Somehow the engine kept going, and Sheldon managed to maneuver close enough to shore for one of the men to clamber aboard. Getting out was almost as hard—backing the plane down the rapids, until he came to another stretch just barely long enough to effect a take-off. Sheldon had to repeat this remarkable performance three more times to get all the survivors out.

Look for the little airstrip, through the trees to the east at Talkeetna. This village is the staging area for almost all expeditions to the top of Denali, and for most it begins with a flight to Kahiltna Glacier at 7,000', where base camp is established and the climbing begins.

DENALI

Early explorers sometimes got a glimpse of a very high mountain to the north of Cook Inlet, a peak the natives of the region called Denali, which meant "The High One." An early prospector named it Mt. McKinley, but most Alaskans today refer to it as simply Denali.

At 20,320 feet, it is the tallest peak in North America. If this mountain were in California, or perhaps Peru, it would be a world class climb, but it wouldn't have the particular challenges that come with its high latitude.

The Alaska Range is a wall between Yukon - Arctic highs and North Pacific lows. The result is a highly volatile microclimate, and a mountain that can basically create its own weather very rapidly. Most climbing fatalities here are caused by rapid weather changes, combining wind, cold, and snow.

"On the northern side of the range there was not one cloud; the icy mountains blended into the rolling foothills, which in turn melted away into the dim blue of the timbered lowlands, that rolled away to the north, growing bluer and bluer until they were lost at the edge of the world. On the humid south side, a sea of clouds was rolling against the main range like surf on a rocky shore."

—Belmore Browne, *Conquest of Mt. McKinley*

Consider yourself lucky if you get a view like this one, from a hill above the Mt. McKinley Princess Wilderness Lodge. That's Denali in the center and 17,400' Mt. Foraker on the left. The Alaska Range essentially forms a barrier between two very different weather systems and climates. The result is that the mountain, unfortunately, is often covered by clouds. Early climbers had to struggle through the lowland forest and rugged lower slopes of the range before the hard part of their climb even began. Today ski-equipped small planes take climbing parties up to the new starting place, at about 7,000 feet up.

"...The storm now became so severe that I was actually afraid to get new dry mittens out of my ruck-sack, for I knew my hands would be frozen in the process... The last period of our climb is like the memory of an evil dream. La Voy was completely lost in the ice mist, and Professor Parker's frosted form was an indistinct blur above me... The breath was driven from my body and I held to my axe with stooped shoulders to stand against the gale; I couldn't go ahead. As I brushed the frost from my glasses and squinted upward through the stinging snow, I saw a sight that will haunt me to my dying day. The slope above me was no longer steep! That was all I could see. What it meant I will never know for certain—all I can say is that we were close to the top."

— Belmore Browne, The Conquest of Mt. McKinley

"I was snowshoeing along about fifty feet back of the sled, with Harry (Liek) right behind me when, without warning, the snow fell away under my snowshoes. I plunged into sudden darkness.

I had time to let out a feeble shout. Then for a couple of long, long seconds I plummeted downward. I remember thinking, 'This is it, fellow!' Then my pack scraped against the slide of the crevasse, my head banged hard against the ice wall and I came to a jarring stop.

When my head cleared and I could look around in the blue darkness, I saw I was on a plug of snow wedged between the ice walls. On either side, this wedge of snow fell away into sheer blackness.

About forty feet above me I could see a ray of sunlight, slanting through the hole I had made in the surface crust. The crevasse was about twelve feet wide up there, it narrowed to two feet down where I was. Below was icy death."

— Grant Pearson, *My Life of High Adventure*

"But in half an hour, we stood on the narrow edge of the spur top, facing failure. Here, where the black ridge leading to the tops of the pink cliffs should have flattened, all was absolutely sheer, and a hanging glacier, bearded and dripping with bergschrunds, filled the angle in between...I heard Fred say, 'It ain't that we can't find a way that's possible, taking chances. There ain't *no* way.'

"We were checkmated with steepness, at 11,300 feet with eight days of mountain food on our hands. But remember this: also with scarce two weeks provisions below with which to reach the coast and winter coming. The foolishness of the situation, and the fascination, lies in the fact that except in this fair weather, unknown in Alaska at this season, we might have perished either night in those two exposed camps."

— Robert Dunn, *Shameless Diary of an Explorer*

"We tried to take some snaps, but had to give it up. For four minutes only did I leave my mittens off, and in that time, I froze five tips of my fingers to such a degree that after they had first been white, some weeks later, they turned black, and at last fell off, with the nails and all.."

— Erling Strom, *How We Climbed Mt. McKinley*

"... My mind was racing. I had to grab the rock near Dave with my left hand; it was bare, no mitten or sock. It would be frozen. I had to. Suddenly my bare hand shot out to grab the rock. Slicing cold.

I saw Dave's face, the end of his nose raw, frostbitten. His mouth, distorted into an agonized mixture of compassion and anger, swore at me to get a glove on. I looked at my hand. It was white, frozen absolutely white."

– Art Davidson, *Minus 148 Degrees, The Winter Ascent of Mt. McKinley*

Opposite: Alfred Lindley and Harry Liek, after their successful ascent of Denali, May 1932. On their way down the mountain they encountered tragedy—two members of another expedition had fallen to their death in the deep crevasses. UAF, Rasmuson Library, 81-208-03 Right: Climber Belmore Brown made three attempts on Denali, but was defeated each time. ASL PCA 01-3441

Many climbing parties have had the bitter experience of getting close to the top, only to be turned back, sometimes just a few hundred yards short of the summit by wind and cold. Experienced Denali climbers know that they can only get near the top and hope that the mountain gods will allow them to tread on the top of the continent.

The Pioneer Climbers—for the first climbers, in the early 1900s, just getting to where they could start their climb was an immense task in itself. The 1912 Browne - Parker expedition left Seward on February 1, with dog teams, and took almost five months to reach within a few hundred feet of the summit, only to be turned around by weather on two different days. When they finally gave it up, and turned to leave that desolate spot, their last memory was of the continual roar of wind from the summit somewhere in the clouds above them.

An Imposter's Claim—One of the oddest episodes in Denali's history was the 1906 claim by Dr. Frederick Cook, a very experienced Arctic explorer, that he and a companion had made it to the top of the mountain, the first to do so, bringing down photographs for proof. Climbers familiar with the mountain doubted Cook's claims, but it wasn't until 1910 that a group, specifically climbing to dispute Cook, found the supposed summit photographed by Cook: 10,000 feet lower and 20 miles away from the actual summit.

"There was no pride of conquest, no trace of that exultation of victory some enjoy over the first ascent of a lofty peak, no gloating over good fortune that had hoisted us a few hundred feet higher than others who had struggled and been discomfited. Rather...that a privileged communion with the high places of the earth had been granted... secret and solitary since the world began. All the way down, unconscious of weariness in the descent, my thoughts were occupied with the glorious scene my eyes gazed upon, and should gaze upon never again."
— Hudson Stuck, in *Mt. McKinley:*
The Pioneer Climbs, Terris Moore

First to the Top—In 1910, a group of hardy Alaskan prospectors, tired of the the controversy stirred by Cook's claims, decided to prove that Alaskans could do the job. This was the so-called "Sourdough Expedition." They reached the top of the North Peak, (actually the South peak was slightly higher but they didn't realize it at the time) put up a 14' pole and flag, and then went back down, and got back to prospecting!

Of course, many folks doubted their claim (until another expedition, years later, saw the pole) and the credit for being the first to climb McKinley went to Alaskans Hudson Stuck, Harry Karstens, and their party in 1913. They were fortunate in having a window of clear and relatively calm, though bitterly cold, weather at the top:

Denali today—The mountain has become a very popular climb, sought each summer by expeditions from all over the world.

However today's climbers face a much easier prospect than the early climbers. Instead of starting on the ground near Talkeetna, and struggling for several days before they even got to the top of the first glacier, they hop a plane from the Talkeetna airstrip and get dropped off at the base camp at Kahiltna Glacier at 7,000 feet. In a typical summer literally hundreds of climbers try to find a break in the weather and make it to the top so, this base camp is a busy place, with a ranger station, aircraft, and climbing parties coming and going. How very, very different from the rigors faced by the mountain's true pioneers!

But Denali should never be taken for granted. It remains an extremely challenging ascent, as witnessed by regular fatalities among those who attempt it.

Opposite: On Denali, 1932. When we look at all the high tech equipment today's climbers consider essential, our respect for the feats of the pioneer climbers grows. And especially since those climbers had to do without the services of pilots like Don Sheldon who with ski-equipped aircraft would drop them on Kahiltna Glacier, 7,000 feet up, saving today's climbers weeks of hiking with all their heavy gear! UAF Rasmuson Library 81-218-07n

These aren't your regular trash cans. At many places in bear country, trash cans are of heavy steel, and bolted to the ground. If you hear a loud banging it's probably just a frustrated bear.

"**September 14, 1997:** I stayed at a big new lodge high on the hills above Talkeetna, and took mule ride tonight with a friend. Our "mule skinner" was a rough-hewn fellow, and as we meandered through the hills behind the lodge, he spoke of his years of experience hunting and trapping in the bush. He promised a Denali view we wouldn't forget, and he was right.

But for the dimmest color in the aspens, the low country was dark when we came to the view point. The sun was way off to the west, and its low slanting light putting all the valleys and low places in shadow. But we could make out Ruth and Tokositna Glaciers, Avalanche Spire, Windy Corner and Karsten's Ridge, all those places that had brought so much difficulty and heartbreak to climbers.

Beyond, and high above, a long snow-capped ridge, touched pink at the top with the sun's rays, rising to a marked high peak at its north end, was Denali, looking like the top of the continent that it was. We dismounted, set up a tripod to catch the moment, and then it was time to go, for the night was coming swiftly.

But on the way down, the mountain was always there, pink, in the fading light, above the trees. And I was reminded of the journals of the early travelers to Tibet and Nepal. Of how wherever they were, Everest was always there, seeming to loom over them."

Trumpeter Swans—the bus driver's tale:

"...I live on a lake, back off the road a bit, just two other cabins on the whole lake. There's always been a pair of trumpeter swans there, each summer as long as I can remember. They mate for life, and they're sort of solitary, so usually you'll just get one pair on a lake.

"But for the last couple of days there's just been one swan out there, honking like crazy. So finally this morning, I went out to where they nest, and found wolf tracks and a bunch of feathers..."

Don't count on stopping a bear with a handgun. In a well-known tale, a particularly large marauding bear terrified natives until they got the local priest to bless and sprinkle holy water over their bullets, finally downing the monster with a lucky shot to the eye. When they skinned him they counted 32 bullet holes in the hide from the bear's adventures over the years.

North of Talkeetna, the railway follows the Susitna River to Gold Creek, then cuts north, through Chulitna Pass, along Summit Lake, and comes in to parallel the George Parks Highway again near **mile 280.** Look for the 918' Hurricane Gulch Bridge, at **mile 284.**

RULES FOR BEAR COUNTRY

Brown, or grizzly (or just 'griz'), as well as black bear are common throughout this part of Alaska. While for the most part bears are content to mind their own business, visitors should remember a few rules.

First, let bears know you're around by talking, singing, wearing bells, etc. when you hike though the woods or wherever visibility is reduced. If a bear knows you're coming, he'll probably want to get out of your way. If however, you surprise one on narrow trail, it could get ugly, for you. Bears react badly to surprise...

Don't get between a mother and her cubs, or a bear and its food. Sometimes people have been mauled when they inadvertently got between a mother and cub, without knowing it, in thick bushes. If you see a bear, assume there are cubs nearby.

Don't run—it could trigger an automatic, "chase food" reaction. Bears may look big and lumbering, but when they want to do so, they can accelerate faster than a man ever could.

Be careful where you put your food. Problems have sometimes arisen from campers carelessly leaving food out or stored near or in their tent or vehicle. Put your food in a container, away from your tent.

Bear encounter: the makings of a dangerous situation. In this case, we were walking down the road when there was a rustling in the bushes, and two bear cubs appeared. At 200 pounds, cuddly they were not. We were taken aback and essentially stopped in our tracks, the bears 50 feet or so ahead. Then the mom appeared, about the size of a Volkswagon, and definitely alarmed about seeing us so close to her cubs. Without turning around and actually running, which could have triggered the 'chase food' reaction, we walked backwards about as fast as we could. My 14-year old son, who was with us, forgot everything we had told him and just started running. When I finally caught up with him later, I told him he'd just flunked the bear test!

The last passenger run of the season arrives at the Denali Station in mid-September. The passenger runs, with the elegant domed cars owned by cruise lines in addition to the Alaska RR cars, coincide with the cruise ship season from mid May to mid September. For the rest of the year the trains on this route carry only freight. Before the Georges Park Highway was completed, passenger trains operated year round, taking home-steaders to their remote homes.

Low and treeless **Broad Pass** at **mile 304** was the major north and south route through these mountains long before roads or trains. Look for little cabins along the lake—they're shelters for stranded travelers and pilots.

The **Continental Divide** crosses Broad Pass some-where in the Summit Lake area, near **mile 312**. This is a significant geographic locale—streams a hundred yards south drain eventually into Cook Inlet, near Anchorage, 140 miles south. But just a hundred yards north the streams drain into the Nenana River, that empties into the Tanana, which, many miles later, flows into the mighty Yukon, to flow to the Bering Sea, 800 miles away.

By the time you hit the Nenana River at around **mile 328**, there's enough slope to get the water moving pretty fast.

DENALI NATIONAL PARK

The park was originally established in 1917 as Mt. McKinley National Park, a wildlife preserve that didn't include the mountain for which it is named. Finally in 1980, the protected area was tripled in size, to include the entire mountain massif along with caribou herd winter range and calving grounds, and renamed Denali National Park and Preserve.

The park has become sort of an icon for vistors, representing all that they have come to Alaska for. Yet, some, especially those who just have time for an overnight or two at Glitter Gulch –the nickname for the lodges/shops area just outside the park entrance–come away disappointed. Hours of bus riding on bumpy, dusty roads, a bear or moose sighting, maybe a glimpse of Denali through the clouds, didn't match up to the promotional material.

A bit of advice: the park's true grandeur lies in its being, as much as is possible with the limited visitor access, an intact subarctic ecosystem. For many, Denali Park is experienced in a bus with a naturalist/driver. For others, a visit might include camping at Wonder Lake, with backpacking through the wilderness. But don't expect a park with the visitor facilities of Yellowstone or the Grand Canyon.

Denali watching at the Eielson Visitors Center, about a three hour bus ride from the main visitors center by the park entrance. Alaskastock The weather isn't always just like this... Below: bear protective equipment is a growth industry here...

263

Opposite page: Moose near Denali. These are big, big animals!
Alaskstock Photo

Glimpsing Denali: If you get a view of the mountain that looks anything like the photos in this chapter, consider yourself very lucky. Denali is so high that it acts as a mixing area for weather from the Gulf of Alaska and the great interior, meaning a lot of cloudy days. Generally in summer, expect two days out of three to be overcast. In reality your best views from the mountain are apt to be from the Georges Park Highway, or from the Alaska Railroad, or from a place like the Mt. McKinley Princess Wilderness Lodge, near Talkeetna.

Take a walk: there are some good trails, like the Horseshoe Lake Trail, near the lodges at Glitter Gulch, so get out there! This is bear country, so while you don't need to be terrified, making noise is good. Remember, in almost all cases, if bears can hear you, they will get out of the way.

Getting around: Private vehicles are only allowed as far as the Savage River checkpoint, about 14 miles in. Shuttle buses: **The ARA Courtesy Shuttle**, a beige bus loops between Glitter Gulch, the park visitor center, and Mckinley Village; schedules in hotels. The **Sled Dog Demonstration Shuttle** loops between the visitor center, Riley Creek campground and the Park Headquarters in time for the sled dog demonstrations at 10, 2, &4. **The Park Shuttle**–green bus– is the main way of getting into the interior of the park, leaving the visitor center every hour for Wonder Lake (5 hr. one way $27 RT) and on the half hour to Eielson (3hr. one way $21 RT). Wildlife is often best viewed early, so consider getting up and onto one of the early buses. Wonder Lake is a spectacular place and the site for many of the photos of Denali, but 10 hours of bus riding is a lot. Your chances of seeing wildlife from a bus are high, and generally unless the animals are so close as to possibly pose a danger, buses will stop and allow passengers out for a photo opportunity.

"**In the bus, Denali National Park, Sept 17, 1997**: We didn't have to wait very long to see wildlife; just five minutes after entering the park, we stopped to watch two very big, brown, and somewhat disheveled-looking moose wandering through the low bushes perhaps 25 yards from the bus. Big is the operative word here. Everyone is concerned about bears, but I wouldn't want to meet a moose face-to-face on a narrow trail either.

A little later our sharp-eyed driver pulled over again and directed our attention to a place on the hillside where something brown could be seen moving. This was nature in the raw—you needed binoculars to see it, but a big 'griz' was chowing down on what looked like a side of Dall sheep. "

The Seventy-Mile Kid: When the park was created in 1917, it was entirely fitting that Harry Karstens, known as the 'Seventy-Mile Kid,' was the first superintendent. Barely 19 when he came north with the Klondike Gold Rush, he got his nickname after he and a buddy pulled a dogsled themselves on a 40-day trip back into the Seventy-Mile River country of the upper Yukon. A few years later he got the 900-mile dog sled mail run contract from Gakona on the Copper River to Fort Gibbons on the Yukon, through the unmapped Alaska interior. His bitterly cold trips along this route became an Alaska legend.

"**Denali National Park, Sept. 17, 1997**, evening: the Nenana rushes by in the canyon below; across it the aspens are all bright orange, and the upper slopes dusted with snow. I feel the shadow of those who struggled in the high country beyond the ridge. Belmont Browne and his group—five months of hard traveling, only to be turned back just a few hundred yards from the top. Art Davidson and his friends—caught in a 130 mph blow, in winter, out in the open, at 18,000 feet, chipping out a cave in the ice and managing to survive. And the many who didn't make it, swallowed up by the sea of crevasses, or simply disappeared. One feels humbled."

Opposite: A tour bus in Denali stops to let a big 'griz' take his time walking across the road. Above: Dall sheep and an early winter snowstorm dust the Alaska Range. Alaskastock photos If you have time consider either a flight-seeing tour or a ride all the way back to Kantishna, 95 miles into the interior of the Park. This town, billing itself as "The Heart of Denali," has around 140 residents in summer and is essentially abandoned in the winter.

Beaver dam on lake just across the river from the lodges at the entrance to Denali.

"On the Alaska Railroad, Sept 18, 1997: The the long mournful horn echoes from the hills and the Southbound pulls into the station. Glad to get in, out of the cold, get a hot "Mt. McKinley"—coffee and Yukon Jack liqueur—and just sit, watching the landscape flow past.

"The silty Nenana boils and rushes through the canyon below us. I imagine the little mining camps back in the draws, the men working all winter, to dig out the frozen earth, and pile it to wait for the spring thaw, when they can process the ore in the sluice boxes. The weather warms and the water begins to flow down through the riffles in the sluices, lifting away the dirt, until only the gold remains. Finally the gold is in the pokes (small canvas bags) and the men pack to go to town, drag the boats down to the shore, and slide into the current, to let the bucking Nenana take them to Tanana, or Fairbanks, with money to spend, maybe even a trip "outside" before winter."

The big weird thing near mile 362, as the train emerges from the Nenana River canyon is the Usibelli coal tipple. Inside is the equipment for filling the coal cars that run north to Fairbanks, or all the way south to Seward to be loaded aboard ships for the Orient.

The country changes substantially here as the trees seem to swallow us up until it seems we're traveling in a leafy canyon. This is all the northern tiaga—a taste of the vast, low, mixed black spruce and birch forests that cover much of the Yukon basin that drains interior Alaska. Plants and trees don't get very big here; the growing season is short and the ground has great frozen areas (permafrost) just below the surface.

The country is so flat here that the Nenana, barely thirty yards wide in places in the gorge, and rushing along faster than a man can run, breaks into many branches like Seventeenmile and Lost Slough, and almost seems to just disappear into the flats before finally rejoining to enter the Tanana River at Nenana. Early travelers on rafts often had to pole tediously through miles of shallows here.

Look for the big black and white wooden tripod (about 30' high), between the tracks and the river at Nenana, mile 411. Each winter this tower is dragged out onto the frozen river for the Nenana Ice Classic, a uniquely Alaskan lottery. What folks are betting on is "Ice Out," the moment in spring when the frozen river breaks up.

THE RIVER COUNTRY

It's entirely fitting that this be celebrated, for the rivers are the lifeblood for most of the towns in the immense drainage of the Yukon River.

Where there are no highways, the arrival of the first freight barge in the spring is always an exciting community event. This freight (usually in 40' containers or vans) usually begins its water journey from Seattle, stacked five and six high on a huge 400' oceangoing barge, towed by a 5,000 horsepower tug. Somewhere near the mouth of the Yukon River, perhaps at St. Michaels, the containers would be hoisted onto a smaller barge, to be pushed upstream. Sometimes, for freight bound for communities on the smaller rivers, the container would be transferred a third time, onto a yet smaller barge, pushed by an even smaller tug.

Navigation is still tough—the river channels sometimes shift every few weeks; there are few buoys or navigational aids. Captains use hand drawn charts passed along from other captains and pilots. Sometimes the only way through is launching a skiff to sound out a particularly tricky channel before you entered it. Even with all these precautions, groundings are routine.

In the shallows of Kotzebue Sound the Saidie transfers a load of freight to the Kobuk River-bound John Reilly, in the fall of 1903. Note the sandbars in the background—navigation was very tricky here. The smaller the river, the smaller the steamboat. Probably the freight destined for the far upper reaches of the Kobuk might be put on an even smaller steamer! Most of of the boats of any size were built 'down south—usual'y Seattle or San Francisco and had to be strong enough to travel up the stormy North Pacific and Bering Sea before getting to the much gentler waters of the Yukon River and tributaries.

Northern Commercial Co's Plant, St. Michael, Alaska, Sept 1908.

Top: St. Michaels, on Norton Sound, in September, 1908. The boats in the foreground are already laid up for the winter. St. Michaels was a major transshipment spot - ocean going steamers would stop here and transfer their loads to smaller, shallower draft paddlewheelers who could navigate the winding maze of shallow rivers that accessed much of interior Alaska. UW Nowell 6037 Opposite page: winter was hard—sometimes the rivers froze quickly, trapping steamers far from any towns, forcing passengers to make their way overland, like this group, on the upper Yukon, in 1912. Yukon Archives, Scillinger Collection.

The river as highway. Despite what you may hear, not everyone who lives out in the bush has a floatplane in their backyard. But the majority of villages and settlements in the vast country between the Alaska Range and the Bering Sea and Arctic Ocean lie along one of the many rivers with native and Russian names like Kitchatna, Tonzona, Kantishna, Hoholitna, and Chilikadrotna, Ugashik, Nushagak, and Kinak. When the ice is out, watercraft ranging from big tugs and barges to outboard jet boats move people and supplies around. When the ice is in, it is usually hard and smooth enough for vehicles.

It was during those in-between months, the short spring and falls, that travel was difficult, as the tale on the left shows...

Suddenly, around mile 466, Civilization appears— houses, streets, and people mowing lawns. After what seems like the endless tiaga forest stretching unbroken to the horizon, coming upon civilization so suddenly is almost a shock. First is College, and the University of Alaska at **mile 467**, and then a few miles later, Fairbanks.

A TALE OF FREEZEUP

"My brother had a hunting lodge, way up the Noatak, with a native partner. One fall, I went up to help them, that first year when they were putting it up. 'Course there's no roads anywhere up there...all the stuff came in by barge to the village and then we had to lug it all up the river in the big Lund outboards, loaded right to the gills with sheetrock, 2x6s, etc. It's almost forty miles up the river from the village to where the lodge is, and we really had to get the main lodge framed up and closed in that fall—we put in a barrel stove [wood stove made from a 55-gallon drum, fairly common in rural Alaska,] and kept working right through October. But then when we headed out to go home, the damn river was half froze up—maybe a hundred yards of ice, then fifty yards of water, then more ice! I thought we were screwed—that we'd have to leave the skiffs on the bank for the winter, and hike the 40 miles back along the shore.

"But my brother's partner, a native, he cruised back and forth when we got to the first of the ice, checking it out, then called over to us, 'If this works, follow me...' I didn't have the faintest idea what he was going to try, but he swung around, got up to full throttle and headed right for the ice. Then, just as he hit, he killed the engine, and pulled it up and that aluminum skiff slid right up on top of that ice and skidded almost all the way across to the next open water! So we swung around, got a good run at it, and up we went too...

"That first time we were a little hesitant, but then after a few more tries we got the hang of it, and we could slide maybe 50 yards if we could get a good run at it...and a lot of them frozen places were 50 yards or less, so we'd just slide all the way across and into the water on the other side and just keep on going.

"What a kick—we got back to the village without having to push those boats over the ice hardly at all. But you could tell—another two or three days and we'd have been totally screwed."

— A friend

Take the time to read the bronze plaques beneath the Pioneer's Memorial in downtown Fairbanks. It's a moving tribute to the courage and perseverance of the early settlers. The winters here are considerably colder than at Anchorage, and the days noticeably longer in summer and shorter in winter. Imagine what it must have been like before electricity, indoor plumbing and central heating! Opposite page: Floatplanes along the shore of the Tanana River.

The Wandering Trader—In the summer of 1901, E.T. Barnette was headed for the upper Tanana with a load of trading goods. Shallow water forced him to unload his goods right in front of what is now the Fairbanks Visitor's Bureau log cabin. He started to build an even shallower-draft vessel to keep going up the river, but when gold was discovered nearby, Barnette decided to build his trading post right where he was and Fairbanks was born.

Fairbanks today has a more stable economy, with a large military contingent from nearby Fort Wainwright and Eielson Air Force Base. For much of the century, however, it went through the many boom and busts that characterize so much of Alaskan economy.

"Thirty below zero this morning. Frost has crept through the walls and caused the bedclothes to stick to the wall on that side and it is mortal agony to crawl out of the warm nest in the center of the bed when daddy called."

— Margaret Murie, *Two in The Far North*

Winter in Fairbanks lasts from October to April, and before the modern conveniences like plumbing, electricity and oil heat, these months were an unrelenting challenge for residents, especially for women, perhaps raising families with their men away. Margaret Murie, who came to Fairbanks in 1911 when she was nine, grew up with a keen memory of the routines and community activities that made life manageable for the women of Fairbanks:

"A regular routine, a definite project for each day, a regular program with other people – all that helps. It is all part of the bulwark the women built, consciously or unconsciously, against the isolation, the wilderness, the cold, the difficulties of housekeeping..."

— Margaret Murie, *Two in The Far North*

The river was the highway, and the nearest town was ten days away by river boat. Between freeze-up in the fall and ice out in the spring, there was only the weekly horse-drawn mail sleigh that traveled a difficult trail through the mountains and over the frozen rivers to Valdez.

This is not the Alaska Railroad! The conductor plays a fiddle tune on the steam train at the Eldorado Gold Mine, where you can pan for gold like the visitors are doing below. Opposite page: Operating on a regular summer schedule from near Fairbanks, the Discovery III offers passengers a glimpse of bush life, here they pause off the homestead of an Athabascan family and their fish wheel.

Ice out was a big event—notices were posted around town to keep residents informed: "Ice moved at Fort Gibbon this morning at 8 a.m.," for the first steamer of the season meant fresh vegetables, followed shortly thereafter by the "slaughterhouse boat" with its pens of cows, sheep, pigs, geese, and chickens, brought up from Seattle.

In a town of log homes that heated with wood, fire was always a worry. A big steam pump at the Northern Commercial Company power plant was always ready to pump river water from under the river ice to fight fires. On at least one occasion, when the wood-fired boilers couldn't keep up with the demands of a big fire, the cry went out to "Bring the bacon"—case after case of oily bacon was brought from the warehouse, thrown into the boilers, the steam pressure rose, the water flowed once more, and the fire was contained.

Today Fairbanks is the most northerly city in North America. There are many of the conveniences found elsewhere, but the long winters are still bitter, bitter cold, with all their unique problems like having your car go bumpity bump in the mornings because of the frozen flat place in the tires from sitting on the street all night long.

THE OIL RUSH

Barge loads of trailers destined as housing for pipeline workers, headed to Alaska in the summer of 1975. Critically important barge deliveries to the Prudhoe Bay oil field were only possible during a brief ice free window in mid summer. Tugs and barges from as far away as Alabama were pressed into service to deliver the many loads that had to be delivered that busy summer. Native land claims had to be resolved before the pipeline permits were issued. This delayed the project for several years.

Every Thursday in Seattle in the winter of 1974-5, there was a curious sight at the Alaska Ferry Terminal at Pier 48. (Before it moved to Bellingham in 1985, the Alaska ferry left each week from downtown Seattle.) Dozens of old beat-up cars pulling trailers, or pick-up trucks with campers on the back, full of whole families and their possessions were lined up, waiting to get on the Alaska-bound ferry. One wondered how many had those $1,200-a-week jobs already lined up, or where those who didn't might end up.

It was no less than another Gold Rush, though with substantially less hardship and a lot more winners.

For Alaska and its citizens, the Oil Rush brought a sea change. The state's budget rose to unprecedented levels, affording programs found in few other states. But to many Alaskans it brought too many people, and too many new rules on what a person could or could not do on public land.

Before the Oil Rush, Federal land managers would sometimes turn a blind eye on squatters or trespassers, as long as they kept a low profile. But the state's new prominence brought many people north that found land or rents too expensive, and naturally wanted simply to set up camp on a piece of that vast land. What had worked for a few didn't for many, and agencies had to crack down.

THE TRANS ALASKA OIL PIPELINE

The 1968 oil strike at Pudhoe Bay brought a new era to Alaska. But first an 800-mile pipeline to the ice-free port of Valdez on Prince William Sound was required to get the oil out. The route had to cross two major mountain ranges, 350 rivers and streams, operate in bitter winter weather, and withstand possible earthquakes.

As well as an engineering challenge, it was a political challenge; taking almost five years for environmental and Native land claim issues to be resolved. In the interval the price boomed as well - from the first estimate of $900 million dollars, to the final tab that would reach almost 8 billion before the first barrel of oil flowed in June, 1977.

The Oil Boom and the revenues it brought transformed the state in many ways, from social (see page to left) to economic. Governor Jay Hammond demonstrated exceptional foresight by creating the Alaska Permanent Fund with excess oil revenues, whose investment income was to be distributed among all Alaskans via an annual dividend check.

Today Prudhoe Bay production is in decline, and despite very high oil prices, Alaska's income from oil royalties has dropped substantially. There is, however, a very large resource of North Slope natural gas, and plans are in the works to construct another pipeline that could bring yet another boom to the state.

Pipeline visitor's area near Fairbanks. The odd structures at the top of the supports are part of a heat transfer system to keep the posts from melting the permafrost and sinking. Note also that the pipeline can move sideways on a track between the posts as it expands and contracts.

A so-called pig, which can be used to separate different kinds of oil passing through the pipeline as well as keeping the inside of the pipe clean.

THE FAR NORTH

Tundra stream and ponds. Much of the north is covered by this kind of terrain. Wide areas are sometimes covered with tussocks, little round elevated bits of soil and vegetation, which are particularly difficult to travel over, summer or winter.

North of Fairbanks, the roads, for the most part, disappear: first they become gravel, then dirt tracks, then they simply stop. The taiga and tundra that covers the vast Yukon basin rises into the Brooks Range, falls away again to become the lonely north slope. Beyond is the austere Arctic—active for a few Brilliant months in summer, but frozen, seemingly abandoned in winter, the Arctic Coast stretches seamlessly from the shore to the very pole itself.

Olaus and Margaret Murie—Beginning in the 1920s, working for the US Fish and Wildlife Service, the Muries traveled through much of the far North, banding birds, exploring animal habitat, making records and writing journals. Eventually becoming head of The Wilderness Society, Murie and others were instrumental in creating much of the vast parkland, monuments, and refuges that today ensure the integrity of Alaska's ecosystems. Margaret Murie's book, *Two in The Far North,* published by Alaska Northwest Books, selections of which follow, gives a wonderful account of their travels together.

On the Trail— The Muries' many dogsled trips give a real flavor of those winter days when dogs and sleds were the only way to get around The North:

"It was...dark when we labored up the last steep pitch to the mail cabin. Twenty four miles from Alatna, dogs pulling and puffing, we pushing and puffing; and when we were within a few yards of the cabin, my legs seemed to go out from under me and I crawled the rest of the way and through the square door hole and collapsed on a straw-strewn bunk. Olaus, who is never 'all gone,' put up the dogs, brought in our beds and grub and started a fire."

Dangers – dog sled travelers were pretty much on their own, dependent on their skill and knowledge in a harsh environment. They also depended on the skills of their dogs. A well-trained dog team would keep its driver away from some of the unique hazards of the trail, like overflows. These were created when river ice reached the river bed causing what water was still liquid to come to the surface of the ice.

"...the overflow is more deadly because it is accompanied by cold weather, and only those who have experienced it can appreciate the horror of a plunge into ice water in forty-below weather. This is another reason for the waterproof match safes and the candle stubs or can of Sterno which Olaus and other mushers carry in the big front pockets of their parkas."

On Northern Rivers – on a goose banding trip to the Old Crow River, the motor of their boat broke, and Margaret watched, day after day, from the confines of a 4'x4' mosquito net with their six-month-old son, as Olaus and Jesse, his native assistant, pulled and poled their boat upstream:

"By leaning forward and putting my eyes close to the netting I could catch glimpses of the outside world. It remained unvaried for five weeks: Jesse's booted legs, the tip of the red painted bow, a green blur of grass and willows on the shore, maybe a bit of sky. Sometimes I caught a view of Olaus, trudging along on shore, the line over his shoulder. He was 'pulling her by the whiskers,' as the trappers say. Jess, experienced with the pike pole, leaned his weight on every stroke, in a steady rhythm all day long."

The Mosquitoes of the Old Crow country were legendary. Mealtimes were a particular challenge:

"Some days we merely went ashore with the tin grub box and ate a bowl of stewed fruit or tomatoes with pilot biscuits or cold sourdough pancakes, and a bit of cheese. Bowl in hand, you loosened the string of the head net, poked the spoonful of food into your mouth and quickly let the net down again. It was the same with all the bites."

Many of Olaus Murie's early trips throughout Alaska were to determine the range and habits of the caribou. Brenda Carney photo.

GLOBAL WARMING

Tidewater glacier in Glacier Bay. This is an active glacier, calving ice into deep water. While at least one glacier in Alaska is advancing, most are receding, raising the possibility that within a few decades or sooner, this kind of close up glacier viewing from yachts and cruise ships might be difficult or impossible.

"It's completely beyond what any of our models had predicted." "I never expected it to melt this fast." Such were the comments among scientists at a recent symposium on the Arctic. There still may be debate in a few quarters about global warming, but not in Arctic Alaska: it's here.

The tidewater glaciers up and down the Alaska coast had been receding slowly for years even before global warming was a household word. But recent events in the Arctic and implications for the future, especially for species dependent on wide areas of sea ice like the polar bear, are sobering.

Up until a decade or so ago, the sea ice covered most of the Arctic in winter, melting and receding a bit in the summer and then refreezing again in the winter. But in recent years the sea ice has receded dramatically in the summer. From 1979-2000, the average area of ice in the Arctic was around 3 million square miles. In August of 2007, that number had shrunk by half, a truly staggering reduction. One scientist predicted that the Arctic would be totally ice free in summer by 2030, just 23 years away!

It may even happen sooner, for as the ice melts, the darker ocean absorbs much more heat than the white ice which reflects the sun's rays, further increasing the melting.

In the changes this brings there would be losers and winners. The Northwest Passage ship route from Atlantic to Pacific would become reality. Vast new areas would be open for mineral and oil exploration. Valuable fish species like salmon and pollock might thrive and move their range further north.

But the polar bear would probably be a loser. They depend on the ice pack for habitat and if it disappeared in the summer, the only polar bears would be in zoos.

Many native villages in the Arctic are built close to the shore, but had been protected from storm seas by the ice. But as the ice recedes, the seas become larger, and villages must either relocate or eventually be swept away. Permafrost–frozen earth close to the surface of the ground–is another huge issue. Most small buildings and houses in the Arctic essentially have permafrost foundations. As the ice in soil melts, the buildings slowly settle into the soggy ground.

Can global warming be stopped? In theory, yes. But the realities of a rapidly developing Asia and a global economy built on high energy use make it unlikely.

So–if you want to see Alaska in its present state, go soon!

Polar Bears on sea ice. These big mammals are dependent on year round ice. If present trends continue, Arctic summer ice may disappear within 30 years, threatening the existence of this species in the wild. Alaskastock photo.

Acknowledgments

I am indebted to a number of unusually talented people, without whom this book would have been far less than what it is.

In particular to my designer, Martha Brouwer, of Waterfront Press, for her skill and grace in taking a sheaf of text, maps and drawings and fashioning them page by page into art.

To my old pen pals, John and Peggy Hanson, for their ideas, and valuable suggestions.

To John J. O'Ryan, for allowing me to quote freely from his unusual book, *The Maggie Murphy*.

To Glenn Hartmann, for his excellent editing and valuable ideas.

To John Pappenheimer, of Waterfront Press, for his continual support, excitement, and direction.

To my family, for encouraging me through a long project.

To many friends and shipmates, in all manner of craft, in many a breezy cove and strait, for sharing so many stories of the coast.

And finally to old Mickey Hansen, passed away but not forgotten, for his kindness in taking a green-horn kid under his wing aboard the old *Sydney*, in 1965, showing him the way of a ship and the true magic of The North.

Bibliography

Allen, Arthur, *A Whaler & Trader in the Arctic*. Anchorage: Alaska Northwest Books,1978.

Armstrong, Robert H. *A Guide to the Birds of Alaska,* Seattle: Alaska Northwest Books, 1991.

Blanchet, M. Wylie. *The Curve of Time*, N. Vancouver: Whitecap Books Ltd., 1990.

Bohn, Dave. *Glacier Bay: The Land and the Silence*. New York: Ballantine Books, 1967.

Bolotin, Norm. *Klondike Lost*. Anchorage: Alaska Northwest Publishing, 1980.

Caldwell, Francis, *Land of the Ocean Mists*, Seattle: Alaska Northwest Books, 1986.

Canadian Hydrographic Service: *British Columbia Pilot, Vol I & II* . Ottowa, 1965

Craven, Margaret. *I Heard the Owl Call My Name.* New York: Doubleday,1972

Eppenbach, Sarah. *Alaska's Southeast*. Seattle: Pacific Search Press, 1990.

Farwell, Captain R.F. *Captain Farwell's Hansen Handbook*. Seattle: L&H Printing, 1951.

Gibbs, Jim. *Disaster Log of Ships*. Seattle: Superior Publishing, 1971.

Goetzmann, William & Sloan, Kay, *Looking Far North, The Harriman Expedition to Alaska*, 1899, Princeton: Princeton Univ. Press, 1982.

Hill, Beth. *Upcoast Summers*. Ganges, British Columbia: Horsdal & Schubart, 1985.

Hoyt, Erich. *Orca: the Whale Named Killer*. Buffalo: Firefly Press, 1990.

Huntington, Sydney, *Shadows on the Koyukuk*, Seattle: Alaska Northwesst Books, 1993.

Iglauer, Edith. *Fishing With John*. New York: Farrar, Straus & Giroux, 1988.

Jackson, W.H. *Handloggers*. Anchorage: Alaska Northwest Publishing, 1974.

Janson, Lone, *The Copper Spike*, Anchorage: Alaska Northwest Books, 1973.

Jonaitis, Aldona, editor. *Chiefly Feasts*. Seattle: University of Washington Press, 1991.

Jonaitis, Aldona. *From the Land of the Totem Poles*. Seattle: University of Washington Press, 1988.

Kent, Rockwell, *Wilderness*, New Haven: Leete's Island Books, 1975.

MacDonald, George, *Chiefs of the Land and Sky*, Vancouver: UBC Press, 1993.

Macfie, Matthew. *Vancouver Island and British Columbia*. London: 1865.

Mckeown, Martha. *The Trail Led North*: *Mont Hawthorne's Story*. Portland, Oregon: Binfords & Mort, 1960.

Moore, Terris, *Mt. McKinley, The Pioneer Climbs*, Seattle: The Mountaineers, 1981.

Muir, John. *Travels in Alaska*. Boston: Houghton, Mifflin Co., 1915.

Murie, Margaret, *Two in the Far North,* Portland: Alaska Northwest Books, 1975.

Murie, Olaus, *Journeys to the Far North*, Palo Alto: The Wilderness Society, 1973.

Newell, Gordon and Joe Williamson. *Pacific Tugboats*. Seattle: Superior Publishing, 1957.

Nicholson, George. *Vancouver Island's West Coast*. Victoria, British Columbia: Moriss Printing, 1965.

Ritter, Harry. *Alaska's History*. Portland: Alaska Northwest Books, 1993.

Rushton, Gerald. *Echoes of the Whistle*. Vancouver: Douglas & McIntyre, 1980.

Ryan, John J. *The Maggie Murphy*. New York: W.W. Norton & Co., 1951.

Sherwonit, Bill, *To The Top of Denali*, Seattle: Alaska Northwest Books, 1997.

U. S. Dept. of Commerce. *United States Coastal Pilot, Vol 8 & 9*. Washington, D.C. 1969.

Upton, Joe, *Alaska Blues*. Anchorage: Alaska Northwest Publishing, 1977.

Upton, Joe, *The Coastal Companion*, Bainbridge Island, WA: Coastal Publishing, 1995

Upton, Joe, *Journeys Through the Inside Passage*. Portland: Alaska Northwest Books, 1992.

Vancouver, George. *A Voyage of Discovery to the North Pacific Ocean and Round the World*, London, 1798.

Walbran, Captain John T. *British Columbia Coast Names*. Ottawa: Government Printing Bureau, 1909.

White, Howard, editor. *Raincoast Chronicles: Forgotten Villages of the B.C. Coast*. Madeira Park: Harbour Publishing, 1987.

Index

Joe and Matthew Upton,
Katmai, Alaska, 1997

Traveling northwest waters as a commercial fisherman since 1965 in small craft and large, Joe Upton gained intimate knowledge of the coast from Puget Sound almost to the Arctic Circle.

In the 1970s Upton lived and fished out of a tiny island community in the roadless wilderness of Southeast Alaska. His first book, *Alaska Blues*, based on those years, was hailed as "One of those books you want to proclaim a classic" by the *Seattle Post Intelligencer*.

In 1995, Upton established Coastal Publishing to produce illustrated maps and guidebooks for Alaska cruise travelers.

Upton lives with his wife, Mary Lou, on an island in Puget Sound, and spends much of his summers traveling and fishing along the northwest coast.